THE
CHRIST-CENTRED
PREACHING
OF
MARTYN
LLOYD-JONES

THE
CHRIST-CENTRED
PREACHING
OF
MARTYN
LLOYD-
JONES

CLASSIC SERMONS FOR
THE CHURCH TODAY

Edited by **ELIZABETH CATHERWOOD**
and **CHRISTOPHER CATHERWOOD**

INTER-VARSITY PRESS
Norton Street, Nottingham NG7 3HR, England
Email: ivp@ivpbooks.com
Website: www.ivpbooks.com

First published 2014

British Library Cataloguing in Publication Data
A catalogue record for this book is available from the British Library.

ISBN: 978–1–78359–102–2

Typeset in the United States of America
Printed and bound in Great Britain by Ashford Colour Press Ltd, Gosport, Hampshire

Inter-Varsity Press publishes Christian books that are true to the Bible and that communicate the gospel, develop discipleship and strengthen the church for its mission in the world.

Inter-Varsity Press is closely linked with the Universities and Colleges Christian Fellowship, a student movement connecting Christian Unions in universities and colleges throughout Great Britain, and a member movement of the International Fellowship of Evangelical Students. Website: www.uccf.org.uk

CONTENTS

INTRODUCTION

Dr. D. Martyn Lloyd-Jones (1899–1981) was one of the greatest preachers of the twentieth century and one of the leading evangelicals in that God-given major renaissance of evangelical life and witness that has been continuing worldwide since his death. He was also keen on the works of the Puritans and was instrumental in the renewed interest in their works after 1945, an enthusiasm that has continued to the present day.

But while Dr. Lloyd-Jones was someone who loved history and enthused friends and family alike with his abiding interest in it, this is not essentially a historical tome or retrospect. Some years ago a book of his collected sermons was published so that those who enjoyed his preaching could have their favorites in a nutshell volume. The purpose of this book, however, is very different.

THE THEME OF THIS BOOK

Dr. Lloyd-Jones ("the Doctor" as he was usually known, and how we shall frequently refer to him here) believed strongly that God's Word is relevant for all time and in all places. His view of the centrality of Scripture in preaching has guided this book. When we met to decide which sermons would be included here, we soon realized that one could not possibly say that any sermon was worthier of a *Best of Martyn Lloyd-Jones* than any other.

But what was true of all of them was that they remain *relevant*, even though they were preached across his decades-long ministerial life, from 1927 when he began as a young preacher in Aberavon in South Wales to his last sermon, preached for a friend's gathering in 1980, when he was already suffering from the cancer that took him the following year.

So what we have in this book is selected sermons from that fifty-three-year period chosen:

- Mainly chronologically, in the order in which they were preached.
- But also thematically, illustrating his preaching style and the eternal relevance of his expositions.

7

- To prove the point that we are making that if you preach in an expository way you always speak to your congregation, and that if you are biblical you are always relevant, so that a sermon on events thousands of years ago speaks as much to the twenty-first century as it did in its own time.

If the new excitement for Reformed theology and for expository preaching—for which we can all thank God—is to continue, it must have a secure base. Otherwise it is but a passing fad whose ending will be of great loss to the evangelical church in the century ahead of us.

The Doctor himself always stressed that his interest in history was not a mere antiquarian fancy but one *with a purpose*: to build up God's people in biblical doctrine from generation to generation.

So this is a book to introduce both the Doctor *and* the truths for which he stood to the twenty-first-century generation. They have, like him, become evangelicals, discovered Reformed theology and expository preaching, and wonder how they can bring those same truths to their own generation as he did to his.

One brief comment is needed about our selection before we enter the biographical part of this introduction.

We have concentrated on *sermons*. No one could have been more enthusiastic about church history than the Doctor, but we have decided that it would be better not to include any of his historical lectures here and emphasize his *preaching* instead. The same also applies to his deeply held views of church government and ecclesiology, which he firmly believed were Scripture based but are perhaps, for the same reason, not appropriate here.

And we also want this book to be irenic. This is very much the case with several core groups in the United States at the moment. For instance, Together for the Gospel is united in its enthusiastic encouragement for the reintroduction of Bible-based, Scripture-centered Reformed theology as the basis for an evangelical renaissance in America today.

HIS LIFE AND THE BACKGROUND TO THE SELECTIONS

So these are sermons with a purpose! We can see how they unfold against the chronology of the Doctor's life because, being the believer in Reformed theology as he was, he knew that all that happened to him unfolded in the providence of God. And as millions worldwide have been influenced by his ministry, the events of his life have changed all of ours as well.

He was not born to wealth or privilege. His father, Henry Lloyd-Jones, was a village shopkeeper, later moving to London when his business went bankrupt. His mother, Magdalen Evans, was a farmer's daughter. Llwyn-cadfor, the family farm in South Wales, was to remain a focal point for the Doctor the rest of his life as he stayed in touch with the cousins who eventually inherited both the farm and also the successful horse-breeding business based there. One could say that he had his father's considerable intellect—in another age Henry Lloyd-Jones would have gone on to a university and a stellar career—and the dynamism of his Evans forebears.

Significantly though, when he died in 1981 he was buried with his *wife's* family, the Phillipses. Martyn's elder brother, Harold, a gifted poet, survived the horrors of the western front in World War I, only to die in 1918 in the huge influenza epidemic that killed millions worldwide. His younger brother became a distinguished High Court judge—Sir Vincent Lloyd-Jones—and a well-known figure in literary and political circles in Wales. Henry Lloyd-Jones, his beloved father, died in 1922. Decades after his father's death, Martyn came close to tears when American theologian Carl Henry asked him if his father had been a Christian, because he simply did not know how to respond.

The Doctor always said that he was never a teenager in the meaning that we understand that today. He nearly died in a fire in his childhood home in Wales, and his father's bankruptcy gave him a sense of responsibility for his family that weighed heavily on him. The Doctor never made jokes from the pulpit, which caused some people to think that he was a somber person. In fact, his sense of humor was infectious and lifelong, never more so than with his family or a close circle of friends with whom he could relax. When he and his brother Vincent launched into their favorite puns, no one could stay glum!

Except for the humor, which was private, and the very profound love and affection he had for his family and close friends, one could say that the public man and the personal were one and the same. His love for debate, for example, and of verbal repartee was no different in a meeting of ministers than around the intimacy of the family table at mealtimes. He was a man who practiced what he preached in whatever context he found himself.

Despite a lack of money for private schooling, the increasingly gifted Martyn was admitted to one of London's best schools, St. Marylebone Grammar (the Old Philologian), located in Westminster, where he would one day become famous.

He became a medical student at a much younger age than usual at St Bartholemew's Hospital in London, one of the top medical training schools in the country, and one of the very oldest. It was joked that "you could always tell a Bart's man, and you could not tell him much." Here he shone, becoming one of their best and brightest students, and at an unusually young age a full doctor of medicine and also chief clinical assistant to Lord Horder, the royal physician to King George V and the top diagnostic physician of the day.

At Martyn Lloyd-Jones's memorial service in 1981 an amicable dispute broke out between two of the speakers on what had influenced their late friend's preaching the most. One of them, Dr. Gaius Davies, a leading London psychiatrist, was surely right to say that the Doctor's *medical* training was used by God to make Martyn Lloyd-Jones into the kind of preacher that he later became. Sin was diagnosed as the disease, and Christ was the only remedy. When one thinks of his great definition of preaching, "Logic on fire, theology coming through a man who is on fire," one can see this clearly—the diagnostic method that he learned as a medical student at Bart's led him to the logic with which he would dissect sin in his evangelistic message or expound the doctrines so clearly laid out in Scripture. His way of preaching both logically and with great passionate conviction was what made his preaching so unique and persuasive. One can easily see why God sent him to medical school first before he contemplated the ministry.

Being in London changed his life in other ways, too. The Lloyd-Jones family began attending a Welsh chapel in the famous Charing Cross Road, where they met the Phillips family. Thomas Phillips was an eminent eye surgeon with a consulting room in Harley Street. He and his wife, Margaret, and their three children—Ieuan, Bethan, and Tomos John—lived in a big house in Harrow. Ieuan would become a preacher in South Wales; Bethan was a medical student at Bart's great rival, University College Hospital in London; and Tomos John would later follow his father and become an eye surgeon. Ieuan and Martyn became lifelong friends, but it was Ieuan's sister, Bethan, whom Martyn noticed! Beautiful and much admired, Bethan was eighteen months older than Martyn, and for many years his feelings for her were unreciprocated. But over the course of time things changed, and in January 1927 they married and, as the famous saying goes, "lived happily ever after!"

Significantly the Phillips family had played a role in the great revivals in Wales both in 1859 and in 1904—indeed Bethan and her older brother had witnessed much of the latter revival personally as their father had sent them there to see and experience it for themselves. Revival was to be a major preoccupation of the Doctor's life. In 1959, one hundred years after the Great Awakenings both in the United States and in Wales, he was to preach one of his most famous sermon series on the subject of revival itself and how the Bible saw it. He longed to see revival himself, and though he witnessed it on a small scale in parts of his ministry in Wales and believed that Christians should pray for it unceasingly, he was never to experience it on the scale of those great outpourings about which he loved to preach.

Martyn would look back to his early days in medicine and say that he was not then a Christian, but the hound of heaven was after him, convicting him of sin, but also working on his conscience in a manner that showed him how man's cures were not God's cures. Many of the Bart's patients were from the top echelons of British society and led lives that were not attractive to behold.

In due time the Holy Spirit worked in him in two different ways. First, he was converted to his own true faith in Jesus Christ. But second, he realized that while he was mixing with educated and privileged people in London, the poor Welsh folk from whom he had come were living in spiritual darkness.

So at the age of twenty-six the Doctor decided to give up what would have been an immensely prominent medical career in London, the capital not just of Britain but of the British Empire at the time, and return to Wales. He would go, not as a doctor, but as a physician of souls, as a pastor for the Welsh Forward Movement, part of the Welsh Calvinistic Methodist group of his childhood.

This move, coupled with his wedding, was so astonishing that it actually made the national press! The newlyweds went to Sandfields in Aberavon, a rundown part of South Wales that after the Great Depression hit was to become poorer still, with many of the local workers—from the steel works and the docks—out of work. Alcoholism was rife among them.

But these were the people in need of the gospel and to whom he had been called. From 1927 to 1938 he had a ministry there that is still spoken of and remembered because of the impact that it made.

Their first child was a daughter, Elizabeth, whose childhood years in such circumstances were to make an impression upon her that has never left her. With the birth of Ann over nine years later, the Lloyd-Jones quartet was completed, giving him the family and emotional security needed as the human base for his God-given ministry, first in Wales and then in London and the world beyond.

What is significant for us now as it was then is that he treated the congregation with the same intellectual courtesy and respect that he would have given his socially eminent patients in London. He knew, as he would often boast, that the ordinary working man (though often unemployed) could, if taught, properly understand God's truth and biblical theology every bit as well as a university professor. He never, throughout his life, condescended or dumbed down the gospel message—something that both students from Third World countries and also children appreciated in later years as he treated all of them as intellectual equals, fully capable of grasping the most complex truths.

If one reflects upon this it is wholly biblical—only Luke and Paul were educated among the writers of the New Testament, and most of the disciples were simple fishermen. Yet it was just such a group of people that turned the world upside down, transformed the Roman Empire, and spread Christianity across the globe.

Note that the sermon we have chosen for this period of time is evangelistic, and then think of the educational background of those listening.

As his wife demonstrates in her small book *Memories of Sandfields*, extraordinary things happened in their time in Wales, with the unlikeliest people becoming gloriously saved. This was no seeker-sensitive church—in fact some of the first things he did was to scrap the choir and abolish the anti drink Temperance League—alcoholics did indeed go on to give up their drunken ways but through being converted and not via well-meaning middle-class good works.

This being a brief summary of his life, we can now say that his fame spread, even across the Atlantic. He came to love the United States, spending as many summers there as possible, preaching in many places. During his recovery from cancer in 1969, he delivered his master lectures on preaching to the students of Westminster Theological Seminary near Philadelphia, one of which appears first in this book.

In 1938 the then eminent preacher J. Campbell Morgan asked him to become his joint minister at Westminster Chapel, one of the biggest Free Churches in Britain and a place with a global reputation. Largely forgotten today, Morgan was one of the pulpit giants of his time. This would be a major change for the Doctor, leaving his successful ministry in Wales.

He decided to accept, and when Morgan retired in 1943 the Doctor became sole minister, remaining there until cancer forced his retirement a quarter of a century later in 1968. It is for his ministry at Westminster Chapel that he is most famous, and most of the sermons in this book were preached there. It was certainly one of the biggest platforms that a non-Anglican could have. But such was the power of his preaching that he soon became renowned for it not just in Britain but also in the United States and in the world beyond. The Chapel might have been his base, but in reality his ministry was soon global, especially after the war.

After 1945 he was in effect able to build up his own congregation, with folk coming increasingly from all over the southeast of England, some from many miles away, to attend Westminster Chapel. So much so in fact that people had to stay all day, arriving in time for the eleven o'clock morning service and not leaving until coffee after the evening service, which lasted until around eight thirty or later. Temporary wartime lunch facilities became permanent, and hundreds of people both lunched there and had tea after the afternoon Bible classes (the British equivalent of an all-age Sunday school in the United States). The Chapel, while geographically disparate, was a community.

It was of course his preaching that drew people in numbers unique for London—only the ministry of John Stott a few miles away at All Souls Langham Place came anywhere near the congregational size that Westminster Chapel witnessed in these years. Indeed some of those listening to the Doctor on Sundays were young curates from All Souls, including a profoundly impressed young Anglican theologian named James Packer. This period, Packer was later to recall, was Martyn Lloyd-Jones at his peak of unmatched excellence.

The Sunday morning sermons were preached to Christians, and the evenings were essentially evangelistic, though as much Scripture-based and expository as those in the mornings. The Doctor would refuse to let his own sermons be regarded as authoritative. Everything had to be proved from the words of Scripture itself.

However, some of the great sermons he gave during this period were on apologetics and on the great doctrines of Scripture. If one is Bible based, there is no clash between apologetics and exposition, since apologetics flows naturally from the truth of God as seen in Scripture as well as from the world that God has made and that we see around us. It is significant that the sermon we have chosen from this time, from *Truth Unchanged, Unchanging*, was one preached in the United States, for he was becoming as well known there as he was back home.

Around this time he also became the first chairman of the executive committee of the International Fellowship of Evangelical Students (IFES), of which he later became the president. IFES was truly global and indeed is more so today than ever, since areas of the world where the gospel was forbidden or unknown are now some of the strongest evangelical regions of the twenty-first century. Studies that concentrate on him as a British figure sadly omit this vital part of his international life and ministry, which was so central to his life for well over a quarter of a century.

The fact that IFES began as a strongly evangelical movement after World War II was very much due to his influence and Bible-centered thinking. While this book concentrates on him as a preacher, one cannot get an over-all perspective on the Doctor and leave so crucial a ministry out of the record.

In 1950 he began what in some circles still remains his best-known sermon series, that on the Sermon on the Mount. This was the period during which he was gaining fame as an expositor both at home and overseas. His preaching was intelligent, reasoned, Scripture based, timeless, and also delivered with passion and total conviction. This was in such contrast to many popular pulpit fillers of his own generation in London, most of whom now lie forgotten, their works dated and their theologies, if they had any, long since discredited.

At the same time, he found that many of his congregation knew the basics—they knew they were saved through Jesus Christ on the cross—but they knew very little actual Christian doctrine as such. Faith without depth is bound to be shallow and is what the apostle Paul described as milk for infants—not the real meat that adults need. So keeping his Sundays clear for straight exposition of particular books of the Bible, he used the Friday night sermons to begin a Scripture-based expository series called Great Doctrines of the Bible.

Sadly, one can argue that we now live in an era in which the serious study of biblical doctrine, or indeed the very thought of doctrine itself, causes so-called evangelicals to shudder. But the need for the study of sound theology is a running theme throughout the New Testament, alongside warnings against ravenous wolves who would devour untaught and theologically shaky believers. In that sense we need Scripture-centered exposition on both *what* we believe and *why* we do so more than ever. So his sermons have even greater relevance more than six decades after they were first delivered to a congregation prepared to often travel many miles into central London on a working day in order to hear someone speak to them on weighty matters for over an hour.

The biblical office is that of *pastor-teacher*. The Doctor was a doctor in more senses than one—both medical and spiritual—and in the case of his congregation and that of the Westminster Fellowship of Ministers (originally Anglican and Free Church and just Free Church later on) he was both. With his acute medical knowledge—which he kept up all his life, reading medical journals for enjoyment to the end of his days—and with his pastoral insights, he could see how a member of the Chapel congregation or a struggling preacher might be run down and depressed *physically and mentally* and therefore more open to *spiritual* attack. He was also aware that while sin sometimes causes spiritual dryness or isolation, it could be that, as with Job, Satan was attacking a faithful and innocent child of God. Maybe God was testing one of his own children for his or her particular good.

All these were possibilities and as a medically trained physician with a deep understanding of human psychology, as well as being a pastor charged by God with the spiritual care of souls, the Doctor knew that the permutations were many and various.

The chapter "Mind, Heart, and Will" shows the Doctor both as an outstanding biblical expositor but also as someone who used the medical training that God had put him through in the 1920s. True preaching appeals, if scripturally understood, to the heart (emotions), to the mind (intellect), and to the will (application). This unique combination is at the heart of his preaching altogether and not just on this subject. Logic on fire and its application with the employment of our will was all tied in together, so unlike the preaching of his own time, which appealed usually to either heart or head but seldom to both, and which never appealed to the human will to implement what was learned in everyday life.

How true that is today as well! Cerebral sermons, emotionally excessive and manipulative, with no application of what kind of life should be lived on Monday morning, are quite common. The importance of the Doctor's very different combination cannot be emphasized enough since this particular combination—*heart, mind, will*—is as important, in many ways, as his actual words and makes the six decades or more between the original sermon and us as readers of it today immaterial.

As the Doctor began, so he continued.

He is best known in the evangelical world for his epic expository sermons, in particular those on Ephesians, which he preached on Sundays, and those on Romans, which he delivered on Friday nights.

While his exposition was biblical, it was also profoundly practical! One of his series was on life as a Christian in marriage, at home, and at work. That volume has been a wedding present for new couples now for decades. The principles outlined by Paul in Scripture do not alter. Human nature does not change, and so marriage and its joys and requirements are the same too—as indeed are the biblical principles upon which we base every waking minute of every day.

But all this has a deep *spiritual* underpinning—God's work of reconciliation on the cross—without which we would be nowhere. So we have chosen a foundational chapter as the one to be represented in this book.

Remember when you read any of these chapters, it is *unction*, the gift of God, at work, enabling the Doctor to preach with the conviction and power provided solely by the Holy Spirit. There is a world of difference between, say, a history lecture and an unction-filled sermon. A history lecturer, or a speaker on modern physics, may proclaim with passion but with *human* endeavor, whereas a preacher equipped by God to preach to the saints does so with a conviction that comes from God alone.

This is vital to recall since no formula will enable one to preach like Martyn Lloyd-Jones.

1

NO SUBSTITUTE

(1969)

From *Preaching and Preachers*

This is a book about Christ-centered preaching. For that reason the great majority of chapters in our volume will be the sermons of Martyn Lloyd-Jones, as outlined in this book's introduction.

However, we do need to know what Dr. Lloyd-Jones actually meant when he employed that term. Thankfully, he has given us a detailed answer in Preaching and Preachers, *a book still in print well over five decades after the original lectures were given.*

As he goes into some depth in "No Substitute," there is not as much need for as full an introduction here as will be the case with subsequent chapters. For him, preaching and giving a lecture were two totally different things—one a God-ordained way of proclamation, the other a human institution. This is why he had the very high notion of what he did Sunday by Sunday and on Friday evenings at Westminster Chapel. He was proclaiming God's Word, not just giving a stream of good ideas that had by chance come to him during the week or while reading the news.

Pastor-teacher is one of the spiritual gifts of the New Testament, and thankfully it is one of those whose continual validity is never contested. It is as vitally necessary in our time as it was in the time of the apostle Paul! Being a preacher was not a human vocation but a calling from God himself. It was God's means of communication, and that being the case there was no possible substitute for it.

Today there is a renaissance in the centrality of preaching, for which we can be thankful to God! But simultaneously there are those who announce that we must find new ways of "doing church" because twenty-first-century people can no longer cope with the supposedly old and outdated methods of the past. A biblically based, Christ-centered defense of preaching has therefore never been more important.

No one can speak more eloquently on this than the Doctor himself.

Let the words that now follow transform you as they did those who heard them spoken in 1969 and the many who have been changed by them since.

In our first lecture I laid down a proposition that preaching is the primary task of the church and therefore of the minster of the church, that everything else is subsidiary to this and can be represented as the outworking or the carrying out of this in daily practice. What I am doing is to justify this proposition, and I am doing so, particularly, in view of the tendency today to depreciate preaching at the expense of various other forms of activity. Having laid down the proposition, I have tried to substantiate it by evidence from the New Testament and also from the history of the church.

I now want to go a step further and to suggest that this evidence from the New Testament itself, supported and exemplified by the history of the church, leads us to the conclusion that the ultimate justification for asserting the primacy of preaching is theological. In other words, I argue that the whole message of the Bible asserts this and drives us to this conclusion. What do I mean by that? Essentially I mean that the moment you consider man's real need, and also the nature of the salvation announced and proclaimed in the Scriptures, you are driven to the conclusion that the primary task of the church is to preach and to proclaim this, to show man's real need, and to show the only remedy, the only cure for it.

Let me elaborate that a little. This is the very essence of my argument. I am suggesting that it is because there are currently false views with regard to these matters that people no longer see the importance of preaching. Take the question of the need, man's need.

NOT A MERE SICKNESS

What is it? Well, negatively, it is not a mere sickness. There is a tendency to regard man's essential trouble as being a sickness. I do not mean physical sickness only. That comes in, but I mean a kind of mental and moral and spiritual sickness. It is not that; that is not man's real need, not his real trouble! I would say the same about his misery and his unhappiness, and also about his being a victim of circumstances.

These are the things that are given prominence today. There are so many people trying to diagnose the human situation; and they come to the conclusion that man is sick, man is unhappy, man is the victim of circumstances. They believe therefore that his primary need is to have these things dealt with, that he must be delivered from them. But I suggest that is too superficial a diagnosis of the condition of man and that man's real trouble is that he is a rebel against God and consequently is under the wrath of God.

Now this is the biblical statement concerning him; this is the biblical view of man as he is by nature. He is "dead in trespasses and sins"; that means spiritually dead. He is dead to the life of God, to the spiritual realm, and to all the beneficent influences of that realm upon him. We are also told that he is "blind." "If our gospel be hid," says Paul in 2 Corinthians 4:3–4, "it is hid to them that are lost: In whom the god of this world hath blinded the minds of them which believe not." Or as Paul puts it again in Ephesians 4:17ff., man's trouble is that his understanding is darkened because he is alienated from the life of God through the sin that is in him. Another very common biblical term to describe this condition of man is the term "darkness." You have it in John 3:19: "This is the condemnation, that light is come into the world, but men loved darkness rather than light, because their deeds were evil." And in 1 John 2:8 you find the same idea worked out. Writing to Christians he says that "the darkness is past, and the true light now shineth." The apostle Paul uses the same idea exactly in Ephesians 5:8. He says, "Ye were sometimes darkness, but now are ye light in the Lord." These are the terms that express the biblical diagnosis of man's essential trouble. In other words we can sum it up in one word by saying that it is *ignorance.* All the terms such as "blindness" and "darkness" are indicative of ignorance. And according to this biblical view of man all these other things, such as unhappiness and misery, even physical illness, and all the other things that torment and trouble us so much are the results and the consequences of original sin and the fall of Adam. They are not the main problem; they are consequences or symptoms if you like, manifestations of this primary, this ultimate disease.

THE KNOWLEDGE THAT SAVES

That being the picture of man's need, it is not surprising that when you turn to the biblical account of salvation you find that it is put in terms that correspond to this expression of the need. The apostle describes salvation in these words: it means "to come unto the knowledge of the truth" (1 Tim. 2:4). It is the will of God that all men should be saved and come to the knowledge of the truth. Salvation is a knowledge of the truth. In 2 Corinthians 5:19–20 he says that the message that has been committed to the preacher, who is an "ambassador for Christ," is to say to men, "be ye reconciled to God." You find it again in the practice of the apostle. We read in Acts 17:23 of him preaching in Athens and saying, "Whom therefore ye ignorantly worship, him declare I unto you." They were ignorant though they were philosophers, and he is the one who can teach them and give them light in this matter.

I am simply showing that the biblical teaching concerning salvation is that it is the result of bringing men to this "knowledge" that they lack, it is dealing with this ignorance. Paul talks about preaching "all the counsel of God," and Peter had the same idea when he says that Christians are people who have been called "out of darkness into [God's] marvellous light." Now these are the biblical terms, and they all, it seems to me, indicate that preaching always comes first and is given priority. If this is the greatest need of man, if his ultimate need is something that arises out of this ignorance of his, which in turn is the result of rebellion against God, then what he needs first and foremost is to be told about this, to be told the truth about himself, and to be told of the only way in which this can be dealt with. So I assert that it is the peculiar task of the church, and of the preacher, to make all this known.

I would emphasize the word *peculiar*—you can use the word *exceptional* if you like or *special*. The preacher alone is the one who can do this. He is the only one who is in a position to deal with the greatest need of the world. Paul says of himself in 1 Corinthians 9:17 that "a dispensation of the gospel is committed unto me." That is what he was called for—this "dispensation of the gospel," this message, had been given to him. And you have the same thing expressed in a very glorious statement in the third chapter of the epistle to the Ephesians, verse 8: "Unto me," he says, "who am less than the least of all saints, is this grace given, that I should preach among the Gentiles the unsearchable riches of Christ." This is his calling, this is his task. He has said before that all this "in other ages was not made known unto the sons of men, as it is now revealed unto his holy apostles and prophets by the Spirit" (Eph. 3:5). This is the message: "And to make all men see what is the fellowship of the mystery, which from the beginning of the world hath been hid in God, who created all things by Jesus Christ: to the intent that now unto the principalities and powers in heavenly places might be known by the church the manifold wisdom of God" (Eph. 3:9–10).

My whole contention is that it is the church alone that can do this, and it is the preacher therefore who alone can make it known. He is set apart by the church, as I am going to show, to serve this particular function, to perform this particular task. This is the thing that is given primacy and is emphasized, and it must surely of necessity be the case. The moment we realize man's true need and see the only answer, it becomes clear that only those who are in possession of this understanding can impart this message to those who lack it.

THE BUSINESS OF THE CHURCH

Let me work this out a little. There are other agencies in the world that can deal with many of the problems of mankind. I mean by that things like medicine, the state, other religions and cults, psychology and various other teachings, and political agencies. These are all designed to help and to relieve, somewhat, the human condition, to ease the pain and the problem of life and to enable men to live more harmoniously and to enjoy life in a greater measure. They set out to do that, and it is not part of our case to say that they are of no value. We must observe the facts and grant that they can do good, and do much good. They are capable in a measure of dealing with these things. But none of them can deal with this fundamental, this primary trouble at which we have been looking.

Not only that, when they have done their all, or when even the church coming down to that level and operating on that level alone, has done her all, the primary trouble still remains. So I would lay it down as a basic proposition that the primary task of the church is not to educate man, it is not to heal him physically or psychologically, it is not to make him happy. I will go further: it is not even to make him good. These are things that accompany salvation, and when the church performs her true task she does incidentally educate men and give them knowledge and information, she does bring them happiness, she does make them good and better than they were. But my point is that those are not her primary objectives. Her primary purpose is not any of these; it is rather to put man into the right

21

relationship with God, to reconcile man to God. This really does need to be emphasized at the present time because this, it seems to me, is the essence of the modern fallacy. It has come into the church, and it is influencing the thinking of many in the church—this notion that the business of the church is to make people happy, or to integrate their lives, or to relieve their circumstances and improve their conditions. My whole case is that to do that is just to palliate the symptoms, to give temporary ease, and that it does not get beyond that.

I am not saying that it is a bad thing to palliate symptoms; it is not, and it is obviously right and good to do so. But I am constrained to say that though to palliate symptoms or to relieve them is not bad in and of itself, it can be bad, it can have a bad influence and a bad effect from the standpoint of the biblical understanding of man and his needs. It can become harmful in this way: by palliating the symptoms you can conceal the real disease. Here is something that we have to bear in mind at the present time because, unless I am greatly mistaken, this is a vital part of our problem today.

Let me use a medical illustration. Take a man who is lying on a bed and writhing in agony with abdominal pain. Now a doctor may come along who happens to be a very nice and a very sympathetic man. He does not like to see people suffering; he does not like to see people in pain, so he feels that the one thing to do is to relieve this man of his pain. He is able to do so. He can give him an injection of morphine or various other drugs that would give the man almost immediate relief. "Well," you say, "surely there is nothing wrong in doing that. It is a kind action; it is a good action. The patient is made more comfortable; he is made happier and is no longer suffering." The answer to that is that it is well-nigh a criminal act on the part of this doctor. It is criminal because merely to remove a symptom without discovering the cause of the symptom is to do a disservice to the patient. A symptom after all is a manifestation of a disease, and symptoms are very valuable. It is through tracking the symptoms and following the lead that they give that you should arrive at the disease that has given rise to the symptoms. So if you just remove the symptoms before you have discovered the cause of the symptoms, you are actually doing your patient real harm because you are giving him temporary ease that makes him think that all is well. But all is not well; it is only a temporary relief, and the disease is there, is still continuing. If this happened to have been an acute appendix or something like that, the sooner it is taken out the better, and if you have merely given the patient ease and relief without dealing with it, you are asking for an abscess or something even worse.

That, surely, gives us a picture of a great deal that is happening at the present time. This is one of the problems confronting the Christian church today. This affluent society in which we are living is drugging people and making them feel that all is well with them. They have better wages, better houses, better cars, every gadget desirable in the home. Life is satisfactory and all seems to be well, and because of that people have ceased to think and to face the real problems. They are content with this superficial ease and satisfaction, and that militates against a true and a radical understanding of their actual condition. And, of course, this is aggravated at the present time by many other agencies. There is the pleasure mania and television and radio bringing their influence right into the home. All these things persuade man that all is well; they give him temporary feelings of happiness, so he assumes that all is well and stops thinking. The result is that he does not realize his true position and then face it.

Then you have to add to that the giving of tranquilizing drugs and the taking of so-called pep pills and hypnotics. People live on these, and all this, very often, not only has the effect of concealing the physical problem but also, and still more serious, the spiritual problem. As man is content with this temporary relief, he tends to go on assuming that all is well and eventually ends in a crash. The form that the crash is taking so often today is drug addiction and so on, and there are many who cannot continue to do their work without this alternation of pep pills and hypnotics, tranquilizers and stimulants. I suggest that many of these agencies to which the church seems to be turning today, instead of carrying out her primary task of preaching, are ultimately having that same kind of effect. While they are not bad in and of themselves, they can become bad, and truly harmful, by concealing the real need.

The business of the church and the business of preaching—and she alone can do this—is to isolate the radical problems and to deal with them in a radical manner. This is specialist work; it is the peculiar task of the church. The church is not one of a number of agencies, she is not in competition with the cults, she is not in competition with other religions, she is not in competition with psychologists or any other agency, political or social or whatever it may chance to be. The church is a special and a specialist institution, and this is a work that she alone can perform.

THE INSTITUTIONAL CHURCH AND THE SOCIAL GOSPEL

I want to support this contention by certain other statements. Here, for instance, is one that to me has an almost amusing aspect to it. These proposals that we should preach less and do various other things more are of course not new at all. People seem to think that all this is quite new and that it is the hallmark of modernity to decry or to depreciate preaching and to put your emphasis on these other things. The simple answer to that is that there is nothing new about it. The actual form may be new, but the principle is certainly not a new one at all; indeed it has been the particular emphasis of this present [twentieth] century.

Take all this new interest in the social application of the gospel and the idea of going to live among the people and to talk politics and to enter into their social affairs and so on. The simple answer to that is that until the First World War that was the real vogue in most western countries. It was then called "the social gospel," but it was precisely the same thing. The argument was that the old evangelical preaching of the gospel was too personal, too simple, that it did not deal with the social problems and conditions. This was a part, of course, of the liberal, modernist, higher-critical view of the Scriptures and of our Lord. He was just a perfect man and a great teacher, a political agitator and reformer, and the great exemplar. He had come to do good, and the Sermon on the Mount was something that you could put into acts of Parliament and turn into legislation. So you were going to make a perfect world. That was the old liberalism of the pre-1914 period. The very thing that is regarded as so new today, and what is regarded as the primary task of the church, is something that has already been tried, and tried with great thoroughness, in the early part of the twentieth century.

The same is true of various other agencies that are coming into the life and activity of the church. What is advocated today as a new approach was practiced by what was then called the institutional church; and this, once more, was done with considerable thoroughness. There were all sorts of cultural clubs in the churches, and the church became the center of social life. There were organized games and clubs of various descriptions. All this was given a most thorough trial in the pre-1914 period.

But we are entitled to ask, surely, whether they worked, how effective they were, and what they led to. The answer is that they proved to be failures. I am not so aware in a detailed way of the position in the United States, which I know is somewhat different from that in Great Britain, but I have no hesitation in asserting that what was largely responsible for emptying the churches in Great Britain was "social gospel" preaching and the institutional church. It was more responsible for doing so than anything else. The people rightly argued in this way: if the business of the church was really just to preach a form of political and social reform and pacifism, then the church was not really necessary, for all that could be done through the political agencies. So they left the churches and went and did it, or tried to do it, through their political parties. That was perfectly logical, but its effect upon the churches was most harmful.

That can be illustrated and shown equally well at the present time. There are two preachers in London who are great advocates of this political-social interest of the church in the man of the world and who contend that this is the way to win him and to help him and to make him a Christian. It is most interesting to notice that these two men who are most given to this teaching in Britain have small congregations on Sundays in their churches in the very heart and most accessible part of London. These are facts that can be verified, and that this should be the case is not at all surprising. People say to themselves that there is no need to go to church to hear that kind of thing. You can get it daily in the newspapers and in the political and social institutions that are designed to do this very thing. One of these two men who gets great publicity because of this interest of his has recently even ceased to have a Sunday evening service at all in his own building. He has had to join his evening service with that of another church on the same street.

Now this is more interesting and most important. When you depart from the primary task of the church and do something else, though your motive may be pure and excellent, that is the result. I am not disputing or criticizing the motives, I am simply showing that actually this theory in practice has the reverse effect from that which it sets out to achieve. I argue that in many ways it is the departure of the church from preaching that is responsible in a large measure for the state of modern society. The church has been trying to preach morality and ethics without the gospel as a basis; it has been preaching morality without godliness, and that simply does not work. It never has, and it never will. And the result is that the church, having abandoned her real task, has left humanity more or less to its own devices.

FADS AND FASHIONS

Another argument that I would adduce at this point is that the moment you begin to turn from preaching to these other expedients you will find yourself undergoing a constant series of changes. One of the advantages of being old is that you have experience, so when something new comes up, and you see people getting very excited about it, you happen to be in the position of being able to remember a similar excitement perhaps forty years ago. We have seen fashions and vogues and stunts coming one after another into the church. Each one creates great excitement and enthusiasm and is loudly advertised as *the* thing that is going to fill the churches, *the* thing that is going to solve the problem. They have said that about every single one of them. But in a few years they have forgotten all about it, and another stunt comes along, or another new idea; somebody has hit upon the one thing needful or he has a psychological understanding of modern man. Here is the thing, and everybody rushes after it; but soon it wanes and disappears, and something else takes its place.

This is, surely, a very sad and regrettable state for the Christian church to be in, that like the world she should exhibit these constant changes of fashion. In that state she lacks the stability and the solidity and the continuing message that has ever been the glory of the Christian church.

But my objection to the substitution of a sociopolitical interest for the preaching of the gospel can be stated more positively. This concern about social and political conditions and about the happiness of the individual and so on has always been dealt with most effectively when you have had reformation and revival and true preaching in the Christian church. I would go further and suggest that it is the Christian church that has made the greatest contribution throughout the centuries to the solution of these very problems. The modern man is very ignorant of history; he does not know that the hospitals originally came through the church. It was Christian people who first, out of a sense of compassion for suffering and illness, began to do something about even physical diseases and illnesses. The first hospitals were founded by Christian people. The same thing is true of education; it was the church that first saw this need and proceeded to do something about it. The same is true of poor law relief and the mitigation of the sufferings of people who were enduring poverty. I argue that it is the church that really has done this. Your trade unions and other such movements, you will find, if you go back to their beginnings, have almost invariably had Christian origins.

My argument is that when the church performs her primary task these other things invariably result from it. The Protestant Reformation, for instance, gave a stimulus to the whole of man's outlook on and activity in life. It can be demonstrated quite satisfactorily that the Protestant Reformation gave the greatest possible stimulus to science and scientific inquiry and study, and it certainly did the same to literature and many other activities of man. In other words, when man truly becomes what he is meant to be under God, he then begins to realize what faculties and propensities he has, and he begins to use them. And so you will find that the greatest periods and epochs in the history of countries have always been those eras that have followed in the wake of great religious reformations and revivals. The other people talk a great deal about the political and social conditions but do very little about them. It is this activity of the church that really deals with the situation and produces enduring and permanent results. So I argue that even from the pragmatic standpoint it can be demonstrated that you must keep preaching in the primary and central position.

PREACHING IS PERSONAL WORK

We turn now to the realm of personal problems. This is a familiar argument today as I have already indicated. People say that the preachers stand in their pulpits and preach their sermons, but that there before them are individuals with their individual problems and sufferings. So the argument runs, you ought to preach less and spend more time in doing personal work and counseling and interviewing. My reply to this argument is to suggest, once more, that the answer is to put preaching into the primary position. Why? For the reason that true preaching does deal with personal problems, so much so that true preaching saves a great deal of time for the pastor. I am speaking out of forty years of experience. What do I mean? Let me explain. The Puritans are justly famous for their pastoral preaching. They would take up what they called "cases of conscience" and deal with them in their sermons, and as they dealt with these problems they were solving the personal, individual problems of those who were listening to them. That has constantly been my experience. The preaching of the gospel from the pulpit, applied by the Holy Spirit to the individuals who are listening, has been the means of dealing with personal problems of which I as the preacher knew nothing until people came to me at the end of the service saying, "I want to thank you for that sermon because if you had known I was there and the exact nature of my problem, you could not have answered my various questions more perfectly. I have often thought of bringing them to you, but you have now answered them without my doing so." The preaching had already dealt with the personal problems. Do not misunderstand me. I am not saying that the preacher should never do any personal work, far from it. But I do contend that preaching must always come first and that it must not be replaced by anything else.

I have often told a story of a remarkable case that illustrates this point. Many years ago I was asked to see, with a doctor and a pastor, a young lady who was said to have been paralyzed in both legs for eight years. I went to see her with them, and I found to my amazement that she was capable of making most extraordinary movements with her legs. This led me at once to diagnose her as a case of hysteria, and so it turned out to be. This supposed paralysis, this functional condition, had come on as the result of a disappointment in her emotional life. She lay there on the bed, and I was not able to help her because she just would not keep sufficiently quiet for the doctor or myself to examine her properly. However, this is what happened afterward. She had two sisters, and her older sister, as the result of this visit of mine, began to attend our church and after a number of months was converted and became a very fine Christian. After a while the second sister began to attend our services, and she in turn became a Christian. Then eventually one Sunday night I saw the so-called paralytic being half-carried into the church by her two sisters. She continued to attend, and in due course she became a Christian. Now the point I want to emphasize is this: I never had another conversation with her about her so-called paralysis; it was never mentioned, it was never discussed, but it completely disappeared. Why? How? As the result of the preaching of the gospel. As she became a Christian this matter was dealt with by the application of the truth by the Holy Spirit without any personal counseling or psychological analysis or treatment.

Now I am not arguing that this will happen every time. My contention is that if the gospel is truly preached, in a most astonishing manner it can be so applied by the Spirit to these individual cases and problems that they are dealt with without the preacher knowing it at all. I could tell you numerous stories to illustrate this very thing and how sometimes even a mere aside by the preacher has been the means of dealing with some person's problem.

In any case I have often found that the preaching of the gospel brings people to talk to the preacher and gives him an opportunity of dealing with their particular condition. It is the best means of introducing them to one another; it forms the link. Something that the preacher has said either gives them the impression that he will be sympathetic and understanding or that he has an insight into their particular difficulty. It is the preaching that brings them to the preacher for this personal help.

Moreover, by doing it in this way, you are able to deal with dozens, and perhaps hundreds, of people at one and the same time. It is quite astonishing to find that in expounding the Scriptures you are able to deal with a variety of differing conditions all together in one service. That is what I meant by saying that it saves the pastor a lot of time. If he had to see all these people one by one, his life would be impossible, he could not do it; but in one sermon he can cover quite a number of problems at one and the same time.

But in any case—and this to me is a very important argument—it is preaching that lays down the essential principles by which alone personal help can be given. Let me illustrate briefly. Someone comes into your room, into your vestry, and wants to consult you about a problem. The first thing you have to do is to discover the nature of the problem. You have to discover whether this person is a Christian or whether he is not a Christian, because that will determine what you are going to do. If a man is not a Christian you cannot give him spiritual help. If he is not a Christian the first thing you have to do is to help him to become a Christian. That is essential first, and it is only then that you can apply your spiritual teaching to the particular problem. If he is not a Christian, it is idle for you to try to apply spiritual teaching. You are wasting your time as a minister of the gospel in dealing with such a man's particular problems and difficulties. I suggest that your duty in that case is to hand him over to someone else whose professional work is to deal with such problems. Your business as a Christian minister

29

is this specialist business of dealing with spiritual problems, so this is the first question you have to decide. It is no use talking to people in a spiritual way unless they have spiritual understanding, and such understanding is the result of a spiritual rebirth, which is generally produced by the preaching of the gospel (1 Cor. 2:10–16; 1 Pet. 1:23). If in your preaching you have brought these people to see that they are not Christians, they will come to you about that, and you will be able to show them that the particular symptom that had worried them was due to the fact that they were not Christians, that they were in the wrong relationship to God. So they come to you, and you can then counsel them and help them and show them the way of salvation. If that does not in and of itself deal with the particular problem, you are now in a position to reason it out with them in a spiritual manner. I maintain that ultimately the only true basis for personal work, unless it is to degenerate into purely psychological treatment, is the true and sound preaching of the gospel.

My contention, then, is that personal counseling and all these other activities are meant to supplement the preaching, not to supplant it, that they are the "carrying on," "follow-up" work if you like, but must never be thought of as the primary work. The moment you get these into the wrong relationship, you are not only asking for trouble in a personal sense, but I suggest also that you are not interpreting the mandate of the church in a true and right manner. So I would sum up by saying that it is preaching alone that can convey the truth to people and bring them to a realization of their need and to the only satisfaction for their need. Ceremonies and ritual, singing and entertainment, and all your interest in political and social affairs and all the rest cannot do this. I am not denying that they can produce effects, I have granted that they can, and that this is where the danger sometimes comes in. What men and women need is to be brought to "the knowledge of the truth." If this is not done you are simply palliating symptoms and patching up the problem for the time being. In any case you are not carrying out the great mandate given to the church and her ministers.

BUT HAVEN'T TIMES CHANGED?

But let me deal with a few objections to this contention and point of view. Someone may say, "Have not the times changed? All you have been saying might have been correct, say, even twenty years ago, still more so, perhaps, a hundred years ago, but have not times changed? Is your method right now in the light of our new conditions?" Or perhaps some in the United States might say, "Well, all you are saying may be all right for Britain, but it does not work in America. Conditions are different here; there is a different background, different cultures, different circumstances, and so on." What is the answer to that? It is quite simple. God has not changed, and man has not changed. I know there are superficial changes—we may dress differently, we may travel at four hundred miles an hour instead of four miles an hour—but man as man has not changed at all, and man's needs are exactly and precisely what they have always been. Not only that, there have been dead and lifeless times in the history of the church before in past ages, as we saw in the first lecture.

There is nothing new about this condition of ours; one of the central fallacies of today is to think that because we are living in the mid-twentieth century we have an entirely new problem. This creeps even into the life and the thinking of the church with all the talk about postwar world, scientific age, atomic age, post-Christian era, etc. It is just nonsense; it is not new at all. God does not change. As someone put it, "Time writes no wrinkle on the brow of the Eternal." And man does not change; he is exactly what he has always been ever since he fell and has the same problems. Indeed I would go so far as to say that never has there been a greater opportunity for preaching than there is today, because we are living in an age of disillusionment. The Victorian age was an age of optimism. People were carried away by the theory of evolution and development, and the poets sang about the coming of "the parliament of man and the federation of the world." We would banish war and all would be well, and the world would be one great nation. They really believed that sort of thing. Nobody believes it by now apart from an odd representative here and there of the old "social gospel" of the pre-1914 era. We have lived to see the fallacy of that old optimistic liberalism, and we are living in an age of disillusionment when men are desperate. That is why we are witnessing student protest and every other kind of protest; that is why people are taking drugs. It is the end of all the optimism of the liberals. It was bound to lead to this because it was wrong in its basic conceptions, in its origin, in its very thinking. We are seeing the end of all that.

Is not this then the very time when the door is wide open for the preaching of the gospel? The age in which we are living is so similar to the first century in many respects. The old world was exhausted then. The flowering period of Greek philosophy had come and had gone. Rome in a sense had passed her zenith, and there was a kind of tiredness and weariness with consequent turning to pleasure and amusement. The same is so true today. Far from saying that we must have less preaching and turn more and more to other devices and expedients, I say that we have a heaven-sent opportunity for preaching.

BUT AREN'T THERE OTHER WAYS?

Then let us look at a second objection. People may say, "Surely with man as he is now, educated and sophisticated and so on, cannot all you want to do be done equally well by reading books and journals? Cannot it be done by television or radio, through discussions particularly?" Of course reading can help and is a great help, as are these other agencies, but I do suggest that it is time we asked the question as to what extent they are really helping and dealing with the situation. I suggest that the result is a disappointing one, and I think I can give the reasons for this. The first is that this is a wrong approach because it is too individualistic. The man sits on his own reading his book. That is too purely intellectual in its approach; it is a matter of intellectual interest. Another thing, which I find very difficult to put into words, but which to me is most important, is that the man himself is too much in control. What I mean is that if you do not agree with the book, you put it down; if you do not like what you are hearing on the television, you turn it off. You are an isolated individual, and you are in control of the situation. Or to put it more positively, that whole approach lacks the vital element of the church.

Now the church is a missionary body, and we must recapture this notion that the whole church is a part of this witness to the gospel and its truth and its message. It is therefore most important that people should come together and listen in companies in the realm of the church. That has an impact in and of itself. I have often been told this. The preacher after all is not speaking for himself—he is speaking for the church; he is explaining what the church is and what these people are and why they are what they are. You remember that the apostle Paul in the first epistle to the Thessalonians makes quite a point of this. It is something that we tend to neglect at the present time. He tells those Thessalonians that they as a church had been a great help to him in his preaching; he put it like this in 1 Thessalonians 1:6–9:

> And ye became followers of us, and of the Lord, having received the word in much affliction, with joy of the Holy Ghost. So that ye were ensamples to all that believe in Macedonia and Achaia. For from you sounded out the word of the Lord not only in Macedonia and Achaia, but also in every place your faith to God-ward is spread abroad; so that we need not to speak any thing. For they themselves shew of us what manner of entering in we had unto you.

The very presence of a body of people in itself is a part of the preaching, and these influences begin to act immediately upon anyone who comes into a service. These influences, I suggest, are very often more potent in a spiritual sense than pure intellectual argumentation.

Not only that, when a man comes into a church to a body of people, he begins to get some idea of the fact that they are the people of God and that they are the modern representatives of something that has been known in every age and generation throughout the centuries. This makes an impact on him in and of itself. He is not simply considering a new theory or a new teaching or a new idea. Here he is visiting or entering into something that has this long history and tradition.

But let me put it in this form: the man who thinks that all this can be done by reading or by just looking at a television set is missing the mysterious element in the life of the church. What is this? It is what our Lord was suggesting, I think, when he said, "Where two or three are gathered together in my name, there am I in the midst" (Matt. 18:20). It is not a mere gathering of people; Christ is present. This is the great mystery of the church. There is something in the very atmosphere of Christian people meeting together to worship God and to listen to the preaching of the gospel.

Let me tell you one story to illustrate what I mean. I remember a woman who was a spiritist, and even a medium, a paid medium employed by a spiritist society. She used to go every Sunday evening to a spiritist meeting and was paid three guineas for acting as a medium. This was during the thirties, and that was quite a large sum of money for a lower-middle-class woman. She was ill one Sunday and could not go to keep her appointment. She was sitting in her house, and she saw people passing by on their way to the church where I happened to be ministering in South Wales. Something made her feel a desire to know what those people had, and so she decided to go to the service, and did so. She came ever afterward until she died and had become a very fine Christian. One day I asked her what she had felt on that first visit, and this is what she said to me, and this is the point I am illustrating. She said, "The moment I entered your chapel and sat down on a seat among the people, I was conscious of a power. I was conscious of the same sort of power as I was accustomed to in our spiritist meetings, but there was one big difference. I had a feeling that the power in your chapel was a clean power." The point I am making is simply that she was aware of a power. That is this mysterious element. It is the presence of the Spirit in the heart of God's children, God's people, and an outsider becomes aware of this. This is something you can never get if you just sit and read a book on your own. The Spirit can use a book, I know, but because of the very constitution of man's nature—our gregarious character and the way in which we lean on one another and are helped by one another even unconsciously—this is a most important factor. That is so in a natural sense, but when the Spirit is present, it is still more so. I am not advocating mob or mass psychology, which I regard as extremely dangerous, particularly when it is worked up. All I am contending for is that when you enter a church, a society, a company of God's people, there is a factor that immediately comes into operation, which is reinforced still more by the preacher expounding the Word in the pulpit, and that is why preaching can never be replaced either by reading or by watching television or any one of these other activities.

2

THE NARROWNESS OF THE GOSPEL

(1935)
Matthew 7:13–14

From *Evangelistic Sermons at Aberavon*

There is a romance about the Doctor's early years in ministry, those spent in the rough, predominantly working-class town of Aberavon (or Port Talbot). He was newly married and launching on what was to be a unique forty-year career as a full-time pastor and teacher. Anyone who reads his wife, Bethan's, Memories of Sandfields *will see that this was an astonishing time of conversions of unlikely people, of a real sense of the power of the Holy Spirit at work among those whom society had often rejected or ignored. It is a wonderful tale.*

It is also important because as the Doctor began, so he continued. He was little known when these sermons were preached, although the sheer God-given, Christ-centered strength of them soon made him famous, first in Wales and swiftly in both the rest of Britain and then the United States. Much of what he did there was entirely counterintuitive, both then and now.

Drunkenness was a major problem in South Wales, and many churches thought that the answer was to have a Temperance Union—a similar instinct but less draconian than Prohibition in the United States. But just as legal enforcement failed in America, so, too, did the well-meaning middle-class efforts to prevent excessive use of alcohol in Wales.

Dr. Lloyd-Jones, while himself a lifelong teetotaler, scrapped the temperance movement in his church, as we saw in the introduction to our book. But what is interesting and should not surprise us spiritually is that countless inhabitants of Aberavon not only gave up alcohol but did so permanently. The reason is that they became Christians through the Doctor's preaching. It was sermons like this one that stopped them from ever wanting to drink again.

Conversion rather than human endeavor changed the lives of scores of people in the chapel in Sandfields in the eleven years that Dr. Lloyd-Jones served there as pastor. Becoming a Christian changes everything, and few things more than lifestyle, since a new believer is a new person in Jesus Christ.

The Doctor understood this. Societies and choirs and all the usual paraphernalia of well-intentioned but spiritually lifeless churches could never effect the inward change that conversion brings. To him the clear proclamation of the gospel was all that mattered. God honored that commitment as the Welsh spiritual equivalents of Saul of Tarsus were gloriously saved and transformed.

What is also significant is that the Doctor never spoke down to his congregation. Precious few of them were as educated as he had been, yet in London he had seen the moral bankruptcy and inner hopelessness of the capital's elite. Sinners were the same whatever their social class or educational achievement, and they all needed the same message of salvation straight from the Bible itself. He would preach no differently to students at Oxford than he would to his working-class and (after the Great Depression began) frequently unemployed congregation in South Wales.

We can thank God that Dr. Lloyd-Jones was faithful to Scripture and to the Bible's answers and ways of evangelism right from the beginning. This sermon shows us why.[1]

> Enter ye in at the strait gate: for wide is the gate, and broad is the way, that leadeth to destruction, and many there be which go in thereat: Because strait is the gate, and narrow is the way, which leadeth unto life, and few there be that find it. (Matt. 7:13–14)

There is no charge that is quite so commonly and frequently brought against the Christian way of life as the charge of narrowness. It is a charge also that is constantly brought against the individual Christian believer by that type of man who, in his desire to show his own breadth of mind, describes himself as a man of the world. He is so broad that nothing but world dimensions can give you a true impression of the width and largeness of his views! He is a man of the world in contrast to this narrow and confined man who calls himself a Christian! I fear at times also it is true to say that there is no charge concerning which the average Christian believer is quite so frightened as this charge of narrowness. To some Christians at the present time, it is more or less immaterial what men may say about them as long as they do not describe them as narrow. Of course, there is a sense in which that is a very good and healthy reaction. God forbid that we should ever really become narrow in the sense that the Pharisees were narrow or that Judaism was narrow. God forbid that we should ever really reduce this glorious gospel of liberty to a mere number of prohibitions and restraints. But that is not our danger at all. Our danger is that in our fear of being thought narrow, we should so swing over to the opposite extreme as eventually to become quite nondescript.

I sometimes feel that a simple, well-known story in *Aesop's Fables* has a good deal to say to many modern Christians. I am referring to the well-known story of the frog and the ox. One day, it says, a little frog in a field suddenly lifted up his head and observed an ox standing nearby. He looked at the ox and began to admire him and wished that he was as broad and as big as the ox. "I am so small and insignificant," he said. "How marvelous it must be to have the breadth and width of that ox." And the story goes on that the frog began to imitate the ox, and he began to expand and to grow larger and larger and broader and broader, and eventually he reached a point at which he just exploded and ceased to be. Now that, unless I am mistaken, is the precise thing that has happened to the so-called faith of many a Christian during the last fifty years. In his desire to become broad and wide, the little Christian faith that man ever had has long since exploded and ceased to be. What the exact explanation of the phenomenon is I am not quite sure, but I think we must recognize that there has been a tendency, particularly during the twentieth century, for the church to pay great respect and regard to the man of scientific knowledge. He has become the last authority on all these questions. The church has gone to very great lengths in order to please him; she has been prepared not to stress certain doctrines in her creed and to delete certain portions of the Bible, and she has in so doing wandered very far from the example set for her by her Lord and Master. I never find Jesus Christ changing his gospel in order to make it suit the people. Rather, I find him changing the people in order to make them fit into his gospel. We can be perfectly certain that there will be no true revival in this country, in spite of what may be happening round about us, until we return to the royal pattern.

My commission is this:

Ye servants of God, your Master proclaim,
And publish abroad His wonderful Name.

Whether men like it or dislike it, our business is to preach the truth that was once and for all committed unto the saints. There is a very real danger that we will develop a kind of inferiority complex in the fear of being thought narrow and ultimately make a shipwreck of our faith. But all this is merely an aside.

My text is not a negative text but a very positive text. It tells us that we must not only not be afraid of being called narrow, but it actually goes on to say that if we really want to be Christians worthy of the name, we must go out of our way to become narrow: we must enter in at the strait gate and walk on the narrow way! Now this, surely, is rather a startling and amazing thing. Is it not wonderful that when our Lord came to choose the designation to express his way of life, he selected the very word by which we are most frightened—that the very word of which we tend to be afraid is the very word in which he exults, the very word that he puts upon his flag? I would say also, for the purpose of encouraging and stimulating any frightened Christian, the next time one of these so-called men of the world tells you that you are narrow, instead of trying to run away, just stand your ground, look him straight in the face, and say, "Of course I am narrow, and it would be a very much better thing for you, and for your wife and children, if you also became narrow and ceased to boast of a largeness and a breadth that are in reality nothing but a cloak for laxity and looseness." He would not worry you quite so frequently in the future!

But why does our Lord speak about entering in at the strait gate and walking on the narrow way? Christ never said anything accidentally. He had all the letters of the alphabet at his command, yet he deliberately chose these words to describe his way of life. He spoke thus because there must be certain respects in which the gospel of Christ is really narrow. I want to try to consider with you some of the respects in which this is so.

The first respect in which we observe its narrowness is this: the gospel confines itself to one particular subject. The gospel of Christ narrows itself down to one question—the soul of man and its relationship to God. In the Bible there is a good deal of history—history of men and nations—and geography, and some people find in it geology and biology. All sorts of subjects are dealt with in this book, and yet it is not an encyclopedia. It is not a book that gives us a little knowledge about many things. It is a book that gives us much knowledge about one thing. It is the textbook of life, the handbook of the soul. It is a manual dealing with one subject, the reconciliation of man with God. If ever there was a specialist's textbook in this world, it is this book. This is true also of the Master of the book. If ever there was a specialist on the face of the earth, it was our Lord Jesus Christ. There is a sense in which he preached only one sermon, and the theme of this sermon was this—the soul of man and its relationship to the eternal Father. All the knowledge and information he possessed he used in order to illustrate this important and vital subject. Let me give you some instances.

One day our Lord was in the country with his disciples standing round about him. And he observes a farmer sowing seed into the ground. Very clearly our Lord was not only interested in agriculture, but he knew a good deal about it. But the sight of that farmer does not prompt our Lord to deliver an address on agriculture. As he watches that farmer he sees an illustration for his sermon. "You see that man," says our Lord. "He is sowing seed into the ground. There are different types of ground into which it is sown, and the ground will be judged by its response to the seed that the farmer is sowing into it. I am like that farmer: I am sowing the seed of the Word of God that leads to eternal life. Ultimately men will be judged by their reaction to that seed sown in their lives."

On another occasion when in the country our Lord beholds various fruit trees in an orchard. It is quite clear that our Lord knew a good deal about horticulture, but that does not lead him to deliver an address on that subject. "Look at those trees," says our Lord. "They may bear either good or bad fruit. Ultimately they will be judged by the kind of fruit that they bear." And turning to his disciples he says, "You are exactly like those trees. By your lives and by your works you will bear either good or bad fruit. So take heed." On another occasion our Lord was in the country and he observed the lilies of the field and the birds of the air. "If God is so concerned about the lilies of the field that he clothes them, and about the birds of the

39

air that he feeds them, how much more is he concerned about you," Christ says. I could go on taking you through our Lord's discourses, and you will find how he is constantly making use of things around him to illustrate his one great theme—the soul of man and its relationship to God.

We hear a good deal nowadays about the simple gospel. The secret of the simplicity of the gospel is this: Jesus of Nazareth, being the Son of God and living in perfect correspondence and communion with his Father, had all knowledge. He knew what was important and what was unimportant, and he ignored the unimportant and gave himself solely and entirely to the important things of life. He disregarded the irrelevant and gave himself utterly and only to the relevant and to that which ultimately matters. The secret of the simplicity of the gospel lies in the fact that he brushed aside everything but the one supreme question of the soul's need. That is clearly an utter contradiction of all our modern ideas and conceptions. We today tend to judge the greatness of a man not by his simplicity but by his complexity. Yet here was the very Son of God, and even little children got something from him, and ordinary fisherfolk followed him—"the common people heard him gladly." Why? Because he always talked about something that they understood. You, my friend, may be very well versed in many of the arts and sciences. You may be an expert on politics; you may be an authority on quite a number of subjects. But I would like to put a very simple question to you—do you know how to live? "What shall it profit a man, if he shall gain the whole world" of knowledge as well as wealth, "and lose his own soul?" (Mark 8:36) "Enter ye in at the strait gate" (Matt. 7:13). Come back to the beginning. The important and vital question is that of the soul.

But the narrowness of the gospel does not end at that point; it is merely a beginning. We discover that the gospel even narrows that. The ancient Greek pagan philosophers were very interested in the soul as a concept, as a thought, and they talked and argued much concerning the soul. But our Lord was not interested in the soul the way the Greek philosophers were. It was the individual soul in which our Lord was interested. Someone says, "I do not like such a gospel—it is so personal." It is profoundly true that the gospel is personal, and on that account it annoys certain people. We find a perfect illustration of the personal nature of the gospel in the fourth chapter of the Gospel according to John in the story of our Lord's meeting with the woman of Samaria at the well. Our Lord that afternoon was very tired, too tired to accompany his disciples into the city to buy food, and he rested by the side of the well. A woman came to draw water, and immediately they had a religious discussion. Did that well really belong to the Jews or to the Samaritans, and where exactly should worship take place? This woman seems to have been very astute; she was certainly an expert in the art of repartee. They were engaged in this religious discussion when suddenly our Lord actually became personal! He turned to the woman and said, "Go, fetch your husband," revealing thereby that he knew all about the kind of life she was living. It was as if he said, "My dear woman, you have really no right, being what you are, to talk about worship and about God. You cannot even manage your own life. You have no right to express an opinion on these great eternal themes. Start with yourself first. Go, fetch your husband. When you put your own life in order, then you will be entitled to speak."

Yes, the gospel is a personal thing. We cannot be saved in families; we cannot be saved as a congregation. We cannot be saved collectively because we are all doing a certain amount of philanthropic work. We are saved one by one. It is a question of you and God. Have you entered in at the strait gate? Are you prepared to meet God face-to-face? Are you ready for the judgment? Do you know in whom you have believed? Is all well with your soul? Have you a personal conviction of sin and a personal knowledge of God?

But the narrowness of the gospel does not end even there. It tends to become still narrower by insisting upon having a say in our conduct and behavior. It is not content merely with bringing the soul into a personal contact with God. It insists upon dictating to us the kind of life we have to live. Someone says, "That is precisely why I have long since finished with organized religion and turned my back upon it. It is too narrow. I maintain that I am entitled to live my own life in my own way. I will not be fettered." Yes, the gospel is very narrow, and it is narrow with respect to this question of conduct and ethics in two main respects: we can call them, if you like, negative and positive. The negative injunctions of the gospel with regard to conduct are perfectly familiar to us all: "Thou shalt not kill." "Thou shalt not steal." "Thou shalt not commit adultery." "Thou shalt not take the name of the Lord thy God in vain." "Abstain from all appearance of evil." If a thing is doubtful, it is wrong, and you must not do it. The gospel goes so far as to say that though a thing may be perfectly right for me, if it is a stumbling block to a weaker brother, I must not do it for his sake. Says someone, "That is exactly why I have no use for such a gospel: it makes life a misery. You have to put on a black suit and walk to church with your head down." But have you realized that if every man and woman were as narrow as the gospel of Christ would have us be, there would be no more drunkenness, no need of divorce courts, no need for the League of Nations? Why? The world would be a paradise. It would be perfect, even as God himself is perfect! The narrowness of the gospel—I speak with reverence—is the narrowness that is in God himself. Oh, that we all became narrow, that we might enter in through this strait gate! "Few there be that find it," says our Lord. It takes an exceptional man to say no to temptation and to restrain and control himself. It takes an exceptional man to deny himself in order to make things easier for others. On the broad way there is a great crowd! "Many there be which go in thereat." It does not take an exceptionally great man to sin. Any fool can sin, and every fool does sin. But that broad way leads to destruction. There is the narrowness of the gospel in its negative injunctions.

But I also want to show you its narrowness in its positive injunctions. This, of course, is the great theme of the Sermon on the Mount. If you would really see the narrowness of the gospel, you must come to the Sermon on the Mount. One of the great words of this generation is the word *love*. But if you really want to see the greatness of the word *love*, you must narrow it down, you must focus it. You do not know what love really means until you love your enemies. The great task that is set before the Christian is to love ugly people until they are made beautiful. Another great word today is the word *brotherhood*. We believe today in doing good and in helping others but if you want to see how great that word really is, you must narrow it down. You must bless those who curse you and pray for those who despitefully use you. The task set before the Christian is to "do good to them that hate you." Another great word is the word *happiness*. There are those who say, "I want to enjoy myself, and I have no use for religion. Why should I bury myself alive?" Again you have a great word, but you must narrow it down and focus it if you would discover its real size. You know not what happiness means until you can "glory in tribulations," until you can be happy even in the midst of persecution. The task for the Christian is to be happy even when the clouds have gathered and the sun has ceased to shine and everything has gone wrong.

There, then, we see something of the essential narrowness of the gospel. It is, in other words, this narrowness of the expert, or if you like, the narrowness of the highest circle of achievement. You are all familiar with the saying that there is always plenty of room for a good man at the top. The higher the circle of achievement, the smaller will be the number found in it. For instance, there are many who can sing remarkably well, but very few Carusos; there are many who can play the violin amazingly well, but very few Kreislers; there are many who paint extraordinarily well, but comparatively few Royal Academicians. That, it seems to me, is the very point that our Lord makes in this text. He says in effect, "Do not be content with living on the ordinary level of life. Come up to the top. Ascend the mount. Live life tremendously; live life as an expert. Live as I live; yea, come to the very summit. Be perfect, even as your Father in heaven is perfect."

But, lastly, if you would see the narrowest and straightest point of all, you must confront the gospel at that point at which it tells you that salvation is only possible in and through one particular person and especially in his death. There is the point at which perhaps the majority tend to object. "I have agreed with you entirely so far," says someone. "I liked your emphasis upon the soul, your emphasis upon personal decision, and your emphasis upon ethics and conduct. But when you tell me now that I can only be saved by believing that Christ died my death, I find it impossible to follow you. The conception is too narrow. I cannot understand it. It seems to me to be almost immoral. I cannot accompany you any further." What has the gospel to say to such a man? It does not argue with him. It challenges him. It turns to him and says something like this: "If you can find God without going via Calvary, do so. If you can find liberation from your besetting sin without the power of the cross of Christ, carry on. If you can find peace and rest for your troubled conscience without believing in the death of the Son of God for you and for your sins, go ahead. If you can lie on your deathbed and think of facing a holy God without fear and without alarm, I really have nothing to say to you. But if ever you should feel lost and miserable and wretched, if ever you should feel that all your righteousness is but as filthy rags, if ever you are filled with terror and alarm as you think of God and his holy law, if ever you feel utterly helpless and hopeless, then turn back to him, the Christ of the cross, with his arms outstretched, who still says, 'Look unto me, and be ye saved, all the ends of the earth' (Isa. 45:22). It is there that the whole of humanity is focused. He is the representative of the whole of mankind. He died for all. But still more wonderful, according to Paul it is also true to say that, 'in him dwelleth all the fullness of the God-head bodily.'" Complete man and complete God and all in one Person! The God-man! In him God and man are indissolubly linked, and through him and in him the way is opened from hell to heaven, from darkness to light, from despair to hope.

Let me show you, as I close, how perfectly this text and all I have tried to say with respect to it can be illustrated from the story of our Lord's earthly life and pilgrimage. Consider his birth and the self-emptying that it involved. Try to think of the narrowness and straitness of Bethlehem, when the Word was made flesh and eternity came into time—"strait is the gate." Then think of him in the wilderness at the commencement of his earthly ministry, tempted forty days and forty nights. Then watch the scribes and Pharisees and Sadducees and Herodians as they spread their net round about him and gradually draw it in—"strait is the gate, and narrow is the way." Then look at him in the garden of Gethsemane—the very Son of God, by whom and through whom all things were created, confined to a garden surrounded by soldiers. And then, in a few hours, in the police court, with a soldier standing on each side. In the garden he could at least walk backward and forward along the path; now he is not allowed to move—"strait is the gate, and narrow is the way." But still it is not finished—see him on the cross nailed to the tree—the Son of God, the Creator of the world—fixed there, unable to move hand or foot. He dies. They take down the body and place it in a grave. Peer into that grave—can you see any light there? Do not the very sides seem to fall in and collapse? "Strait is the gate, and narrow is the way." It leads to death, the grave, darkness, utter desolation.

And there we should have to end if we but believed what so frequently passes as gospel at the present time. But—blessed be the name of God—the gospel goes on. It does mean Bethlehem, it does mean the wilderness and temptation, it does mean enemies and persecution, it does mean Gethsemane, trial, cross, death, yea and the grave. But on the morning of the third day, behold, the resurrection! He bursts asunder the bands of death and rises triumphant o'er the grave! The darkness leads to dawn and to the light of endless day! "Strait is the gate, and narrow is the way"—but it "leadeth unto life."

If you accept the gospel and yield yourself to it, it will mean another birth for you. It will mean trial and temptation; it will mean persecution; it will mean the crucifixion and death of an old man that is in you. But it will lead to life that is life indeed, life more abundant, yea, the very life of God himself.

"Enter ye in at the strait gate." Come onto the narrow way!

3

THE FINAL ANSWER TO ALL OUR QUESTIONS

(1939)
Romans 8:28

From *Why Does God Allow War?*

Britain in 1939 was facing a major struggle with Germany only twenty-one years after the end of the previous conflict. For them the message to the Romans was of the profoundest contemporary relevance. This is why Lloyd-Jones in his preface to Why Does God Allow War? *says that he allowed his sermons to appear in book form, his first excursion into print.*

World War II was the greatest conflict in the history of humanity. This struggle killed at least fifty million people. The key difference from previous wars was that most of those who died were not soldiers in battle but civilians, many of whom died in bombing raids on their own homes. The Lloyd-Jones family was in London at the beginning of the war and at its end. The family was evacuated, like thousands of families, for some of the time, but they were actually back in London for the second wave of air attacks in the last year of the war.

In 1939 these attacks were still some way into the future. It is probably just as well that in the "phoney war" period, which lasted until the spring of 1940, his congregation had no idea that they would be an object of Hitler's direct wrath or that thousands of Londoners would be killed in the air raids, or blitz, of the autumn of 1940.

It is significant that when this sermon was published, the book in which it appeared did not have the present title of Why Does God Allow Suffering? *but* Why Does God Allow War? *Thereby we see the timeless relevance of the Doctor's sermons. The book was reissued when Britain was fighting Argentina in 1982, but when the current US edition came out, it could be changed to a work on the whole issue of suffering without any change to what you are about to read.*

As Dr. Lloyd-Jones shows, the basic truth is always theological. The Romans to whom the apostle Paul was writing were suffering considerably for their faith, and as we know, Paul himself would die a martyr's death. It was the trials and sorrows of these first-century Christians that the apostle was addressing. Yet as he shows, the answer is always theological and spiritual, God centered and not human oriented. In today's therapeutic culture we concentrate so much on ourselves that we forget that God even exists. But without him we have no hope. As the Doctor showed, what matters is not how we feel or what our particular circumstances might be but our relationship to God through Jesus Christ. Compared to this, the rupture of relations between Britain and Germany was as nothing. While everyone felt uneasy about how the war would turn out, God's action in our lives is wholly independent of external circumstances.

In this sermon Martyn Lloyd-Jones speaks to us in our uncertain world with as much biblical authority and theological insight today as he did back in 1939. Preach from Scripture and you are always contemporary, as we now discover.

And we know that all things work together for good to them that love
God, to them who are the called according to his purpose. (Rom. 8:28)

Here, perhaps in the briefest compass, we have the most comprehensive and the most final answer to all the various questionings and complaints that tend to rise within our minds and our hearts during a time of trial and of difficulty. The apostle was writing to men and women who were suffering hardships and experiencing trials and tribulations. These things were trying and testing their faith. They wondered why they were being allowed to endure them, and they were still more baffled as to how these things could be reconciled with the promises that had been held before them in the gospel. Paul deals with the whole question in this mighty passage. He has, in the earlier part of the chapter, been working out the results and the fruits of the gospel in the personal life of the believer. He has shown how, as the result of the working of the Holy Spirit, the believer is enabled to become more than a conqueror over all the assaults of flesh and sin. Then he proceeds to show how the Holy Spirit, in addition to that, also gives us the assurance of son-ship, testifying with our spirit that we are the children of God and therefore heirs and joint-heirs with Christ. Then suddenly at verse 18 he introduces the statement, "For I reckon that the sufferings of this present time are not worthy to be compared with the glory which shall be revealed in us."

Why does he say that? The answer must be that he imagines someone in Rome arguing in the following manner: "It is all very well for you to hold before us that glorious vision and to tell us that we are heirs of God and joint-heirs with Christ. But look at our situation, see the things that are happening to us and the things that are threatening us in the future! Do they indicate that God is taking a special interest in us? Do they augur a future bright with promises? Everything seems to be against us. Far from occupying the customary position of heirs, we are confronted daily by tribulation, distress, persecution, famine, nakedness, peril, and the sword. How are these things to be reconciled with the great and precious promises of which you write and of which you speak? Have we any guarantee that in spite of all that is happening to us what you say will ultimately come to pass?" That being the difficulty, either actual or conceivable, in the minds of the Christians at Rome, Paul proceeds to deal with it and to give the answer to it.

This is surely one of the most magnificent passages that is to be found in his writings. As a piece of literature it is superb. As apologetic, as an eloquent and at the same time reasoned and logical statement of a case it is masterly. And above all there breathes through it a spirit of devout wor-ship. It is not an academic or theoretical discourse on a problem. The writer himself has experienced untold difficulties and trials. He has been in prison frequently, has been beaten with stripes above measure, has several times been face-to-face with death, has from the Jews five times received forty stripes save one, has been beaten with rods and stoned, has three times suf-fered shipwreck and has been in the deep "a night and a day," has been "in perils of waters, in perils of robbers, in perils by mine own countrymen, in perils by the heathen, in perils in the city, in perils in the wilderness, in perils in the sea, in perils among false brethren; in weariness and painful-ness, in watchings often, in hunger and thirst, in fastings often, in cold and nakedness" (2 Cor. 11:25–27). That has been his experience, and he writes

49

to men and women who, while they had not suffered in the way that he had, nevertheless were having a very difficult time.

There is a sense in which we should consider the entire passage as a whole. But the text before us focuses attention on the central principles, which are taught not only here but also everywhere else in the New Testament. This passage is typical of the New Testament method of comforting and consoling believers. It is vitally important that we should observe carefully and precisely what it does say and also what it does not say. We must be careful not to allow the writer's eloquence to carry us away and not to be content merely with some general feeling. We must analyze the statement and see exactly what it has to say. But before we do that, there is something else that we must do and that, in a sense, is quite as important. We must observe not only the actual statement but also the way in which the statement is made. Or, if you prefer, the method of the theodicy is as important as the details of the theodicy. Or, to use still another form of expression, we must grasp the principles on which the statement is founded as well as the details of the statement. Indeed, if we fail to do this, whatever effect these words may produce upon us will be false and entirely foreign to what was in the apostle's mind.

There are two main principles that are absolutely vital to a true understanding and grasping of the New Testament teaching with respect to this whole matter of consolation and comfort. The first is that the comfort it imparts is always *theological*. That statement may well arouse feelings of surprise and indeed of annoyance in many, for it cuts right across what we should naturally expect, and it is certainly the extreme opposite of what has been the popular attitude toward religion for some time. We have referred already, several times, during our consideration of this general theme of theodicy to the opposition to theology and to systematic teaching and thinking. Experience and results have been unduly exalted, and any attempt to stress the vital importance of a true foundation has been resented and has been dismissed as indicative of a rational or legalistic outlook. But apart from the general opposition to theology, there are many who, I say, are surprised and pained at the thought that theology should have a vital place in this matter of comfort and of consolation. Their position is that they can well see the importance of having a basis to one's life and that there is undoubtedly a need for theology and definition. "Such," they argue, "may well occupy our time and attention during a time of peace and of tranquillity. But during a time of trial and affliction, a time of crises and of stress," they proceed, "what one needs is not a theological thesis or reasoned statement but comfort and consolation. When nerves are frayed and minds are tired, when feelings are wounded and hearts are at the breaking point, it is surely cruel to present men and women with some sort of a compendium of theology. They need to be made to feel happier and brighter; they need help to forget their problems and their troubles. They need to be soothed and eased. Theological terms at such a time are an impertinence, however right they may be during normal times."

This is a very widespread feeling. But how terribly and tragically wrong it is, how utterly false to the New Testament, is shown plainly in this great passage. It is surely one of the most highly theological passages in the Bible. Listen to some of the terms that are used: foreknowledge, predestination, justification, glorification, the elect! These are the great and characteristic words of theology, the words that have been hated and abominated so heartily by all who demand and insist upon "a religion that does something." Yet these are the words that are used by this loving apostle as an integral part of his message, he who had himself suffered so much, as he writes to men and women who were exposed to sufferings and trials that we can scarcely imagine. He conveys his comfort and consolation to them in this passage that probably contains more pure theology and that has probably led to more argument and discussion and disputation than any other individual passage in the whole of the Bible. Why does he do that? And what does it mean? The answer is twofold.

It means that the New Testament never isolates the problem of happiness and never deals with it as if it were something separate and special that could be handled on its own. We, desiring happiness as we do, tend to do the opposite. We approach happiness directly and immediately. We fail to realize that happiness according to the New Testament is always the result of something else, and that what determines, therefore, whether it is true or false is the nature of the agent that produces it. According to the New Testament there is but one real happiness or joy, and that is the happiness that is based upon a true relationship to God, the happiness that is the result of the righteousness that God gives us through Jesus Christ his Son. It is because we have false notions of happiness and base it upon false and insecure foundations that we so constantly experience alternating periods of elation and dejection, joy and despair. The only joy that never fails is that which is given by the Lord himself according to his promise. The way to obtain it and to retain it, therefore, is to understand and to grasp the conditions on which he gives it. And that implies thought and theology.

The other reason why Paul offers his consolation in this way is that he was anxious that they should grasp the method whereby he consoled and comforted himself, in order that they might apply it to themselves whenever and wherever occasion might arise in the future. He was not out to comfort them and to make them feel happy merely while they were reading the letter or while they were still under the influence of his personality. For that would have meant that he would have to write to them regularly at intervals. But he might not be alive to do so, and they might be scattered and cast into prison and be beyond the reach of letters. He desires, therefore, to introduce them to the method that can be applied always and everywhere and in spite of all circumstances and conditions. The happiness of the Christian, he would have them see, is not to be something that is produced artificially and that is dependent upon circumstances and surroundings that may be constantly changing. It is to be the result of an acceptance of certain truths and the working out of a reasoned, logical argument on the basis of these truths. It is not to be something vague and general and intangible, which varies with one's moods and feelings or with the precise situation in which one finds oneself. It is not to be dependent even upon regular attendance at the house of God and the effect of its atmosphere or the preaching of its preachers. It is to be the result of an argument, the end and conclusion of a logical series of positions that any believer can, and must, work out for himself. If we depend upon anything save an understanding of the truth, we are doomed ultimately to disappointment and unhappiness. But if we accept the truth and grasp its teaching, we will be able to apply it to our needs at all times and in all places. The primary business of the church with respect to believers is to teach the doctrines of the faith and not merely to try to enthuse or to comfort in general.

The second principle that is always in evidence in the comforting and consolatory passages of the New Testament is the view that it takes of life. That view is what is generally termed otherworldly or spiritual. Failure to realize that this is so surely accounts for much of the unhappiness in the lives of Christian people and also for much of the sense of disappointment that they feel when certain unpleasant experiences fall to their lot. And yet there is nothing that is quite so characteristic of the Bible as this view that it takes of life. This is seen very clearly in this passage with which we are dealing. Christians, according to Paul, are "heirs." They have not yet inherited fully, they are waiting, they are expecting. There is "the glory which shall be revealed," and they look forward to it. They are "waiting for the adoption, to wit, the redemption of our body." They have not yet gathered in the great harvest, but they have received "the firstfruits." They have not yet seen fully their great inheritance, but they have seen and known sufficient to make them hope for the remainder, and hoping for that, they "with patience wait for it." And it is because of all this that Paul can say with such confidence, "I reckon that the sufferings of this present time are not worthy to be compared with the glory which shall be revealed in us." Though he lives in the present, it is clear that the Christian, according to Paul, is meant to live for the future. That is why he tells him elsewhere to "set your affection on things above, not on things on the earth" and exhorts the Ephesians to know "what is the hope of his calling, and what the riches of the glory of his inheritance in the saints" (Eph. 1:18). This is also the view that we find in the Epistle to the Hebrews, especially in chapters 11 and 12. And in like manner we remember how Peter talks about "a lively hope" (1 Pet. 1:3). Indeed, it is the view of life found everywhere in the New Testament and also in the Old Testament. The true believers in Israel regarded themselves as "strangers and pilgrims" on the earth, mere sojourners in this land of time. They were all looking forward and looking ahead; they were pilgrims on their way to God and to eternity.

That is the view of life held everywhere in the Bible, and that view is vital to its comforting and consolatory teaching. Indeed, without this there is no comfort at all. The New Testament is primarily interested in the condition of our souls, not our bodies; its concern is with our spiritual welfare rather than with our material condition, and over and above and before it begins to consider our relationship to men and what they may do to us, it stresses the all-importance of a right relationship to God. The result is that it seems to ride very loosely to this present life and to this present world, and face-to-face with the worst conditions conceivable it can boldly say, "The Lord is my helper, and I will not fear what man shall do unto me"

(Heb. 13:6), and "For our light affliction, which is but for a moment, worketh for us a far more exceeding and eternal weight of glory; while we look not at the things which are seen, but at the things which are not seen: for the things which are seen are temporal; but the things which are not seen are eternal" (2 Cor. 4:16–18). That is its attitude toward life. We need not indicate how totally different this is from the modern view, which is almost altogether this-worldly. Looking and hoping for things in this life and in this world, men and women are disappointed and in turn tend to blame God and the gospel. And when they are reminded that it is their life and worldviews that are false and not true to the biblical teaching, they reply by stating that the otherworldly view is nothing but a manifestation of escapism and at the same time is guilty of neglecting present conditions and problems.

The answer to that charge cannot be given fully in a passing word, but we must show that it is an entirely false charge. This we can do by first reminding you of certain historical facts. Can the people whose lives we find recorded in the Old Testament be described as men and women who avoided the problems of life—Abraham, Jacob, Moses, David, and all the others? Can it be said of the apostles, and especially of Paul, that holding this otherworldly view they just escaped from and avoided the problems and the responsibilities of life in this world? And afterward can that charge be leveled at the Puritans who, perhaps above all others, exemplified this view of life?

That Christians who hold the otherworldly view refuse to become excited about and to work for ideas and schemes that are based upon the precise opposite view of life does not mean that they are unconcerned about life and what happens in it. Their position is that they have learned that the greatest of all snares is to be bound by this world and to live only for this life. They have had a vision of things that "eye hath not seen, nor ear heard, neither have entered into the heart of man" (1 Cor. 2:9). They live for these things and their ultimate attainment. These are the things that enthuse them. Indeed, these are the things by which they live. But that does not mean entire indifference to this world. It means and implies a very pessimistic view of this world accompanied by efforts to make it as tolerable as possible.

Are we as concerned about our souls as we are about our bodies? Do we experience as much agony of spirit as we contemplate the terrible spiritual warfare that is going on in this world at all times as we do with respect to the physical wars that take place from time to time? Can we say that we grieve as much about the wrong relationship of men to God as we do about broken national and international relationships? If our view of life is not that of the New Testament, we shall not only experience grievous disappointments in this world, but we shall also fail to be comforted and consoled by its teaching.

Having considered in that way the vitally important background to our text, we can proceed to look at its specific and detailed teaching along the following lines. In the face of all kinds of trials and tribulations and difficulties, it announces that "all things work together for good to them that love God, to them who are the called according to his purpose" (Rom. 8:28). This is both a statement and a promise.

I.

Let us look for a moment at *the all-inclusiveness of the promise*—"all things work together for good." It is generally agreed that the "all things" has special reference to trials and tribulations. Here is one of the most remarkable claims ever made for Christianity. Here is certainly the boldest justification of God's ways to man. Let us observe exactly what it says. Perhaps we shall best be able to grasp its significance if we approach it along the negative route. We see clearly that as Christians we are not promised an easy time in this world. Our Lord himself in his teaching told the disciples that they would have tribulations and trials and sufferings. And in the same way Paul teaches that "unto [us] it is given on the behalf of Christ, not only to believe on him, but also to suffer for his sake" (Phil. 1:29). The Christian's view of life and of the world is realistic, not romantic. He does not avoid troubles and problems. Neither does he try to minimize the seriousness and the greatness of the troubles and problems. There are those who think that the business of any ministry of comfort and of consolation is to try to show that the trials and the afflictions are not really as bad as they appear to be. There are well-meaning people who always try to take up that attitude and that line when they try to help their friends. It is true, of course, that there may be a tendency in all of us to exaggerate our difficulties and thereby to increase our problems, and it is surely right that this tendency should be checked and controlled. But it is not only fatuous but also dishonest to try to make light of what is actually serious trouble. To tell a man who is writhing in agony that the pain is not quite as bad as he thinks it is is both insulting and annoying. The intention may be good, but the result will be not only not to help the man but to add to his trials by producing an additional source of irritation! That is not the method of the gospel. It takes the facts as they are. It faces them honestly. It covets no cheap victory or success by belittling the problem.

In the same way its message to us is not just to tell us to clench our teeth and to be courageous. There are many who confuse faith with courage and who would depict the Christian as one who in spite of everything just decides and determines to hold his head erect and to go forward come what may. Courage as a virtue has been highly extolled during the past years. And let us agree that there is something very noble in the picture that is drawn. It is manly, it is upright to refuse to grumble and complain, to maintain one's poise and equanimity in spite of everything, to go on to the end unbroken and unbent—there is something truly noble and heroic in it all. But that is essentially a pagan virtue that has nothing whatever to do with Christianity. Paul does not call upon these people merely to be courageous. His appeal is not merely that they should hold on and hold out in spite of everything. As we shall see, his whole emphasis is not upon what they are to do but upon what God *has* done, *is* doing, and *is going* to do for them. They are to continue not by clenching their teeth in a spirit of courageous determination but rather by "setting their affections on things above." Courage in its real essence, and if it is the only thing that sustains us, is really a confession of hopelessness. It is the attitude of the man who refuses to give in though all is hopeless. But the Christian is saved by hope and lives by his hope.

Neither is the Christian message just some vague statement to the effect that God loves us and that therefore somehow everything must work out right at the end. For that means that a gap is left between the love of God and the condition in which we find ourselves. It is virtually to avoid the problem altogether, to turn our backs upon it, to forget it, and to think of something else. To be morbidly preoccupied with the problem is thoroughly bad, and it is always good to dwell upon the love of God. But the Christian position is not one that oscillates between these two positions, for that is not a real solution. It is a dualism that fails to connect the love of God with the difficulty and the problem. Now the whole glory of the gospel is that it faces the whole situation without shirking anything and yet shows the way out. Some of the older versions bring out this feature in our text very clearly by adding the word "God" to "all things work together for good," i.e., that "God works all things together for good to them who love him." And that is undoubtedly what the apostle teaches. These trials, difficulties, and tribulations are not to be ignored, neither are they without any explanation whatsoever. God uses them and employs them and guides them in such a manner as to promote our good. There is therefore no irreconcilable opposition between belief in God and the difficulties and trials of life. God uses them to our advantage and employs them in order to bring his own great purposes to pass. "All things work together for good to them that love God, to them who are the called according to his purpose." That then is the ultimate justification of God's ways; that is the ultimate answer to all our questions as to why God allows certain things to happen.

II.

We have but time for a passing word on what we might call the *limitation to the promise*. "All things work together for good *to them that love God, to them who are the called according to his purpose*." In the original that is emphasized by placing "to them that love God" at the commencement of the sentence. "We know that to them who love God all things work together for good." The promise is definitely limited. It is not universal as to the people included. As we have had occasion to point out repeatedly, the popular idea of the love of God is the very antithesis of this. He is regarded as promising to bless all in exactly the same way. That he does so in his providential dealings with mankind in general is true. But following that, there is a great fundamental division and distinction everywhere in the Bible between the saved and the unsaved, between those who have entered into a covenant relationship with God in salvation through Jesus Christ and those who have not, or to use the words of our text, "the called" and those who have not been called. Salvation is the result of the operation of special grace, and there are special promises to those who have received this grace.

The gospel has but one word to speak to those who do not believe on the Lord Jesus Christ. It is to exhort them to repent and to believe. It holds out to them no special promises until they have done so. Indeed, it threatens them with doom and disaster. It does not tell them that "all things work together for good" for the reason that it instead tells them that they are "condemned already." As we have seen in our first section, special promises and comforts and consolations are not obtained directly. They are the consequences and results of salvation, of believing on the only begotten Son of God. They are offered only to those who "love God." We must mark the word "love." It is not mere general assent to a number of statements about God, neither is it some sentimental feeling. The word used for "love" involves the idea of a love that is anxious to do the will of God and to serve God, a love that is anxious to glorify God and to please him in all things because he is God.

There is something truly terrible and alarming in our text. It tests us to the very depths. It carries the definite implication that for us to question and to query God and his actions with the slightest suspicion of arrogance just means that we are outside the promise. Those who love God know that "all things work together for good." That does not mean that at times they may not be in a genuine difficulty as to the precise explanation of what is happening. But their spirits are always healthy and sound, though their minds may be baffled. They do not cease to love God. By our questions we often proclaim what we are and where we stand. The one vital question for us is, do we love God? Without being in that relationship to him we cannot possibly understand his ways, and we are outside the scope of his gracious promises. The promises are all conditional, and before we allow ourselves even to raise the question of *his* faithfulness, we had better examine *ourselves* and make sure that we have observed the conditions.

III.

But we must look at what I choose to call *the mechanism of the promise*, the way in which it works. The apostle says that "all things work together for good to them that love God, to them who are the called according to his purpose." He says that we "know" this, that it is something that is well-known and acknowledged, something that to the Christian is self-evident. How is this so? The answer is partly doctrinal and partly a matter of experience. The doctrinal answer has already commenced at the end of our text— "to them who are the called according to his purpose"—and continues right until the end of the chapter. We know that all things work together for good to believers because their whole position is dependent upon God and his activity. Our salvation is God's work. Listen to the argument: "For whom he did foreknow, he also did predestinate to be conformed to the image of his Son, that he might be the firstborn among many brethren. Moreover whom he did predestinate, them he also called: and whom he called, them he also justified: and whom he justified, them he also glorified" (Rom. 8:29–30). There is nothing accidental or fortuitous or contingent about God's work. It is all planned and worked out from the beginning right until the end. In our experience it comes to us increasingly, but in the mind and purpose of God it is all already perfect and entire. Nothing can frustrate it, and that is why Paul asks his definite question, "What shall we then say to these things? If God be for us, who can be against us?" (v. 31). But it is not merely a matter of such high doctrine. There is a fact that confirms and substantiates it all: "He that spared not his own Son, but delivered him up for us all, how shall he not with him also freely give us all things?" (v. 32). Is God, who actually delivered up his only Son to that cruel death on Calvary's cross for us and for our sins, likely to allow anything or anyone to stand between us and his ultimate purpose for us? It is impossible. With reverence we say that God, having thus done the most impossible thing, must of necessity do all else. If God did that for our salvation, he will surely do everything else that is necessary. And if the death of Christ, with all that is so true of it, is the final cause of our salvation, surely everything else that we may experience, however bitter and cruel, must work to the same great end. God turned sin's most desperate action into the means of our salvation, and whatever lesser suffering we may have to bear as the result of the activity of sin and evil will be turned to the same glorious end. If we believe that we are in God's will, if we know that he loves us, and if we love him in return and as a consequence of his love, then we can be certain that all things, whatever they may be, are working together for our good.

But God be thanked, we can also answer the question with regard to the mechanism of this glorious promise in an experimental manner, from the realm of experience. That our text is true is the universal testimony of all the saints whose histories are recorded both in the Bible and in the subsequent history of the Christian church. The ways in which this promise works out are almost endless, but the principle that is common to them all is the one that we have emphasized already, namely, that there is but one ultimate good—the knowledge of God and the salvation of our souls. Holding that in mind, we see that trials and tribulations and difficulties and distresses work out in the following ways:

(*a*) They awaken us to the fact of our overdependence on earthly and human things. Quite unconsciously, oftentimes we become affected by our surroundings, and our lives become less and less dependent upon God, and our interests become more and more worldly. The denial of earthly and human comforts and joys often awakens us to the realization of this in a way that nothing else can do.

(*b*) This also reminds us of the fleeting nature of our life here on earth. How easy it is to settle down in life in this world and to live on the assumption that we are here forever. We all tend to do so to such an extent that we forget "the glory which shall be revealed," and that, as we have shown, should be the frequent theme of our meditation. Anything that disturbs our sloth and reminds us that we are but pilgrims here, therefore, stimulates us to "set [our] affection on things above."

(*c*) In the same way, great crises in life show us our weakness, helplessness, and lack of power. Paul illustrates that in this very chapter of Romans in the matter of prayer. "We know not what we should pray for as we ought" (v. 26). In a time of peace and of ease we think that we can pray, that we know how to pray. We are assured and confident, and we feel that we are living the religious life as it should be lived. But when trials come, they reveal to us how weak and how helpless we are.

(*d*) That, in turn, drives us to God and makes us realize more than ever our utter dependence upon him. This is the experience of all Christians. In our folly we imagine that we can live in our own strength and by our own power, and our prayers are often formal. But troubles make us fly to God and cause us to wait upon him. God says of Israel through Hosea, "In their affliction they will seek me early" (5:15). How true that is of all of us. To seek God is always good, and afflictions drive us to do so.

(*e*) But all this is mainly from our side. Looking at it from the other side, we can say that there is no school in which Christians have learned so much of the loving, tender care of God for his own as the school of affliction. While all is well with us, in our self-satisfaction and self-contentment we shut God out of our lives; we do not allow him to reveal to us his solicitude for us even in the details of our lives. It is only when we are so troubled that "we know not what we should pray for as we ought" that we begin to realize that "the Spirit itself maketh intercession for us with groanings which cannot be uttered" (v. 26). And it is to those who were in the depths that the sense of the presence of God has been most real and the realization of his sustaining power most definite.

The widow of a German Moravian bishop told me a few months ago that the universal testimony of all the Christians in Germany who had suffered untold hardships on account of their faith was, in her experience, that they would have missed none of these things, that indeed they thanked God for them. By these things they had been awakened to a realization of the poverty of their Christian lives and experiences; by these things also they had their eyes opened to the wonders of his grace. That is their modern way of expressing what the psalmist puts thus: "It is good for me that I have been afflicted; that I might learn thy statutes" (Ps. 119:71). It is but the reecho also of Paul's reaction to God's pronouncement: "My grace is sufficient for thee: for my strength is made perfect in weakness," which led him to say, "Most gladly therefore will I rather glory in my infirmities, that the power of Christ may rest upon me. Therefore I take pleasure in infirmities, in reproaches, in necessities, in persecutions, in distresses for Christ's sake: for when I am weak, then am I strong" (2 Cor. 12:9–10). Is that our experience? If we but "love God" and submit ourselves to him, it most certainly will be, for again I would remind you that "all things work together for good to *them that love God*, to *them who are the called according to his purpose.*"

4

IS THE GOSPEL
STILL RELEVANT?

(1947)

From *Truth Unchanged, Unchanging*

We live in an age of the New Atheism. Writers such as Richard Dawkins or the late Christopher Hitchens deride the gospel and dismiss Christianity as a dangerous disease that ought to be eradicated.

Plus ça change . . .

There have always been such critics of the Christian faith. Similar detractors existed when Dr. Lloyd-Jones gave a series of lectures in 1947 at Wheaton College in Wheaton, Illinois. While these talks were, strictly speaking, not sermons, we have included one of them in our book because it gives fascinating insights into how he preached and why he preached on the great intellectual issues of his time.

In his training as a medical doctor, he learned the scientific method in order properly to diagnose illness. In that sense calling him simply "the Doctor" is a description as well as an affectionate moniker. He was a scientist. One could say that it was precisely because he was trained to think logically that he had seen for himself that the condition of the world was entirely hopeless. Only through what God had done through Jesus Christ crucified and risen was there any hope for humankind. Medicine and science alone most certainly cannot save us.

At his memorial service in Westminster Chapel in 1981, one of his friends said that Dr. Lloyd-Jones was primarily a preacher, and another that he always remained a medical doctor. In fact, both descriptions were true, and the one greatly helped the other.

Above all he was someone with entirely biblical convictions about the true nature of the human condition. In his lectures he touched on the subject of apologetics. As a preacher he maintained a somewhat ambivalent attitude to the true usefulness of apologetics as an evangelistic tool. But *be that as it may, what he says in the lecture was what informed his evangelism and the entire worldview that he possessed of how to approach the non-Christian world.*

These were three core convictions:

a) Humans have always been exactly the same.
b) God is always exactly the same.
c) God's attitude to the human race is always the same.

These are all eternal verities. So, too, is the gospel, as relevant in the twenty-first century as it was in the first and in the middle of the twentieth. This should have a major impact upon how we proclaim it today. As he jokes, a first-century man would travel at four miles an hour, a twentieth-century person at four hundred miles an hour, but both of them were traveling, and as people one was identical to the other!

Non-Christians will always condemn us for being old-fashioned and out-of-date, of believing in a book that is two thousand years old. But as Francis Schaeffer used to put it, there is such a thing as true truth. The Doctor's expression of truth unchanged, unchanging says the same thing. Truth never changes, however ancient it might be. We are sinners and in need of reconciliation with God through Jesus Christ. Our main goal is not happiness or self-fulfillment or whatever the latest fad might be. It is to be saved through Jesus Christ. Nothing else matters, as anyone who reads the following lecture will see.

The gospel of Jesus Christ confronts and challenges the modem world with the statement that it alone has the answer to all man's questions and the solution to all his problems. In a world seeking a way out of its tragedy and its troubles, the gospel announces that the solution is already available. In a world feverishly looking to the future and talking about plans for the future, the gospel proclaims that the search is not only mistaken in direction but is also quite unnecessary. It denounces the fatal habit of pinning our hopes on something that is going to happen. It announces that all that people, individually and collectively, need has been at the disposal of mankind for nearly two thousand years. The central message of the gospel is to tell people that everything necessary for their salvation is to be found in the person of Jesus Christ of Nazareth, the only begotten Son of God. He, it proclaims, is the full and final revelation of God. It is in him, in his life and his teaching, that we see what we are meant to be and the kind of life we are meant to live. It is in his death upon the cross that we see the sin of the world finally exposed and condemned. It is through his death that we see the only way whereby man can be reconciled to God. It is from him alone that we can derive new life and obtain a new beginning. It is only as we receive power from him that we can live the life God intended us to live.

Indeed, the gospel message goes further and assures us that Jesus Christ is seated at the right hand of God, reigning in power, and that he will continue to reign until his enemies have been made his footstool. The gospel proclaims that the time is coming when at the name of Jesus every knee shall bow, "things in heaven, and things in earth, and things under the earth" (Phil. 2:10). Thus the gospel of Jesus Christ confronts man and urges him to turn back, to look back to this unique person who was here on earth nearly two thousand years ago, in whom alone salvation is to be found.

But we are well aware of the fact that the orthodox idea of the atonement of Christ is highly distasteful to the modern mind. There is no reason that is so frequently adduced today for the rejection of the gospel as the fact that it is so old. The average modern-day individual regards those who are still Christian as being in that position either because they are woefully ignorant or else because they have made themselves deliberately obscurantist and are refusing to face the facts. Nothing to the modern man is so utterly ridiculous as the suggestion that all he needs today is something that has been offered to mankind continuously for nearly two thousand years. Indeed, he regards it as insulting to be told that he, with all his knowledge and advancement and sophistication, is still essentially in the same condition spiritually as men have been throughout the long history of mankind. He assumes that anything that is so old cannot be adequate to meet the needs of the modern situation. For this reason the vast majority of people do not even consider it. Anything so ancient cannot, they argue, be relevant today.

Now what has the gospel to say to such an attitude and to such a criticism? In the first place, we can show that such an attitude is utterly unreasonable and is nothing but the manifestation of sheer prejudice. Were it not that we are dealing with the most serious and important matter in life, it would be simple enough to show that some aspects of this question are most ludicrous. At any rate we shall be able to point out that people who thus reject the gospel out of hand and who refuse even to consider it simply because it is so old can be convicted of failing to apply their own supposed reason and logic. We shall be able to show that many of their own arguments recoil upon their own heads.

For instance, there is nothing that such persons are so fond of claiming for themselves as that they have what they delight to call an open mind. They like to contrast themselves with religious people whose minds, they tell us, are cramped and confined. They charge us with considering but one book and but one person. They, on the other hand, and according to their claim, have kept the windows of their minds open in every direction, and as a result they have garnered so much knowledge and information as to make it quite impossible for them to accept the ancient message of the Bible. They claim to have open minds, to be freethinkers.

But surely before one can claim that a mind is truly open he must be able to prove that it is open in all directions. That mind alone is truly open that is exposed to the north and the south and the east and the west, to the past, the present, and the future. A mind that is deliberately shut in any one direction is no longer an open mind. Surely, therefore, when a man dismisses and rejects the gospel without even considering it, simply because it is old, he is admitting that he has deliberately closed his mind to the past. That is not reason. That is not thought. That is not logic. That is nothing but the demonstration of sheer prejudice. Anyone, therefore, who rejects the gospel on the ground of its antiquity alone has no right whatsoever to claim that he has an open mind.

But we can also show that an individual with his type of mentality is guilty of setting up a false standard in these matters. It is clear that his ultimate and most important criterion is age, not truth. And yet surely what is important when we are discussing truth is not the age of truth but its veracity.

This point can be illustrated quite easily. A man who is a seeker in any respect is a man who speaks in the following way. "My object," he proclaims, "is to arrive at that ultimate goal and destination for which I have set out. I am so anxious to arrive at that goal that I am prepared to receive advice and information from anyone or from any quarter. I care not whether the advice comes from the past or the present or whether it will come from

the future. Anything that helps me arrive at the goal, I welcome and I value."
For such a man to inquire as to the age of his informant or as to the date
upon his truth is surely to introduce an utter irrelevance into the discussion.
If I say that alone can be true that is new and modern and that could not
have been known by those who belonged to the past, then clearly my whole
idea of truth is changed, and I have set up a standard that has become more
important than truth itself—namely, modernity.

Sometimes, of course, the standard of dates and age may be quite le-
gitimate. There are those, for instance, who make a hobby of collecting old
furniture. In that case they are, no doubt, more interested in the age of the
furniture than in its quality. Now as long as it is just a matter of furniture,
we are not disposed to quarrel with those who set up such a criterion. But
when we are discussing man and God, when we are concerned about morality, chastity, purity, when we are thinking in terms of life and death, of
eternity and the whole future condition of mankind, surely to introduce
this question of age and of date is a pure irrelevance, the intrusion into the
discussion of something quite extraneous.

Regretfully we must indicate that those who are thus prejudiced against
the gospel give the impression that their real concern is not with truth itself
but with being considered modern and up-to-date. Their ultimate interest
is not in reality but in modernity.

For our final exposure of this prejudice displayed by rejection of the
gospel simply because it is old, we turn to science, a realm of which the
modern man thinks most highly and that is most popular at the present
time. Much of the case against religion and the Bible claims that it has
arrived at its position through the employment of the scientific method of
inquiry. It tells us that religion belongs to the realm of the imagination and
of fancy, the world of romance and of make-believe. Religion, it affirms,
must be put into the category of folklore or fairy tales, into the whole world
of unreality created by fear and fancy. Utterly opposed to this, they tell us,
is the scientific method, which is concerned only with facts.

Now it is not our concern at the moment to argue that matter out thoroughly, but we must indicate at any rate the following points in connection
with this argument. One is that the truly scientific spirit is always careful
to differentiate between theory and fact, between supposition and truth,
between hypothesis and that which can be proved and demonstrated. The

THE CHRIST-CENTRED PREACHING OF MARTYN LLOYD-JONES

true realm of science is that of phenomena which can be seen and touched, felt and handled; and the moment the scientist moves out of the realm of the tangible, he becomes a philosopher with no more authority than any other thinker.

Now one of the greatest tragedies in the world today is the way in which theories are being equated with facts, and mere hypotheses are being accepted as truths. Many who disbelieve in the very being of God and who deny the deity of Christ, the miraculous, and the supernatural do so on the word of certain well-known scientists who refuse to believe such truths. The dogmatic assertions of such scientists are being accepted as solid facts, though in reality they are nothing but theory. No scientist has proved, or can prove, that there is no God, that Jesus of Nazareth was not in a unique sense the Son of God, and that he did not work miracles. No one can prove that there is no life after death, no judgment, no hell. They can simply say that they do not believe such facts. But their disbelief, however loudly and confidently proclaimed, is not demonstration. There is nothing, therefore, more unscientific than the way in which men and women are thus confusing hypotheses with truth and theories with facts.

This unscientific lack of discrimination may be demonstrated in another way also. What is the truly scientific method of research? It is almost invariably something like this: a young man who is given a piece of scientific research work is generally placed under the care and in the charge of an older man, and he goes to this older man to seek advice. What has the old man to say to the young man? Does he tell him to start by burning and destroying every book that has ever been written on the subject in the past? No; he does the exact opposite. He advises the young man, before he makes a single experiment, to go to the library and study all the past literature on the subject, to understand it, grasp it, make full use of it. And this is obviously a wise method. Why should a man waste his time rediscovering that which has already been discovered? Furthermore, as the young man reads the old literature, he will find many fruitful items of information for his own research work.

The truly scientific method is not one that turns its back upon the past. It is one that starts with the past, studies it, and builds upon it. In other words, there is nothing more thoroughly unscientific than the way the average person today dismisses the Bible and the whole of the Christian gospel and the Christian church without ever reading the Bible, without being familiar with the case for the gospel, without reading the history of the church. Whatever else may be claimed for the method of such an individual, it stands convicted as the very antithesis of the truly scientific one.

We thus have been able to show that the rejection of the gospel merely in terms of its antiquity is something that, far from being based on thought and reason and knowledge and logic, is nothing but the manifestation of sheer prejudice against the past. But someone may object that the modern case is not yet met. Someone may suggest that he agrees entirely that to dismiss the gospel without even considering it, simply because it is old, is nothing but the manifestation of prejudice. But he goes on to suggest that his case is somewhat different. He may speak like this: "I am not a Christian. Though I do not believe the gospel, I think I can prove that my rejection of it is based upon reason and demonstration."

And this is the case that he puts forward: "The more I look at life in every respect and in every department, the more clearly do I see that there is a universal law running through the whole of life. It is the law of growth, of progress, and of development. I see that everything is advancing and moving forward. For instance, I look at my garden in the spring and see the seed that has been sown now sprouting. But the seed doesn't stop at that. It grows, blossoms, reaches its full maturity, and then dies. Likewise, when I take a walk in the country in the spring, I see the little lambs gamboling in the fields. But they do not remain lambs. They likewise develop and mature. I observe also in the country the modern farmer plowing his ground with a tractor. I remember days when men used to plow with horses drawing iron plows. I have read of days when men used to plow with oxen drawing wooden plows, and in still earlier times I know that men used to dig the ground themselves. These examples are manifestations of the same law.

"Again, I look at the modern city with its amenities and contrast it with the rude mud huts in which our forefathers used to live. I compare and contrast the modem physician and surgeon with the barber-surgeon of the eighteenth century and the witch doctor of still more primitive times and peoples. Ever, always, I see the same law. Indeed, I have but to pick up a textbook on any subject and to compare it with a textbook on the same subject of some twenty years ago to see at a glance that there has been a great advance in knowledge and information. Indeed, I compare the way in which World War II was fought with World War I, and even there I see the same law. Everything in life is developing, advancing, moving forward. It is the universal law of life and of being.

"But when the most vital and important matter of all—namely, man, his problems, and his salvation—is mentioned, you Christians suddenly ask us to reverse that process, to turn back and look to the past for the answers and for the solutions. Your position is utterly irrational. It is like asking a modern man when he is taken ill to reject the help of the latest advances of scientific knowledge and to be treated by a barber-surgeon or a witch doctor. It is like asking the modern farmer to refuse the offer of a tractor and to continue to dig the ground himself. You are turning back the clock of time, reversing the essential process found in nature. You are asking man to commit intellectual suicide. I often wish that I could believe your gospel and that I could become a Christian, but in view of what I have said, it is impossible and would be an act of sheer irrationality."

Such is the case put forward at the present time by large numbers of people. What are we to say to this argument? We start by agreeing entirely with the facts that have been adduced. It is not part of the preaching of the gospel to deny facts, and the believer in the gospel is not an utter fool. He is aware of the advances that have been made in many realms of knowledge. He is well aware of the developments that have taken place in many departments of life, but he still believes in the old gospel. "How do you reconcile these two contradictory positions?" asks the modern man.

We do so in the following manner. We agree entirely with the facts, but we believe that we can demonstrate that the argument deduced from the facts is false.

But let us, rather, put this in a positive form. Let us give our reasons for still believing in the message of the old gospel in the modern world. Our first reason for doing so is that man himself as man has not changed at all. All the changes about which men boast so much are external. They are not changes in man himself but merely in his mode of activity, in his environment. This statement can be proved in many ways. It is, for instance, an accepted fact that the really great classic literature of the world is always ageless and timeless. The reason is that it deals with man as man and not merely with certain aspects of men's lives at certain periods. The Greek tragedies are still being translated. The plays of Shakespeare are always contemporary, for Shakespeare, with his profound insight and understanding, was not simply describing Elizabethan man but man as man. The result is that as we read his plays, we feel we are reading about representative modern man.

The case is the same with the Old Testament. It is a very old book, yet its characters are essentially modern. Look, for instance, at Cain, a man who was so jealous of his brother that he murdered him. Are there no such men in the modern world? Then consider a man like Esau, who seems to have been interested only in food and drink. Are there no Esaus in the modern world? One has but to listen to the conversations of people in the dining cars on trains and in restaurants to discover the answer. Then look at a man like Jacob, who was anxious to succeed and to prosper and whose avarice was so great that he did not hesitate to defraud his own brother. Has Jacob become an extinct type? Then consider David, king of Israel. You remember how one day, seated on the roof of his house, he saw another man's wife. He was pleased by her. He desired her. He determined to have her. And he brought about the death of her husband in order that he might obtain her. Are there no men of that type in the modern world? And we could go on through the entire list of Old Testament characters. In almost every single instance we could be looking at a typical modern man.

"But surely," asks someone, "there is some mistake. Have you not seen the modern man traveling in his airplane at four hundred miles an hour? Are you suggesting that he is identical with the man who used to travel on foot at the rate of four miles an hour?" But wait a moment. Let us look at the two men. There they go, one at four hundred miles an hour, the other at four miles an hour. The vital question to answer in each case is: what is the object of the traveling? The remarkable thing is that it is precisely the same in both cases. The individuals are going to make love, or to make war, or to do business, or they are intent upon pleasure. There is but one real difference between the two men. It is the rate at which they travel to the same goal. What in reality is the precise difference between the pride that the modern man takes in his culture and the sophistication and pride of those men who at the very dawn of history tried to build the tower of Babel up to heaven?

But perhaps we can prove this point most clearly by indicating that the modern man with all his cleverness and ability seems to be quite incapable of inventing a new sin. It is no part of our purpose to detract or to derogate from the power and the ability of modern man. Truly, his knowledge and ability are very great. He has succeeded even in splitting the atom. Nevertheless, it is the simple truth to say that he has been quite incapable of thinking of a new sin. All the sins that are being committed in the modern world you will find mentioned in the Old Testament. Or, conversely, all the sins mentioned in the Old Testament you will find being committed by people today. Man as man does not change at all. He still remains the same contradictory person he has been ever since the original fall. That is our first reason for continuing to present to him the ancient gospel of Jesus Christ.

Our second reason for so doing is infinitely more important. God hasn't changed! And it is when we realize, as we have been trying to show, that man's ultimate problem is his relationship to God, that we see the final futility of introducing this question of age and of dates. It is at this point we see most clearly how fatuous it is to reject the gospel simply because of its antiquity. Someone has well put this point by saying, "Time writes no wrinkle on the brow of the Eternal." Of course, there have been advances and developments, but do these in any way affect the being and the character of God? Does the fact that we have an internal combustion engine and that we have succeeded in splitting the atom in any way abrogate God's laws or in any way lessen his detestation of sin and wrongdoing?

No; the most urgent, vital question confronting man is still the question asked of old by Job, "How should man be just with God?"(Job 9:2). Certainly there is a new setting to problems—whether they are economic, political, or educational; whether they deal with the shortage of houses or the proper treatment of strikes. But all these problems are temporary. Behind and beyond them all remains that unavoidable situation in which we shall be face-to-face with the eternal God, "the Father of lights, with whom is no variableness, neither shadow of turning" (James 1:17).

The ultimate problem for man is not himself, his happiness, or the conditions that surround him while he is here on earth. His ultimate problem is his relationship to God both in time and in eternity, and God is eternal, changeless, absolute. How foolish it is, therefore, to argue that modern man needs a new remedy or a new type of salvation rather than "the glorious gospel of the blessed God" (1 Tim. 1:11), which is to be found alone in our Lord and Savior, Jesus Christ.

Our third and last reason for commending this ancient gospel is that there is nothing better than it or, more positively, that it is still the only thing in the world that can adequately deal with the problem and the condition of man. Let us agree wholeheartedly with the modern man when he says that he believes always in having the best. The man who does not desire the best is a fool. Let us by all means have the best, whatever it may cost and whatever its source may be. Further, it is true to say that in many realms and departments of life the latest is undoubtedly the best.

Let us take but one illustration. Of all the amazing and phenomenal advances that were made in World War II, none is in any way comparable to the advances made in the prevention and treatment of the ills of the physical body. We are all aware that by means of preventive inoculation our children can be safeguarded from the ravages of such diseases as whooping cough and diphtheria. We know, too, how men in the services, on going abroad, were given a preventive inoculation against typhoid fever. Likewise, we know of the chemical treatment of diseases by means of the sulfa drugs and by the so-called miracle drug, penicillin. These advances were truly astounding. Their potency is not just a question of opinion or of theory; it can be proved statistically. It is a fact, for instance, that in the South African war more men died of typhoid fever than were killed in the fighting. Yet in the last two world wars there were scarcely any deaths from this disease, solely as the result of preventive inoculation. Likewise, we can compare the mortality rate in diseases like meningitis and pneumonia before and since the introduction of these drugs. The change is truly astonishing. There can be no question at all but that in the treatment of the ills and diseases of the body the latest is the best.

But can the same be said about the prevention, treatment, and cure of the ills of the soul? Is there some wonderful inoculation that can be given to young men and women that will render them immune to the insinuations and suggestions of sin that meet them on the streets, in the movies, in the books and magazines they read? Can they be protected entirely against temptation? Is there some wonderful drug that can be given to a man tormented by an accusing conscience and who is acutely aware of a sense of sin and of failure? Is there a tonic that can be given to him that will strengthen his feeble will and make him more than conqueror over the enemies that assail him? Is there some magical potion that can be given to a man who on his deathbed realizes his sinfulness and is afraid to meet his God and Eternal Judge?

What are the facts? We have seen already that the case for the latest treatment in the physical realm can be proved and established by statistics. But what of this other realm? Let us be realistic and face the facts. In spite of the phenomenal increase in education, knowledge, and culture during the past hundred years—in spite of all the acts of Parliament that have righted wrongs and mitigated injustices and that have been designed for social amelioration in almost every respect—what are the actual conditions prevailing today?

The answer is to be found as we look at the striking figures of the increase in juvenile delinquency, drinking, gambling, immorality, and marital infidelity leading to separation and divorce. Indeed, the results are to be seen in the whole lowering of the moral tone and level of life in most countries, in the sex mania, and in the increasing tendency to live only for pleasure and superficial enjoyment. The fact is that the modern world is desperately ill, that man is perhaps more unhappy than he has ever been.

There is but one cure for the ills of man. When my conscience accuses me, there is but one thing I know of that can give me rest and peace. It is to know that Jesus of Nazareth, the Son of God, who bore my sins "in his own body on the tree" (1 Pet. 2:24), has forgiven me. It is to believe and to know that because he loved me and died for me, I am clear of accusation. And conscious as I am of my weakness and failure and my lack of power to live a life worthy of the name, I am again driven back to him. It is only from him and the power of the Holy Spirit that he imparts that I can be made more than a conqueror. And as I contemplate myself lying on my deathbed and going on to meet my Maker and my Judge, my only hope is that I shall be clothed with the righteousness of Jesus Christ and that he will take me by the hand and present me "faultless before the presence of his glory with exceeding joy" (Jude 24). It is always and only in Christ that I find satisfaction. It is only in him that my problems are solved. The world with all its methods cannot help me at the moment of my greatest need. But Christ never fails. He satisfies always and in every respect. The more I contemplate him, the more do I agree with Charles Wesley when he said:

> Thou, O Christ, art all I want;
> More than all in Thee I find! . . .

Just and holy is Thy Name,
I am all unrighteousness;
False and full of sin I am;
Thou art full of truth and grace.

He still remains the only hope of individual man, the only hope for the whole world. Is the gospel still relevant? Is its ancient message still adequate? The answer is that it alone is relevant. It alone can deal with and solve the problems of man.

5

PRACTICING THE SERMON ON THE MOUNT

(1950–1952)
Matthew 7:28–29

From *Studies in the Sermon on the Mount*

The series that Martyn Lloyd-Jones preached on the Sermon on the Mount in 1950–1952 was at a time when, as J. I. Packer has put it, he was on a "plateau of supreme excellence." The power of these sermons has resonated down the decades, and well over half a century after they were published in 1959 and 1960, they remain in print and widely read. Indeed of all his many series, it is this one that is perhaps the most well-known outside not just his main Reformed constituency but even beyond evangelicalism itself. Many ministers who have this on their shelves have never owned Ephesians or any other series published after his death in 1981.

Yet what is so fascinating about the chapter we have chosen here is that it completely demolishes the liberal view that you can have morality without the Bible, the Sermon on the Mount without the cross. Never has modernist theology looked so incomplete and woolly as he shows it up to be here.

We live in different times, but the kind of theological liberalism exposed here has not really gone away. Nor has the idea, even if it is no longer religiously based, that humanity can improve itself and turn a nasty world into a better one on its own. As is obvious from Scripture, we cannot by definition ever achieve the standards that the Sermon on the Mount sets for us. We are incapable of it. Christ's words, rather than being a blueprint, are in reality a condemnation, because we are all sinners. To obey all that he commands us would mean that we are perfect, which none of us can ever be.

Christ and his mission is thus at the heart of the message. He speaks with a unique authority. He is not the good teacher, a first-century Gandhi (my analogy, not the Doctor's). He is God come down to earth, the Savior, bringing salvation to people who cannot possibly save themselves.

This message is as unpopular today as it was in the 1950s. Since the members of the early church were thrown to lions, it has always been unpopular! Today is no different. Time and again professing believers try to adapt the message and tone it down. The self-satisfied liberalism of the Doctor's day aimed to have a faith emptied of anything spiritual. In our own day there are the attempts of some to get rid of the atonement while still earnestly professing to be Christians. The strategy might be altered, but the basic fallacy is identical. We are all sinners, and we can only be reconciled to God by the work of Christ upon the cross.

So may nonevangelicals continue to read Studies in the Sermon on the Mount! But may those of us who own that allegiance remember never to dilute the message. Christ-centered preaching is at the very heart of the gospel itself, as the chapter you are about to read will show you.

In the last two verses of the chapter [Matthew 7] we are told by the sacred writer what effect this famous Sermon on the Mount produced upon its auditors. They thus provide us at the same time with the opportunity of considering in general what effect this sermon should always produce upon those who read and consider it.

These two verses are by no means an idle or useless kind of epilogue. They are of great importance in any consideration of the sermon. I have no doubt that was the reason why the writer was led by the Holy Spirit to record the effect of the sermon, because we are directed here to the preacher rather than to the sermon. We are asked, as it were, having considered the sermon, to look at the One who delivered it and preached it. We have spent much time considering in detail the teaching of the sermon, and in the later chapters, especially, we have been considering the urgent appeal that our Lord addressed to those who had been listening. He besought them to put it into practice. He issued a terrible warning against self-deception, against merely admiring the sermon and commending certain things in it, and failing to realize that, unless we are indeed practicing it, we are outside the kingdom of God and shall find that all on which we have been resting will suddenly be taken from us on the day of judgment.

But the question many may be tempted to ask is, why should we practice this sermon? Why should we pay heed to this terrible warning? Why should we believe that unless we are indeed making our lives conform to this pattern, we shall be without hope as we come face-to-face with God? The answer to all that is the subject to which we are directed by these last two verses. It is the person himself, the person who uttered these sayings, the One who has delivered this teaching. In other words, as we consider the Sermon on the Mount as a whole, having gone into its various parts, we must realize that we must not concentrate only upon the beauty of the diction, the perfect structure of the sermon, the impressive pictures, the striking illustrations, and the extraordinary balance that we find in it, both from the standpoint of material and the way in which it is presented. Indeed, we can go further. When we consider the Sermon on the Mount, we are never to stop even with the moral, ethical, spiritual teaching; we are to go beyond all these things, wonderful though they are, and vital as they all are, to the person of the preacher himself.

There are two main reasons for saying that. The first is that, ultimately, the authority of the sermon derives from the preacher. That is, of course, what makes the New Testament such a unique book and gives uniqueness to the teaching of our Lord. With all other teachers that the world has ever known, the important thing is the teaching; but here is a case in which the teacher is more important even than what he taught. There is a sense in which you cannot divide and separate them from one another, but if we are to give priority to one, we must always put the preacher first. So these two verses coming at the end of the sermon direct our attention to that fact.

If any man asks, why should I pay heed to that sermon, why should I put it into practice, why should I believe that it is the most vital thing in this life? the answer is, because of the person who preached it. That is the authority, that is the sanction behind the sermon. In other words, if we are in any doubt as to the person who preached this sermon, that is obviously going to affect our view of it. If we are in doubt about his uniqueness, about his deity, about the fact that here was God in the flesh speaking, then our whole attitude toward the sermon is undermined. But, conversely, if we do believe that the man who spoke these words was none other than the only begotten

Son of God, then they have an awful solemnity and added authority, and we must take the teaching as a whole with all the seriousness that must ever be given to any pronouncement that comes from God himself. There, then, we have a very good reason for considering this matter. The ultimate sanction behind every expression in the sermon is to be found there. When we read it, therefore, and are tempted perhaps to argue against it or to explain certain things away, we must remember that we are considering the words of the Son of God. The authority and the sanction are derived from the speaker, from the blessed person himself.

But quite apart from such a general deduction, our Lord himself insists upon our paying attention to it. He calls attention to himself in the sermon. He repeats tests that are obviously designed to focus our attention upon himself. That is the point at which so much that passes for gospel differs from the real gospel. There is a tendency for some people to create a division between the teaching of the New Testament and the Lord himself. That is an essential error. He is always calling attention to himself, and we find that abundantly illustrated in the particular sermon. The ultimate trouble, therefore, with people who emphasize the teaching of the Sermon on the Mount at the expense of doctrine and at the expense of theology is that they never realize that point. We have often referred, in passing, to the case of those who say they like the Sermon on the Mount and who put the Sermon on the Mount over against the teaching about the atonement and the death of Christ and all the high doctrines of the epistles because, they say, the Sermon on the Mount is something practical, something that can be applied to life and become the basis of the social order and so on. The real trouble with such people is that they have never truly read the Sermon on the Mount, for if they had done so, they would have found that they were being directed continually to this person. And immediately that raises crucial doctrine. In other words, the Sermon on the Mount, as we have seen so many times, is really a kind of basic statement out of which everything else comes. It is full of doctrine, and the idea that it is moral, ethical teaching and nothing else is an idea that is quite foreign to the teaching of the sermon, and particularly to the point that is emphasized here in these last two verses.

We see, then, that our Lord calls attention to himself, and in a sense there is nothing in the sermon that is quite so remarkable as the way in which he does that. So, having looked at the whole sermon we find that all the instructions he gave become focused together in him. We look at him in a special way in the Sermon on the Mount, and any study of it should always lead us to that. Here in these two verses we have a very wonderful way of doing so. We are told about the reactions of these people who had the great and high privilege of looking at him and listening to the sermon. And we are told that their reaction was one of astonishment. "And it came to pass, when Jesus had ended these sayings, the people were astonished at his doctrine [or at his teaching]: for he taught them as one having authority, and not as the scribes."

Let us try to recapture this if we can, for there is nothing that we should enjoy—I use the term advisedly—as much as looking at him. There is no value in all other teaching if we are not right about him. Essentially the vital point of all teaching, of theology, and of the whole Bible is to bring us to a knowledge of him and into relationship with him. So we look at the blessed person, and we must try to picture this scene. Here is a great crowd of people. First of all, it was just our Lord and his disciples when he sat down to teach, but by the end it is obvious that there was a great crowd. Here, sitting before all these people on that mountain, is this young man, apparently just a carpenter from a little place called Nazareth in Galilee, an artisan, a common, ordinary person. He had had no training in the schools. He was not a Pharisee or a scribe. He had not been sitting at the feet of Gamaliel or any of the great authorities or teachers. Apparently he was just a very ordinary person who had lived a very ordinary life. But suddenly he bursts forth upon the countryside in an extraordinary ministry, and here he sits and begins to teach and to preach and to say the things we have been considering together. It is not surprising that these people were astonished. It was all so unexpected, so unusual in every way, so different from everything they had ever known. How difficult it is for us, because of our sheer familiarity with these facts and details, to realize that these things actually happened nearly two thousand years ago and to realize what the effect must have been upon our Lord's contemporaries. Try to imagine their utter astonishment and amazement as this carpenter from Galilee sits and teaches and expounds the law and speaks in this extraordinary manner. They were amazed and astonished and dumbfounded.

The thing for us to discover is exactly what caused the astonishment.

The first thing, clearly, is the general authority with which he spoke—this man who talked to them with authority and not like the scribes. That negative is interesting—his teaching was not after the manner of the scribes. The characteristic teaching of the scribes, you remember, was that they always quoted authorities and never uttered any original thoughts; they were experts not so much in the law itself as in various expositions and interpretations of the law that had been put forward since it was first given to Moses. Then, in turn, they were always quoting the experts on these interpretations. As an illustration of what this means, we have but to think of what so often happens in the law courts when a case is being heard. Various authorities are quoted; one authority has said this, and another authority has said that. Other textbooks are produced, and their expositions are given. That was the manner or practice of the scribes. They were always arguing, but the chief feature was the endless string of quotations. This still happens today. You can read or hear sermons that seem to be nothing but series of quotations from various writings. That kind of thing gives the impression of learning and culture. We are told that the scribes and Pharisees were very proud of their learning. They dismissed our Lord with derision and said, "How knoweth this man letters [learning], having never learned?" (John 7:15). That points to the fact that the outstanding characteristic of his method was the absence of endless quotations. In other words, the surprising thing about him was his originality. He keeps on saying, "I say unto you"; not "So-and-so has said," but "I say unto you." There is a freshness about his teaching. His whole method was different. His appearance was different. His whole attitude toward teaching was different. It was characterized by this originality of thought and of manner—the way in which he did it as well as what he did.

But, of course, the most astonishing thing of all was the confidence and certainty with which he spoke. That appeared at the very beginning, even as he was uttering those great Beatitudes. He begins by saying, "Blessed are the poor in spirit" and then, "for theirs is the kingdom of heaven" (Matt. 5:3). There is no doubt about it and no question; this is no mere supposition or possibility only. This extraordinary assurance and authority with which he spoke was something that was manifested from the very beginning.

I imagine, however, that what really astonished these people over and above his general authority was what he said, and in particular what he said about himself. That, most surely, must have amazed and astonished them. Think again of the things he said, first of all about his own teaching. He keeps on making remarks that call attention to his teaching and to his own attitude toward it. Take, for instance, the frequency with which in the fifth chapter he said something like this: "Ye have heard that it was said by them of old time . . . but I say unto you" (Matt. 5:27–28). He does not hesitate to correct the teaching of the Pharisees and their authorities. "Them of old time" stood for certain Pharisees and their exposition of the Mosaic law. He did not hesitate to put that aside and to correct it. This artisan, this carpenter who had never been to the schools, says, "I say unto you." He claims that authority for himself and for his teaching.

Indeed, he does not hesitate to assert in that phrase that he, and he alone, is able to give a spiritual interpretation of the law that was given through Moses. His whole argument is that the people had never seen the spiritual intent or content of the law given by Moses; they were misinterpreting it and reducing it to the physical level. As long as they did not actually commit physical adultery, they thought it did not matter. They did not see that God was concerned about the heart, the desire, the spirit. So he stands before them as the only true interpreter of the law. He says that his interpretation alone brings out the spiritual intent of the law; indeed, he does not hesitate to speak of himself and to regard himself as the Lawgiver: "I say unto you."

Then you remember how at the end of the sermon he puts this in a still more explicit manner. "Therefore," he says, "whosoever heareth these sayings of mine, and doeth them . . ." You notice the significance he attaches to his own sayings. As he says that, he is saying something about himself. He is using this terrifying picture of the two houses. He has already spoken about judgment, and he puts it all in terms of "these sayings of mine." He says in effect, "I want you to listen to these, and I want you to practice them—'these sayings of mine.' Do you realize who I am and the importance, therefore, of what I say?" Thus we find that in what he said about his teaching he is making a tremendous pronouncement about himself. He claims unique authority.

But we are not left simply with interferences and implications; his references to himself are not only indirect. Have you ever contemplated the direct references that he makes to himself in the Sermon on the Mount? Let us take them in the order in which they appear. First, in 5:11, when he has just finished the Beatitudes, he goes on to say, "Blessed are ye, when men shall revile you, and persecute you, and shall say all manner of evil against you falsely, for my sake." What an astonishing and amazing thing that is. He does not say, "Blessed are you when men shall revile and persecute you for the teaching's sake," or "Blessed are you people if, in your desire to implement this high and exalted teaching, you suffer persecution and perhaps death itself." He does not say, "If you suffer like this for the name of God your Father in heaven, you are blessed." Rather he says, "for my sake." What unutterable folly it is for people to say that they are interested in the Sermon on the Mount as ethical and moral and social teaching only. Here, before he comes to "turning the other cheek" and the other things they like so much, he tells us that we ought to be ready to suffer for his sake, and that we are to endure persecution for his sake, and that we may even have to be ready to die for his sake. This tremendous claim comes at the very beginning of the sermon.

Then he goes on to do the same thing by implication immediately afterward. "Ye are the salt of the earth," and "ye are the light of the world." Do you see the implication of that? He says in effect, "You people who are my disciples and my followers, you who have given yourselves to me even to the extent of enduring persecution for my name's sake, and if necessary death for my sake, you who are listening to me and are going to repeat my teaching and propagate it throughout the world, you are the salt of the earth and the light of the world." There is only one real deduction to draw from that: they are going to be a very special and unique people who, because of their relationship to him, become the salt of the earth and the light of the world. It is the whole doctrine of rebirth. They are not just people who listen to teaching and then repeat it and so have the effect of salt and light. They themselves are going to become salt and light. We have here the doctrine of the mystical relationship to and the union of his people with him, he dwelling in them and imparting his nature to them. Therefore, they in turn become the light of the world as he is the light of the world. So it is again a tremendous statement about him. He is here asserting his unique deity and his Saviorhood. He is asserting that he is the long-expected Messiah.

So as we look at these two striking statements before we come to his detailed teaching, we are driven to ask, as these people must have asked, who is this person who talks like this? Who is this man, this carpenter from Nazareth, who asks us to be ready to suffer for him and tells us we will be blessed indeed of God if we do, who says, "Rejoice, and be exceeding glad: for great is your reward in heaven" if you suffer injustice and persecution "for my sake" (Matt. 5:12)? Who is this? And who is this who says he can make us the salt of the earth and the light of the world? He gives the answer to the question in 5:17, where he says: "Think not that I am come to destroy the law, or the prophets: I am not come to destroy, but to fulfil." Look for a moment at this extraordinary expression, "I am come." He speaks of himself and of his life in this world as being different from that of anybody else. He does not say, "I have been born, therefore this or that." He says: "I am come." Where has he come from? He is one who has arrived in this world; he has not only been born, he has come into it from somewhere. He has come from eternity, from heaven, from the bosom of the Father. The Law and the Prophets had said that he was to come. They said, for instance, "The Sun of righteousness [shall] arise with healing in his wings" (Mal. 4:2). They were always talking of someone who was to come from the outside. And here he says of himself, "I am come." It is not surprising that these people as they sat and listened said, "What does he mean, and who is this man, this carpenter who looks like ourselves?"

He is always saying, "I am come." He is telling them that he does not belong to this realm but that he has come into this life and into this world from glory, from eternity. He is saying, "I and the Father are one." He is referring to the Incarnation. What tragic folly to regard this sermon as just a social manifesto and to see nothing but ethics and morality in it. Listen to what he says about himself: "I am come." This is no human teacher; this is the Son of God.

But furthermore he says that he has come to fulfill and not to destroy the Law and the Prophets, which means that he has come to fulfill and to keep God's holy law, and also that he is the Messiah. He is claiming here that he is sinless, absolutely perfect. God gave his law to Moses, but not a single human being has ever kept it—it was given so "all the world may become guilty before God" (Rom. 3:19). "There is none righteous, no, not one" (Rom. 3:10). All the saints of the Old Testament had broken the law; none had succeeded in observing it. Yet here is One who stands and says, "I am going to keep it; not one jot or one tittle of this Law will I break; I am going to fulfill it, I am going to keep and honor it perfectly." Here is one who claims to be sinless, to be absolutely perfect. Not only that, he does not hesitate to claim for himself what Paul puts in the words, "Christ is the end of the law for righteousness to every one that believeth" (Rom. 10:4). In other words, he fulfills the Law by carrying it out; he honors it by absolute perfection in his own life. Yes, but he bears the punishment it metes out upon transgressors also. He has satisfied every demand of the law of God. He has fulfilled the law for himself and others.

But he claims that he is fulfilling the prophets also. He claims that he is the One to whom all the Old Testament prophets pointed. They had been talking about the Messiah; he says, "I am this Messiah." He is the One who fulfills in his own person all the promises. Again the apostle Paul sums it up by putting it like this: "For all the promises of God in him are yea, and in him Amen" (2 Cor. 1:20). God's promises are all fulfilled in this wonderful person who here says of himself that he is the fulfiller of the Law and the Prophets. Everything in the Old Testament points to him; he is the center of it all. This is the coming One, the One expected. He says all that in the Sermon on the Mount, this sermon that we are told has no doctrine, and that people like because it is not theological! Can there be a more tragic blindness than that which causes men to speak in such a foolish manner? The whole doctrine of the incarnation of Christ, his person and his death, is all here. We have seen it as we have gone through the sermon, and we are looking at it again now.

Another great statement pointing in the same direction is the one we found in 7:21: "Not every one that saith unto me, Lord, Lord, shall enter into the kingdom of heaven." He does not hesitate to say that people will address him as Lord, and that means that he is Jehovah, that he is God. He says here quite calmly that people are going to say to him, "Lord, Lord." They are saying it now, in a sense, and on that great day they will say "Lord, Lord" to him. But the emphasis is upon the fact that they will say that to "me"—not to the Father who is in heaven, but to "me," the one speaking there on the mountain. He does not hesitate to ascribe to himself and to take to himself the highest term used in the whole realm of Scripture for the eternal, absolute, blessed God.

He even went a step further and announced at the end of the Sermon that he is to be the Judge of the world. "Many will say to me in that day,

Lord, Lord," etc. Notice the repetition. "And then will I profess unto them, I never knew you: depart from me, ye that work iniquity" (Matt. 7:22–23). Yes, the judgment is being committed to the Son. He is claiming that he is to be the Judge of all men and that what matters is our relationship to him, his knowledge of us, his concern about us, and his interest in us. As someone once put it very well: "The One who sat there on the Mount to teach is the One who at the end will sit on the throne of his glory, and all the nations of the world shall appear before him, and he will pronounce the judgment upon them." Was ever anything more astounding, more astonishing, uttered in this world? Try again to capture the scene. Look at this apparently ordinary person, this carpenter, sitting there and saying in effect, "As I am sitting here now I shall sit on the throne of eternal glory, and the whole world and the nations and all the people will appear before me, and I will pronounce judgment." He is indeed the Eternal Judge.

Thus we have gathered together the main statements he makes about himself in this famous Sermon on the Mount. As we leave it, therefore, I ask you this simple yet profound question: what is your reaction to it all? We are told that these people "were astonished at his doctrine: for he taught them as one having authority, and not as the scribes" (Matt. 7:28–29). We are not told that their reaction went any further than that, but we are told that they were astonished and amazed because of his manner, because of the very form of his teaching, and because of the astounding teaching itself, and especially some of these things that he said about himself. There are many people who are not even astonished by this sermon. God forbid that that should be true of any of us. But it is not enough that we should be merely astonished; our reaction must go beyond astonishment. Surely our reaction as he speaks to us should be to recognize that this is none other than the Son of God himself who has been speaking to us in the words we have considered, the very incarnate Son of God. Our first reaction should be that we recognize again the central truth of the gospel, that God's only begotten Son has entered into this world of time. We are not concerned here with a mere philosophy or outlook upon life but with the fact that the preacher was the Son of God Almighty here in the flesh.

Why did he come, why did he preach this sermon? He has not just come to give another law. He was not merely telling people how to live, because the Sermon on the Mount (we say it with reverence) is infinitely more impossible to practice than even the law of Moses, and we have already seen that there had not been a single human being who had been able to keep that. What then is the message? It must be this. In this sermon our Lord condemns once and for all trust in human endeavor and natural ability in the matter of salvation. He is telling us, in other words, that we have come short of the glory of God and that however great our efforts and striving from now until our death, they will never make us righteous or fit us to stand in the presence of God. He says that the Pharisees have been reducing the real meaning of the law, but that the law itself is spiritual. He is saying what Paul came to see and to say later: "I was alive without [apart from] the law once: but when the commandment came, sin revived, and I died" (Rom. 7:9). In other words, he is saying that we are all condemned sinners in the sight of God and that we cannot save ourselves.

Then Jesus goes on to say that we all need a new birth, a new nature, and a new life. We cannot live a life like this as we are by nature; we must be made anew. And what he is saying in this sermon is that he has come in order to give us this new life. Yes, in relationship to him we become the salt of the earth and the light of the world. He has come not merely to outline the teaching. He has come to make it possible. In this sermon, beginning with the Beatitudes, he has given an account of his people. He has stated what they will be like in general and has given a more detailed account of how they will act. The sermon is a description of Christian people, people who have received the Holy Spirit; not of natural man striving to make himself right with God, but of God making his people anew. He has given us the gift of the Holy Spirit, the promise made to Abraham, "the promise of the Father," and having received this promise, we become people conformable to this pattern. The Beatitudes are true of all who are living the Sermon on the Mount, of all who are Christians. That does not mean that we are sinless or perfect; it means that if we look at the general tenor of our life it corresponds to this, or as John puts it in his first epistle, "Whosoever is born of God doth not commit sin" (3:9). There is this difference. Look at a man's life in general. As you look at the believer he conforms to the Sermon on the Mount. He wants to live it, and he does his utmost to do so. He realizes his failure but prays to be filled with the Spirit; he hungers and thirsts after righteousness, and he has the blessed experience of the promises being realized in his daily life.

This is the true reaction to the Sermon on the Mount. We realize that this was none other than the Son of God and that in the sermon he has been saying that he has come to start a new humanity. He is "the firstborn among many brethren"; he is "the last Adam"; he is God's new man, and all who belong to him are going to be like him. It is astounding doctrine, it is astonishing, amazing doctrine, but thank God, we know it is the truth. We know that he died for our sins, that our sins are forgiven. "We know that we have passed from death unto life, because we love the brethren" (1 John 3:14). We know that we belong to him, because we do indeed hunger and thirst after righteousness. We are conscious of the fact that he is dealing with us, that his Spirit is working within us, revealing to us our shortcomings and imperfections, creating longings and aspirations within us, working "to will and to do of his good pleasure" (Phil. 2:13). Above all, in the midst of life, with all its trials and problems and tests, indeed amidst all the uncertainties of life in this atomic age and the certain fact of death and the final judgment, we can say with the apostle Paul, "For the which cause I also suffer these things: nevertheless I am not ashamed: for I know whom I have believed, and am persuaded that he is able to keep that which I have committed unto him against that day" (2 Tim. 1:12).

> In every high and stormy gale
> My anchor holds within the veil. . . .
> When all around my soul gives way,
> He then is all my hope and stay.
> On Christ, the solid Rock, I stand;
> All other ground is sinking sand.
> All other ground is sinking sand.
>
> EDWARD MOTE, "THE SOLID ROCK"

"For other foundation can no man lay than that is laid, which is Jesus Christ" (1 Cor. 3:11). "Nevertheless the foundation of God standeth sure, having this seal, The Lord knoweth them that are his. And, let every one that nameth the name of Christ depart from iniquity" (2 Tim. 2:19).

6

MIND, HEART, AND WILL

(1963)
Romans 6:17

From *Spiritual Depression*

Few books can ever have been said to originate in the bathroom! Yet this is precisely the case with one of Dr. Lloyd-Jones's most well-known books, Spiritual Depression: Its Causes and Cure. *As he told his biographer Iain Murray, the idea came to him one morning while shaving as the words of Psalm 42, "Why art thou cast down, O my soul?" came to him and convinced him that there was a major pastoral need for his congregation to hear a series of sermons on the vital issue of spiritual unhappiness.*

It is ironic that a man who so disliked paperbacks saw this book, in paperback form, become such a major international bestseller, a work that has been in print more than fifty years since he first preached these sermons at Westminster Chapel in 1963. Much of this is due not just to the subject matter but to the passionate advocacy of George Verwer, the founder of Operation Mobilization. For over four decades he has told audiences around the world that Spiritual Depression *is "the greatest Christian book of all time."*

This sermon series is especially interesting for two reasons:

a) It uses the fact that Lloyd-Jones was a medical doctor as well as a preacher.
b) It was based on passages from different parts of the Bible rather than being a straight exposition of a single book of the Bible, which was his invariable preference.

As is obvious from the title of the chapter, he believed that Christian faith and practice involved both the heart and the mind, and thus also the will. This should be obvious, yet this total biblical picture is so seldom seen in contemporary Christianity. Arid intellectual preaching appeals to the mind only, and exploitative or therapeutic preachers reach out solely to the heart. The Bible involves both the heart and the mind, and this makes the crucial difference to our wills as we go through the ups and downs of everyday life.

Martyn Lloyd-Jones once described preaching as logic on fire, and how perfectly we see this in the chapter that follows. As he concludes, "May God make us balanced Christians." How much we need to hear that today, and how relevant it remains to a Christianity in which we still so easily divide that which God has united.

But God be thanked, that ye were the servants of sin, but ye have obeyed from the heart that form of doctrine which was delivered you. (Rom. 6:17)

That is the statement as it is to be found in the Authorized Version. In the Revised Version you will find that instead of "form of doctrine" you have "standard of teaching." But obviously, as we shall see, that means the same thing, and I call your attention to this verse because I want, by means of it, to continue our consideration of the cause and cure of spiritual depression.

As we do so, we must be impressed by the fact that the forms that this particular condition may take seem to be almost endless. It comes in such different forms and guises that some people stumble at that very fact. They are amazed that there can be so many symptoms or manifestations of this one disease, this spiritual condition; and, of course, their ignorance of the problem in and of itself may lead to the very condition we are considering. The kind of person who thinks that once you believe on the Lord Jesus Christ all your problems are left behind and that the rest of the story will be "they all lived happily ever after" is certain sooner or later to suffer from this spiritual depression. We are brought into this marvelous life, this spiritual condition by the grace of God. But we must never forget that over and against us is another power. We are citizens of the kingdom of God, but the Bible tells us that we are opposed by another kingdom, which is also a spiritual kingdom, and that all along we are being attacked and besieged. We are in "the good fight of faith," and "we wrestle not against flesh and blood, but against principalities, against powers, against the rulers of the darkness of this world, against spiritual wickedness in high places." And since that is so, we must be prepared for the occurrence of this condition that we are considering, and we must be prepared for its manifestation in all types of people and in all kinds of ways.

There is nothing that so characterizes all the activities of Satan as his subtlety. He is not only able and powerful, he is subtle; indeed the apostle Paul tells us that he can transform himself into "an angel of light" if necessary. The one thing he desires to do is to ruin and destroy the work of God, and there is no work of God that he is more anxious to destroy than the work of grace in and through our Lord and Savior, Jesus Christ. Therefore, from the moment we become Christians we become the special object of Satan's attention. That is why James says: "My brethren, count it all joy when ye fall into divers temptations" (James 1:2). We are to rejoice because it is a proof of our faith. The moment we become Christians the devil is particularly concerned to get us down, and he has no more successful way of doing that than to make us miserable or to make us suffer from what Charles Lamb has described as "the mumps and measles of the soul." Such Christians are like severely undernourished children, not growing, not manifesting health and vigor, and any Christian in that condition is more or less a denial of his own faith, and Satan is pleased. For that reason he is particularly concerned to produce this condition in us, and there is no end to the ways in which it may affect us and in which it may show itself in us—we must expect the manifestations of the condition to be protean.

I call your attention now to another general cause of this condition. It is the one that is described in the verse that we are looking at. Now this verse is a positive description of the Christian, but we can use it in a negative way. The absence of conformity to the description that we have in the verse is one of the common causes of all spiritual depression. Here we have an absolute description of the Christian. Paul says in essence: "You were the servants of Satan; you were under the dominion of Satan. That is where you were, but you are no longer there." He thanks God that he can say this about them, that though they were once in that position, now, he says, they are no longer there. Why not? For this reason: "ye have obeyed from the heart that form of doctrine which was delivered you," or "unto which you were delivered." That is the apostle's description of a Christian.

You notice that the point he is concerned to emphasize is the wholeness of the Christian life, the balance of the Christian life. It is a life in which one has "obeyed"—there is the will—"from the heart"—there is the emotion, the sensibility—"that form of doctrine" that came to the mind and to the understanding. So in describing the Christian the thing he is emphasizing is that there is a wholeness about his life. The whole man is involved—the mind, the heart, and the will, and a common cause of spiritual depression is the failure to realize that the Christian life is a whole life, a balanced life. Lack of balance is one of the most fruitful causes of trouble and discord and disquietude in the life of the Christian man.

Once more I have to indicate that the cause of this lack of balance can be laid, I fear too often, to the charge of the preacher or the evangelist. Lopsided Christians are generally produced by preachers or evangelists whose doctrine lacks balance or rotundity or wholeness. More and more as we proceed with our studies we shall see how vitally important are the circumstances of the birth of the Christian. I sometimes think that some-one should take this up as a matter of research and should investigate the relationship between the subsequent course of Christians and the particular means or methods employed in their conversion. It would, I am sure, be both significant and interesting. Children generally partake of the charac-teristics of their parents, and converts tend to take on certain characteristics of the ones who were used of God in their conversion. But not only that, the type and kind of meeting in which people come into the light, indeed all circumstances of the new birth, tend to influence the subsequent history of these converts more than we often realize. We noticed it in a previous chapter, and it is certainly very important with respect to the matter that we are considering now. It is this that explains the existence of different types of Christians showing certain characteristics. All the members of any one group are very much alike and have a certain stamp upon them, while oth-ers are different. Now the extent to which this is true, the extent to which we have these peculiar characteristics associated with a particular type of ministry, is the extent to which we are likely to be the victims of this lack of balance that ultimately will manifest itself in unhappiness and in misery.

The apostle Paul takes this up because it always raises a practical prob-lem. He was writing to the Christians at Rome. We cannot be sure whether he imagined this position in order to refute it or whether it did actually obtain in Rome. It may be that there were people who were actually saying, "Shall we continue in sin, that grace may abound?" or it may be the case that the apostle, having established his doctrine of justification by faith only, suddenly says to himself, "Now there is a danger in leaving it like that: some people may say: 'Very well, shall we continue in sin, that grace may abound?'" for he has been saying that "where sin abounded, grace did much more abound." There were people in the early church that did argue like that, and there are still many who tend to do the same thing. Their attitude is: "Very well, in the light of that doctrine it does not matter what a man does, the more he sins, the more God will be glorified in forgiving him. Since I'm a Christian, it doesn't matter what I do—I will be covered by grace." What does the apostle say to that? His answer is that you can only say a thing like that if you do not understand the teaching. If you understood the teaching, you would never draw deductions like that; it would be impossible. He answers at once in summary: "God forbid. You who are dead to sin (that is what I have been preaching) can no longer live therein." The Christian is now "in Christ"; therefore he has not only died with him but has also risen with him. Only a man who has never really grasped the teaching can ask such terrible questions as "shall we continue in sin, that grace may abound?" The apostle's whole object in this chapter is to show the importance of grasping the balance of truth, the importance of taking hold of the whole gospel and of seeing that if one but grasps it truly, it leads inevitably to certain consequences.

Let me try to divide up the subject briefly. There are certain principles enunciated here. The first is that spiritual depression or unhappiness in the Christian life is very often due to our failure to realize the greatness of the gospel. The apostle talks about "that form of doctrine which was delivered you," the standard of teaching. Now people are often unhappy in the Christian life because they have thought of Christianity and the whole message of the gospel in inadequate terms. Some think that it is merely a message of forgiveness. You ask them to tell you what Christianity is, and they reply, "If you believe in the Lord Jesus Christ your sins are forgiven," and they stop at that. That is all. They are unhappy about certain things in their past, and they hear that God in Christ will forgive them. They take their forgiveness, and there they stop—that is all their Christianity. There are others who conceive of it as morality only. Their view of themselves is that they do not need forgiveness, but they desire an exalted way of life. They want to do good in this world, and Christianity to them is an ethical, moral program.

Such people are bound to be unhappy. Certain problems will inevitably arise in their lives that are strictly outside morality—someone's death, some personal relationship. Morality and ethics will not help at that point, and what they regard as the gospel is useless to them in that situation. They are unhappy when the blow comes because they have never had an adequate view of the gospel. It has been but a partial view; they have simply seen one aspect. There are others who are interested in it simply as something good and beautiful. It makes a great aesthetic appeal to them. That is their way of describing the gospel, and the entire message is to them just something very beautiful and wonderful that makes them feel better when they hear it.

I am putting all these incomplete and partial views over against what the apostle here refers to as "that form of doctrine," "the standard of teaching," the great truth upon which he elaborates in this epistle to the Romans with its mighty arguments and propositions and its flights of spiritual imagination. That is the gospel, all the (if I may borrow a phrase from Thomas Carlyle) "infinities and immensities" of this epistle, and of the epistles to the Ephesians and to the Colossians. We must have an accurate view of these things. But someone may say, "When you talk about the epistle to the Ephesians or the epistle to the Colossians, surely you are not talking about 'the gospel message.' In the gospel message you just tell people about forgiveness of sins." In a sense that is right, but in another sense it is wrong. I received a letter from a man who had been here on a Sunday night, and he said that he made a discovery. The discovery he had made was that in a service that was obviously evangelistic there was something for believers. He said, "I had never understood that could happen. I never knew that it was possible that in one and the same service an evangelistic message could be preached to unbelievers and yet there could also be a message for believers that would disturb them." Now that man was making a great confession. He was telling me what his view had been hitherto of the evangel. It was a partial, incomplete view, just selecting one or two things. The way to evangelize is to give "all the counsel of God." But people say they were too busy or they cannot follow all that. I would remind you that the apostle Paul preached that sort of thing to slaves. "Not many mighty, not many noble, are called" (1 Cor. 1:26). That is what he gave them—this tremendous presentation of truth.

The gospel is not something partial or piecemeal; it takes in the whole life, the whole of history, the whole world. It tells us about the creation and the final judgment and everything in between. It is a complete, whole view of life, and many are unhappy in the Christian life because they have never realized that this way of life caters to the whole of man's life and covers every eventuality in his experience. There is no aspect of life but that the gospel has something to say about it. The whole of life must come under its influence because it is all-inclusive; the gospel is meant to control and govern everything in our lives. If we do not realize that, we are certain sooner or later to find ourselves in an unhappy condition. So many, because they indulge in these harmful and unscriptural dichotomies and only apply their Christianity to certain aspects of their lives, are bound to be in trouble. It is quite inevitable. That is the first thing we see here. We must realize the greatness of the gospel, its vast eternal span. We must dwell more on the riches, and in the riches, of these great doctrinal absolutes. We must not always stay in the gospel. We start there, but we must go on; and then as we see it all worked out and put into its great context, we shall realize what a mighty thing the gospel is and how the whole of our life is meant to be governed by it.

That brings us to the second point, which is that in the same way as we often fail to realize the greatness and the wholeness of the message, we also fail to realize that the whole man must likewise be involved in it and by it—"Ye have obeyed from the heart that form of doctrine which was delivered you." Man is a wonderful creature; he is mind, he is heart, and he is will. Those are the three main constituents of man. God has given him a mind, he has given him a heart, and he has given him a will whereby he can act. Now one of the greatest glories of the gospel is that it takes up the whole man. Indeed, I go so far as to assert that there is nothing else that does that; it is only this complete gospel, this complete view of life and death and eternity, that is big enough to include the whole man. It is because we fail to realize this that many of our troubles arise. We are partial in our response to this great gospel.

Let me suggest some details in order to substantiate my point. There are some people in whose case the head only seems to be in use—the intellect, the understanding. They tell us that they are tremendously interested in the gospel as a point of view, as a Christian philosophy. These are the people who are always talking about the Christian outlook or, to use present-day jargon, Christian insights. It is something purely philosophical, something entirely intellectual. I think you will agree that there are large numbers of people in that position at the present time. Christianity is to them a matter of tremendous interest, and they believe and proclaim that if only this Christian point of view could be applied in politics, in industry, and in every other circle all our troubles would be solved. It is entirely the intellectual attitude and point of view.

There are others, not so many today perhaps as there used to be, whose sole interest in the gospel is their interest in theology and doctrine and metaphysics and in great problems, arguments, and discussions. I speak of past days, days that are gone. I do not want to defend them, but they were infinitely preferable to the present position. There were people then whose only interest in the gospel was their interest in theological problems, and they argued about them and discussed them. Their minds were very much engaged; this was their intellectual hobby and interest. But the tragedy was that it stopped at that interest, and their hearts had never been touched. Not only was there an absence of the grace of the Lord Jesus Christ in their lives, but there was often an absence of the ordinary milk of human kindness. Those men would argue and almost fight about particular doctrines, but they were often hard men to approach. You would never go to them if you were in trouble; you felt that they would neither understand nor sympathize. Still worse, the truth they were so interested in was not at all applied in their lives; it was something confined to their studies. It did not touch their conduct or behavior at all but was confined entirely to the mind. Obviously they were bound, sooner or later, to get into difficulty and to become unhappy. Have you ever seen a man like that facing the end of his life? Have you seen him when he can no longer read or when he is on his deathbed? I have seen one or two, and I do not want to see another. It is a terrible thing when a man reaches the point when he knows that he must die, and the gospel that he has argued about and reasoned about and even defended does not seem to help him because it has never gripped him. It was just an intellectual hobby.

But there are others in whose case the gospel seems to affect the heart only. This is more common today. These are the people who feel that they have had an emotional release; they have passed through an emotional crisis. I do not want to disparage this, but there is a real danger in having a purely emotional experience only. These are people who may have some problem in their lives. They may have committed some particular sin. They have tried to forget it, but they cannot get away from it. At last they hear a message that seems to give them deliverance from that one thing, and they accept it, and all is well. But they stop at that. They wanted this particular release, and they have had it. That can be obtained from an incomplete presentation of the gospel, and it leads to a partial and incomplete experience. Such people, because they desire that primarily, have had an emotional experience and nothing else.

Or it may be that they were naturally interested in mysticism and mystical phenomena. Some people are born natural mystics; there is something rather otherworldly about them, and they are interested in the mystical. There is great interest in this at the present time, in psychic phenomena, in extrasensory experience. There have always been people who have been interested in that kind of thing. They are natural mystics, and they are drawn to something that seems to be offering a mystical experience. They come to the Scriptures because they feel that in them they are going to find satisfaction for this longing and desire for mystical experience. They seek for that, and they get that. And they get nothing else.

Or it may be that certain people are in this position simply because they are moved aesthetically by the presentation of the gospel, by the atmosphere of the church, the painted windows, the monuments, the ritual, the hymns sung, the music, the sermon—any one or all of these things. Life has been hard and cruel to them, and they have been embittered by circumstances. But they go to a particular service, and somehow they find themselves comforted and soothed, and they feel happy and contented. That is all they wanted. They have it, and they want nothing more. They feel happy, and away they go. But as certainly as they do so they will find themselves in a predicament and in a position where that will not help them. One day they will have to face some crisis and to see it through. But they have never learned to think things through; they have been content to live on their feelings.

Others again are in this one-sided position because they have responded to an appeal in a meeting. I remember a number of ministers telling me of how they worked in the inquiry room of a famous evangelist who once visited this country and who is now an old man and retired from the ministry. They would ask the people who came to the inquiry room why they had come. Very often they got the reply that the person did not know. "But," they said, "you have come to the inquiry room. Why did you do so?" And the reply was, "I have come because the preacher told us to come." That preacher had a marvelous and exceptional gift for telling a story. He could dramatize, and he often ended his address with a moving story. Then he appealed to people to come forward, and almost in a kind of trance they walked down the aisle and went to the inquiry room, though they did not know why. They had been moved, they had been fascinated, but there seemed to be no conception of truth; there was no relationship at all to "that form of doctrine which was delivered." Moved emotionally but by nothing else, they had arrived in the inquiry room. Now it is quite inevitable that such people should at some time or other find themselves in trouble. They will be unhappy and miserable; they will get depressed. These are people who have something in the heart, but their head is not engaged at all, and oftentimes, unfortunately, neither is the will. They are content to go on enjoying themselves emotionally and to experience feelings and are not at all concerned about the application of truth to the mind and to the will.

Then, finally, you have the same thing in those whose will alone is involved. It is possible, and it has happened unfortunately, for people to be persuaded to take up Christianity. They say they believe that it is a good life, and they solemnly decide to take it up. I think we should abolish the word *decision* in this context. I do not like it. It seems to me that to talk about deciding for Christ is a denial of the text that we are considering, as I will show you. Making a decision has often happened as the result of an appeal. If a great bombardment is made upon the wills of men, there are certain wills that are sure to respond. They will decide because they have been called upon to decide, because they have been pressed to decide. Pressure has been put on the will. They have been told that they must decide, and they do decide, but they do not always know why they do so. And later on they will begin to ask questions; the devil will see to it that questions are raised in their minds. And they will find that they do not have an answer.

Let me sum up this point by putting it like this: these are the people who decide to take up Christianity instead of being taken up by Christianity. They have never known this feeling of constraint, this feeling of "I can do no other, so help me, God," that everything else has to be excluded, that the truth has so come to them that they must accept it. That is what Paul is saying in this chapter. He says in essence, "What are you talking about? Do you not realize what the truth is? How can you say, 'Shall we continue in sin, that grace may abound?' That means you do not know what grace is." It is only people who have understood the truth who desire to do it. The tragedy of the others is that they have never seen it.

That, then, is the cause of the condition. But let me emphasize, sometimes, as I have been showing, you will find people who have one part of their personality engaged only—head only, heart only, will only. We will agree that they must be wrong. Yes, but let us be clear about this, it is equally wrong to have any two only. It is equally wrong to have the head and the heart only without the will, or the head and the will without the heart, or the heart and the will without the head. That is the thing I think the apostle is impressing upon us. The Christian position is threefold; it is the three together, and the three at the same time, and the three always. A great gospel like this takes up the whole man, and if the whole man is not taken up, think again as to where you stand. "Ye have obeyed from the heart that form of doctrine which was delivered you." What a gospel! What a glorious message! It can satisfy man's mind completely, it can move his heart entirely, and it can lead to wholehearted obedience in the realm of the will. That is the gospel. Christ has died that we might be complete men, not merely that parts of us may be saved—not that we might be lopsided Christians but that there may be a balanced finality about us.

But not only that, if we lack this proportion we shall be in trouble later on because man has been made by God in this balanced way. Have you ever thought of that? It is an interesting matter in psychology to notice how God has put these three powers within us—the mind, the heart, and the will. And what tremendous powers they are. You would have thought that it would be impossible for the three to coexist in one person, but God made man perfect. You see it all perfectly in the Lord Jesus Christ, and the object of salvation is to bring us to that perfection, to be so conformed to his image that the effects and traces of sin will be removed and destroyed.

Let me say a final word about this balance. These things must always come in the right order. There is a definite order about this verse, and the order is obviously this: these people were servants held by sin, but they are

no longer. Why not? The apostle says the form of doctrine came to them—
"ye have obeyed from the heart that form of doctrine which was delivered
you." They had been in slavery. What brought them out? The truth has been
presented to them! They were not simply moved emotionally in the realm
of the heart; it was not merely an appeal to the will. No, the truth was presented. We must always put these things in the right order, and it is truth
first. It is doctrine first, it is the standard of teaching first, it is the message
of the gospel first. We are not concerned simply to attract people emotionally or in the realm of the will; we are concerned to "preach the word." The
apostles were not sent out simply to produce results and to change people.
They were sent to preach the gospel, to preach the truth, to preach and declare Jesus and the resurrection—this message, this form of doctrine, the
deposit! Those are the terms used in the New Testament, and the church is
certain to produce spiritual monstrosities when she fails to put that first.

The Christian should know why he is a Christian. The Christian is not
a man who simply says that something marvelous has happened to him.
Not at all; he is able and ready to give "a reason of the hope that is in
[him]" (1 Pet. 3:15). If he cannot, he had better make sure of his position.
The Christian knows why he is what he is and where he stands. He has had
doctrine presented to him; he has received the truth. This "form of doctrine
[sound teaching]" has come to him. It came to his mind, and it must ever
start with his mind. Truth comes to the mind and to the understanding en-
lightened by the Holy Spirit. Then having seen the truth, the Christian loves
it. It moves his heart. He sees what he was, he sees the life he was living,
and he hates it. If you see the truth about yourself as a slave of sin, you will
hate yourself. Then as you see the glorious truth about the love of Christ
you will want it, you will desire it. So the heart is engaged. Truly to see the
truth means that you are moved by it and that you love it. You cannot help
it. If you see truth clearly, you must feel it. Then that in turn leads to this:
your greatest desire will be to practice it and to live it.

That is Paul's whole argument. He says in summary: "Your talk about
continuing in sin is unthinkable. If you only realized your unity with Christ,
that you have been planted together in the likeness of his death and have
therefore risen with him, you could never speak like that. You cannot be
joined to Christ and be one with him and at the same time ask, 'shall we
continue in sin?'" Does this great truth give us license to go on doing those

things that formerly appealed to us? Of course not. It is inconceivable. A man who knows and believes that he is risen with Christ will inevitably desire to walk in newness of life with him.

So Paul puts forth his mighty argument and demonstration, and from this I draw my final conclusion: in this realm we must always realize, when we talk to others, that the heart is never to be approached directly. I go further: the will is never to be approached directly either. This is a most important principle to bear in mind both in personal dealings and in preaching. The heart is always to be influenced through the understanding—the mind, then the heart, then the will. We have no right to make a direct attack upon the heart either in ourselves or in anybody else. I have known evil-living men who found false comfort, to their own damnation, in the fact that they could still weep and be moved emotionally in a religious meeting. "I cannot be all bad or else I would not respond like this," they have argued. But it is a false deduction—their emotional response was produced by themselves. Had it been a response to truth their lives would have been changed. We must never approach the heart or the will directly. Truth is received through God's greatest gift to man—the mind, the understanding. God made man in his own image, and there is no question but that the greatest part of this image is the mind with its capacity for apprehending truth. God has endowed us with that, and God sends truth to us in that way.

But God forbid that anyone should think that it ends with the intellect. It starts there, but it goes on. It then moves the heart, and finally the man yields his will. He obeys, not grudgingly or unwillingly, but with the whole heart. The Christian life is a glorious perfect life that takes up and captivates the entire personality. Oh, may God make us balanced Christians, men and women of whom it can be said that we are obviously, patently obeying from the heart the form of doctrine that has been delivered unto us.

7

MY PURPOSE AND METHOD

(1952)
Deuteronomy 29:29

From *Great Doctrines of the Bible*

As we saw in the biographical introduction, Dr. Lloyd-Jones loved to hold weeknight meetings for members of his congregation who wished to discover the relevance and application of the Bible to their everyday lives and problems.

Once the war was over, it was possible for him to do the same at Westminster Chapel, and many traveled substantial distances on what for them had been a normal working day.

Initially it was like a question-and-answer time, but by 1952 he realized that the free-flowing approach now needed a change. The Doctor had always relied on the commentaries of the great Reformed thinkers and theologians. But as the introduction to the Great Doctrines of the Bible series states, so many of the congregation were asking him questions on the very basic doctrines of the Christian faith that he felt compelled to move from the auditorium in which the discussions had begun into the main church. Then followed this series and after that his magisterial sermons on Romans that took up Friday nights for the rest of his thirteen years as minister of Westminster Chapel.

But as he himself says in our extract, he was always a preacher who had to have a text. So what we see here is not a university-style seminar or lecture but a sermon.

He once said to his family that he was a "Bible Calvinist, not a system Calvinist." How true that was! Everything in the earlier Friday night discussions had to be proved from Scripture. Even if John Calvin, John Owen, or Jonathan Edwards had said something, his statement had to be proved from the words of the Bible itself. So also was it the case in the doctrine sermons he preached to his congregation: all of it was Scripture based.

The importance of this cannot be exaggerated today as well as then!

One of the most exciting developments of recent years has been the re-discovery of Reformed theology by a whole generation of younger people in the United States. In fact, neo-Calvinism has attracted so much media attention that even the wholly secular Time *magazine has deemed it one of the biggest trends in the United States today. This is very similar to the massive interest in Reformed theology among university students in Britain after the Second World War, a renaissance in which the Doctor was to play a leading part.*

But, to ask his question, is it Bible Calvinism or system Calvinism? Surely if it is the latter it will soon fizzle out or go astray. How many formerly Reformed denominations are now spiritually lifeless? The evident answer reveals the dangers, of which the Doctor himself, with his acute knowledge of church history, was well aware.

Sound doctrine and its importance is rightly one of the hallmarks of evangelical Christianity. Without it one can slide into theological liberalism, or these days into postmodern mush. Doctrine must be Bible based. We can construct all sorts of systematic theologies, but if they are not firmly centered on Scripture, then our faith and practice is based not upon the Word of God but on the constructs of mere mortals.

Dr. Lloyd-Jones defended the need for sound doctrine to the end of his days. But as time progressed he realized that evangelicals could check all the right doctrinal boxes yet not have what one of his closest Welsh associates, Hywel Jones, called life. As we saw earlier in this book, the Doctor believed in theology on fire. It is wonderful that Reformed truth is coming back and influencing the lives of countless thousands. Doctrine is important again. But, he would ask, are they on fire? That, not just soundness of belief, is vital.

It is always good for us to start with a text. Not that I am going to preach, but I do want us to begin with some words that will give the background of all I propose to say now and will explain what I am proposing to do in this series of studies on biblical doctrines. I refer to Deuteronomy 29:29: "The secret things belong unto the LORD our God: but those things which are revealed belong unto us and to our children for ever, that we may do all the words of this law."

Now, inevitably, we shall have to begin with introductions; that is necessary, I think, for several reasons. One is that some people may question the rightness of what we propose to do. We live in an age in which we do not hear very much about doctrines, and there are some people who are even foolish enough to say that they do not like them, which seems to me to be a very pathetic and regrettable attitude. Lectures or sermons on biblical doctrines were once very common, but they have become comparatively uncommon, especially during this [twentieth] century. However, though we shall not deal with that criticism directly, it makes a good starting point, and it leads me to say that there are certain things that we must have quite clear in our minds. We shall consider three things: what we are going to do in these studies, how we are going to do it, and why we are going to do it.

What, then, are we going to do? This is to be a series of studies on biblical doctrines. What do we mean when we talk about a biblical doctrine? The answer is that the Bible is particularly concerned about teaching certain truths, and nothing is more important than that we should grasp that and that we should start with it. The Bible is a book that has a very definite objective. All its teaching is designed to a certain end; it is concerned with putting before us its doctrines, the particular truths that it wants to emphasize and to impress upon the minds of all of us.

Let me put that more clearly in the form of a negative. The Bible is not, for instance, a general history of the world. We do not always remember that, but notice how it crowds two thousand years into just eleven chapters in Genesis. The Bible is not primarily interested in world history; it has another object.

Or let me put forward another negative. The Bible is not even concerned to give us a complete history of everything that God has ever done—he has done many things that are not referred to in the Bible—but it selects certain things that help to bring into focus its own purpose and plan. The four Gospels, for instance, do not pretend to be a complete biography of the Son of God, our Lord and Savior, Jesus Christ. No; they are concerned about presenting certain truths about him. For instance, they only deal with about three years of his life—there is very little apart from that. They tell us about his birth, for example, but the main emphasis in the Gospels is his public ministry—what happened to him after the age of thirty.

John in his Gospel puts this very clearly to us. He tells us, "And many other signs truly did Jesus in the presence of his disciples, which are not written in this book." Then, "But these are written, that ye might believe that Jesus is the Christ, the Son of God; and that believing ye might have life through his name" (John 20:30–31). John did not set out to give us an exact, detailed account of our Lord's life. He had an object in view, and the last verse in his Gospel says, "And there are also many other things which Jesus did, the which, if they should be written every one, I suppose that even the world itself could not contain the books that should be written" (John 21:25).

"What, then, is the Bible about?" asks someone. Surely there can be no hesitation about answering that question. The Bible, in its essence, is the grand story of redemption. It is the history of what God has done about men and women as the result of their sin, and everything else that we find in the Bible is, in reality, incidental to that. The Bible is concerned with presenting to us the message of redemption by God and from God in a way that we can understand and see and believe. So when we talk about biblical doctrines, we mean these aspects of redemption that are unfolded to us in the Bible. They are the various truths that we find in the Bible about this great question.

Now there are many classifications, but let me suggest to you some of the doctrines that we are, therefore, of necessity bound to consider. One is, of course, the book itself. Why do we pay attention to this book? Why do we confine ourselves to it? What does the Bible teach us about itself? Clearly we must start with that. We cannot go on to consider the doctrines of the Bible unless we have a clear idea as to what the Bible itself is and what it claims to be.

Then, of course, having accepted our authority, our standard, we start with the great doctrine that always must come before every other doctrine, and that is the doctrine of God. "In the beginning God . . ." (Gen. 1:1). We meet God here. It is his revelation. So as we come to the Bible we learn the truth about him, and strictly speaking, that is what is meant by the term *theology*.

Next, obviously, is the doctrine of man. I have said that the business of the Bible is to teach us about redemption, and redemption is what God is doing about man. That is what is called anthropology.

Then we come to the doctrine of our Lord and Savior, Jesus Christ—

Christology—because, after all, all redemption is in him and in him alone. Everything that happens in the Old Testament looks forward to him. He is the climax, and the Bible has a great deal to tell us about him.

But having found how redemption has been provided, the next matter that occurs to us is: how is this doctrine applied to us? The Bible has great teaching about this, the doctrine of applied salvation or soteriology.

Then, what happens to us when we are redeemed? Well, we are brought into the church and are made members of the mystical body of Christ. So, clearly, you would expect the Bible to tell us something about the church, and it does. This is called ecclesiology—the doctrine of the *ecclesia*, the church.

And then, naturally, we ask this question: here we are, the redeemed, members of Christ, of his body, the church. What for? What is going to happen to us? What will it lead to? The Bible meets us again at this point because it has its doctrine of the last things, which is called eschatology. Biblical teaching is all leading up to something, to a grand climax and con- summation. There remain certain, ultimate last things, and you find a great deal about that in the Bible.

Now those are some of the truths that, God willing, we hope to consider together, and that is all I am proposing to do. So let nobody think that we are concerned here with giving a general survey or synopsis of the Bible and its contents. That is a perfectly good thing to do, but that is not what we shall be doing. I have given you the general outline of these doctrines, and we shall address ourselves to that. We shall find the doctrines in the text, in the Word, and our business is to extract them and study them.

But let us now look at our second question: how are we going to do this? And here again we must be careful to have a good definition and to be clear in our minds as to what it is we are really attempting, because there is often a good deal of misunderstanding at this point. Let me again put it as a negative. I am not going to give a series of lectures on theology. I wonder whether that comes as a surprise to anybody. I wonder whether anybody thought, "Well, surely you cannot lecture on biblical doctrines without giv- ing lectures on theology!" I suggest to you that the two things are not the same, and it is important that we should know the difference as we con- template this series of addresses. We must of necessity confine ourselves to what the Bible says and to what the Bible alone says.

Now theology does not do that; it addresses biblical doctrines in a wider field. Theology starts by saying that God has not only revealed himself in the Bible but in history. He reveals himself experimentally in experience, and theology says that before it gives you biblical doctrine, biblical dogma, it must take into consideration these other aspects of revelation. Of course, theology includes that as well, but theology includes more than the Bible. In other words, the theologian does something like this: he goes to the Bible; he studies it; he traces and extracts its doctrines or he considers what somebody else has already done. He then proceeds to reflect upon these doctrines; he thinks about them and analyzes them. He tries to bring them into a scheme. He brings in philosophy, which means human thought and thinking, and he takes all these things together and reflects upon them, and the end of that process is what is called theology.

So I trust that I am making it clear that is not what I propose to do. It is not that I do not believe in theology—I do. But when I say I am going to give a series of addresses on biblical doctrines, I do not mean that I am going to give lectures on theology.

Let me give you an example to explain precisely what I mean by this. There was a famous Bible lecturer and expositor in America at the end of the nineteenth and the beginning of the twentieth century who published a booklet called *The Great Doctrines of the Bible*. Now I was very interested when I turned to that book to see what this author had to say, for instance, on the doctrine of God. To my amazement I saw that his first heading was this: "Proofs of the existence of God." The moment I saw that I said to myself, "He should not have put that title in his book; he should have said that it was a book on Christian theology, because you do not find proofs of the existence of God in the Bible."

What I mean by these proofs is this. People argue that you can arrive at a belief in God by just looking into your own conscience. You say to yourself, "I think, so there must be . . . I think of God, but the idea must have come from somewhere, there must be something corresponding to my thought. Therefore there should and there must be God, and so on." Then they take the argument from nature. They say that you look at nature, and as you do so you see the order and design, and you say that it all must have come from somewhere—there must be a creator. A very good argument.

Again, there is the moral argument. I recognize that there is good and better in this world, and that suggests to me that there must be a best somewhere, there must be an absolute perfection, and that is what is called the moral argument for the existence of God. Now this writer to whom I referred goes through all that in his book and many other arguments, but that is something that the Bible never does. Here is a man who tells us that he has written a book about the great doctrines of the Bible but who is behaving as a theologian!

I am not saying there is no value in those arguments for proving the existence of God, but I do want to emphasize that you do not find them in the Bible. And it is interesting to observe how this man, who gives a text for everything he says, suddenly has no text whatsoever in this particular section. So he has gone beyond what he had said he was going to do.

But we shall deal with biblical doctrines. The Bible does not give us proofs of the existence of God, it proclaims him; it just tells us about him. Also, though, as I have said, it is not that I do not believe in theology, yet I do want to say in passing that we must remember that there is a danger in connection with theology. The moment you bring in philosophy and speculation and your own thoughts and human reason, you are beginning to do something that may be dangerous, not of necessity, but it may be. Now we shall avoid all that.

We shall also avoid something else. We shall not attempt to defend these doctrines. That, again, is a perfectly good thing to do—it is called apologetics. But we are not concerned to defend the doctrines, and I say this because some of you, when we go on to particular doctrines, may be disappointed that I am not doing so. For instance, when we come to the doctrine of creation, the whole question of evolution arises, but it will not be my primary purpose to deal exhaustively with it. Biblical doctrine does not make you do that. Of course, we shall have to refer to evolution, but primarily we shall be expounding positively what the Bible itself has to say.

So the position we occupy is that, again, of Deuteronomy 29:29: "The secret [the ultimate explanation of] things belong unto the LORD our God." Again we shall be dealing with the doctrine of sin, and somebody will want to know, "Where does evil come from?" I cannot tell you. The Bible does not tell us. You can speculate, you can reason, but that is not biblical doctrine. We must confine ourselves to the things that have been revealed, not to the secret things that are ultimately in the mind of God.

That, then, is more or less a definition of the way in which we are proposing to consider these doctrines. And that brings us to the last point: why do we believe this should be done? Now these are some of the answers I would suggest to that question. The first is that the Bible itself does it, and therefore we are bound to do it. I told you at the beginning that the Bible is not merely a general history. It is a book that is concerned to bring certain particular truths clearly before us, and those truths are doctrines. So to read my Bible properly means that I must consider doctrine. The Bible wants me to grasp its doctrine. In other words, I may know my Bible very well, but unless I realize the importance of grasping its doctrines, my knowledge of the Bible may be quite useless to me.

Let me put it to you like this. Is that not exactly what the prophets did? You read about them in the Old Testament. What were those men doing? Well, they were taking hold of those doctrines—the doctrine of the law in particular—and they were enforcing them. They were applying the law. They went to the nation, and they said, "You people think that because you have the law you know it, but you don't!" They said, "The law is bringing this before you, and this is what you have to grasp and to understand." They preached doctrine to the people. Is this not also exactly what our Lord himself did? What was he really doing in the Sermon on the Mount except this very thing? He said, "Ye have heard. . . . But I say unto you . . ." (see Matt. 5:27–28). He took the law and expounded it in the form of doctrine. He explained it. He said that a mere general acquaintance with the law was of no value; you must know exactly what it says. He extracted the principles, and he applied them and enforced them.

This is also, obviously, the very thing that was done by the apostles. Read the book of Acts and observe the preaching of those first Christian preachers. What did they do? Well, you do not find that they took a text and then gave its exact meaning in the Greek and the Hebrew and then analyzed it and so on. No, no! Their way of preaching was to proclaim doctrines. They had a message, and they presented that to the people; they used their Scriptures to show that this was the doctrine.

And, of course, that is what is meant by preaching; that is the purpose and function of preaching. It is not merely an opportunity for a man to express his own thoughts. It is not merely to give an alternative translation of the Scriptures. No; its purpose is to bring truth to the congregation. The apostles did that, as preaching in its essence always does.

Or take the epistles of the New Testament. What are they? Well, in these epistles certain great doctrines are taken and are underlined and enforced. There was a particular need of that in particular churches. So the writer of the epistle brings his doctrine and applies it in a practical manner. All along you see that they are concerned with the expression and elucidation of doctrine. That is my first reason, therefore, for doing this. I argue that the Bible demands it. It does so in itself, and it exhorts us to do so.

Another reason is that it is dangerous for us to study the Bible without doing this. We talk, do we not, about missing the forest because of the trees, and what a terrible danger that is! The real trouble with the Jews at the time of our Lord was that they stopped at the letter and never arrived at the spirit. In other words, they never got at the doctrine. They were content with a general familiarity with the words, but they did not get the Word. And this is something that we all have to realize as a terribly dangerous possibility for us, for if we stop at the letter only, it profits us nothing; it even misleads us. It may be the cause of the damnation of our souls. Not to arrive at your doctrine after you have studied your Scriptures means that your study is thoroughly unprofitable. It may be very intellectual. It may be a good way of spending your time. I have known people who have used the Bible as others have used crossword puzzles or even jigsaw puzzles, for fitting things together, but they have never arrived at doctrine. Their study is of no value. It is profitless.

But another reason for studying biblical doctrine is that the church throughout the centuries has always found that it is essential to emphasize the doctrines of the Bible. In the very first days of the church no one was received into church membership without making the confession, at all costs, that Jesus is Lord. But the moment you say, "Jesus is Lord," you are making a doctrinal statement. Then after a while the early Christians found that it was not enough merely to say, "Jesus is Lord"; they found it necessary to introduce what was called a baptismal formula. Candidates for baptism were catechized; they were asked certain questions, and they had to be able to answer them.

But do you remember what happened? Very soon heresies began to arise; people within the church began to say things that were not correct. They were quite genuine and sincere, but many were saying things that were wrong and that were harmful. And these heretical and false teachers, of course, not only caused confusion within the church, they were also misleading people outside the church. The rise of heresy within the church led the early church to draw up what we commonly call the creeds—for example, the Apostles' Creed, the Nicene Creed, and the Athanasian Creed.

Those creeds became essential because there was so much error and heresy in the church, and the church, under the guidance of the Holy Spirit, said, "We must make it quite clear as to what we do believe and what we do not believe. It is not enough merely to give people an open Bible. Perfectly sincere and genuine and able men and women may read this book and say things that are quite wrong. We must define our doctrines," and the definitions of doctrines are what we call the creeds.

Then, of course, after a while the church, which in a sense had been one, was divided into two—into the Eastern and the Western church—but, more or less, the doctrine was the same. The church was dead, I know, but it was governed by these three great creeds.

Then came the Protestant Reformation. New life, new vigor, new understanding came in, and again the church found that it was absolutely essential to extract its doctrines and to state them in a perfectly clear and definite manner. So you had what is commonly called among Protestants the great Confessions. These are nothing but a listing together and an exposition of the doctrines of the Bible. The leaders, again, said, "It is not enough to give people an open Bible. We must guide them. We must help them. They are liable to go astray. So we must tell them that we believe this about God and that we do not believe that. We must tell them about Christ and about the church and so on." The Church of England had its Confession, which is called the Thirty-Nine Articles. There were also many famous Confessions on the European Continent—those, for example, of the Moravian Church and the Reformed Church. And then there was the great Confession that was drawn up in Westminster Abbey in the seventeenth century and is therefore known as The Westminster Confession. It is the Confession of the Church of Scotland and of all Presbyterian churches everywhere throughout the world.

Now all these Confessions, and the catechisms that go with them, are nothing but a statement of biblical doctrines, so that people within the church might know exactly what to believe and what not to believe and the reasons for this belief. They were all designed to build us up in the faith and to enable us to know exactly where we stand.

Now if all that was necessary in the early days of the church, if it was necessary at the time of the Reformation and in the seventeenth century, surely it is something that is urgently needed at this present hour. Today the church is surrounded by cults; these people come to your doors speaking, as they say, "from the Scriptures." They say they believe the Bible that we teach. The moment they make a statement you feel instinctively that there is something wrong with it, but you cannot answer them. Now one of the purposes of studying biblical doctrines is to enable us to discover together the error in such teachings. Not that I am going to lecture on the cults. What I shall do is this: I shall remind you of what the Bible does teach. Then, having a firm grasp and knowledge of that, we can test every other teaching presented to us.

Not only are there all these errors and cults around the church, but even in the church herself there is terrible confusion. There is an absence of doctrine; there is a lack of clear definition and a readiness to allow anybody to say anything they like. And this means there was never a time when it was more urgently necessary that Christian people should consider together the doctrines of the Bible. We must know the ground on which we stand and be able to withstand every enemy that comes to attack us, every subtle foe, every ploy used by the devil who comes disguised as an "angel of light" to ruin our souls.

But I have a higher reason for considering these doctrines with you. Ultimately it is the only way truly to know God, to come into his glorious presence, and to learn something of the wonders of his ways with respect to us. Yes, let us go on reading our Bibles and studying them, but let us not get lost in the detail. Let us pick out these great, mighty mountain peaks of doctrine and realize there who God is and what he has done for us in the person of his dear Son and in spite of our sin.

That, at any rate, is the object that I have in my mind. I am not doing this in order to give you some intellectual knowledge or information that you did not have before. God forbid that I should attempt to do that or that anybody should think of what we are doing in that way. "Knowledge," says Paul, "puffeth up, but charity edifieth" (1 Cor. 8:1). So the atmosphere of this series of discourses or discussions on biblical doctrines will not be that of the classroom. There will be no examinations at the end to determine how much you have learned and no diplomas given to you! No, no. We are concerned with God—to know him. Any consideration of the Bible is worship, and to me there is nothing so dangerous as to approach the Bible and its teaching in the same way you approach any other textbook.

People often say to me, "What is wrong with these theological colleges? I have known many a good man who has gone in all right, but look at him when he comes out!" Now that may not always be true—people often say things like that—but if it is true sometimes, I think I can tell you why. It is because in such places they far too often approach the Bible as if it were a textbook. They far too often approach these great doctrines as if they were human thoughts and ideas. They do not come to them always in the atmosphere of worship and of awe. They are interested in translation and in intellectual knowledge. That is essential, but we must not stop at that.

The doctrines of the Bible are not a subject to be studied; rather, we should desire to know them in order that, having known them, we may not be "puffed up" with knowledge and excited about our information but may draw nearer to God in worship, praise, and adoration because we have seen, in a fuller way than we have ever seen before, the glory of our wondrous God. May he give us cause to do this and grant that as a result of these doctrines we may all come to know him, the only true and living God, and Jesus Christ whom he has sent, and as a result may all be revived. And so I express the hope that through us and others like us the whole church may be revived and that we may witness again in our midst the manifestation of God's glorious power.

8

THE CHRISTIAN MESSAGE TO THE WORLD

(1954–1962)
Ephesians 2:4

From *God's Way of Reconciliation*

Although this sermon is formally known by its longer title, it is loved worldwide under the shorter name of "But God."

This is perhaps the most popular of all his sermons at Westminster Chapel, and that is the main reason for its inclusion in our book. But it is also a wonderful apologia pro vita sua, the ultimate defense of his method of expository preaching.

The Ephesians series was delivered on Sunday mornings from 1954 to 1962, with the break in 1959 for his sermons on Revival. It is the embodiment of his method on how to preach in an expository way through an entire Bible book, and so important did he rank it that it was the first series that he began to edit for publication when he retired in 1968. Our sermon here was edited by him in his lifetime and was published in 1972.

As was so often the case during the Cold War, the threat of a nuclear Armageddon loomed large. The year in which he preached "But God" was no exception, and there are fleeting references in it to one of the many failed peace discussions, along with mention of some of the earliest talks on Vietnam and Korea. (As I write this, North Korea is again threatening dire action, which shows how the Doctor was so right to say that nothing human ever changes.)

But as he points out, that is not the issue! Indeed it is never the thing that matters most. All that truly counts is the activity of God himself, and as he shows, the very words "but God" are a nutshell of the entire gospel itself.

This sermon was preached to a morning congregation; therefore, most of them would have been at least professing Christians. However, he realized people were converted in morning services, and it is hard to read this without thinking of it as a powerful evangelistic sermon.

What is also interesting is that he could not have known, when he began his series on Ephesians back in 1952, that his sermon on this verse would occur during a major international crisis. But this goes to demonstrate his entire point—namely that if one preaches in an expository way, the Bible is by its very nature always completely relevant, since it is God's living Word to us. Sometimes the application will be personal to an individual in the congregation and at other times to all of them. The fact that it remains his most popular and listened to sermon over six decades after it was first delivered shows this to be the case.

We could only choose one sermon from his magisterial Ephesians series, but in fact any one, or indeed all of them, would prove the same point. In "But God" he makes explicit his dislike of topical addresses and expounds a view of Scripture that shows that it is always a God-centered, Scripture-based approach that makes all the difference.

In doing so he was utterly unlike many of the famous preachers of his time. Martyn Lloyd-Jones preached the Word of God and is still read by millions decades after his death, as are Spurgeon, Edwards, Whitefield, and other great giants of the faith. All of them, and the Doctor, have stood the test of time, every one of them a Christ-centered expository preacher.

But God . . . (Ephesians 2:4)

We now come to look at two wonderful words—"But God." These words obviously suggest a connection with something that has gone before. The word "but" is a conjunction, and yet it suggests always a contrast; and here we have the connection and the contrast. Look at them in their context: "And you hath he quickened, who were dead in trespasses and sins; wherein in time past ye walked according to the course of this world, according to the prince of the power of the air, the spirit that now worketh in the children of disobedience: among whom also we all had our conversation in times past in the lusts of our flesh, fulfilling the desires of the flesh and of the mind; and were by nature the children of wrath, even as others. But God . . ."

With these two words we come to the introduction to the Christian message, the peculiar, specific message that the Christian faith has to offer to us. These two words, in and of themselves, in a sense contain the whole of the gospel. The gospel tells of what God has done, God's intervention; it is something that comes entirely from outside us and displays to us that wondrous and amazing and astonishing work of God that the apostle goes on to describe and to define in the following verses.

We shall take these words now in a general manner only. I do so for several reasons. One is that the text itself compels one to do so, but there are also certain special reasons for doing so. A charge frequently brought against the Christian message, and especially the evangelical form of that message, is that it is remote from life, that it is irrelevant to the immediate circumstances in which men and women find themselves. In other words, there is an objection on the part of some to the expository method of preaching the gospel; it is that it never seems to come to grips with the realities of the situation in which men and women find themselves from day to day and that it is irrelevant to the whole world situation in which we find ourselves. I desire to show, therefore, that such a charge is entirely unfounded, and further that the idea that the business of Christian preaching is just to make topical references to contemporary events is indeed, in a sense, to depart from the Christian message altogether. I would go so far as to say that there is nothing that really does deal with the contemporary situation save Holy Scripture, when its doctrines are understood, believed, and applied.

That is what I propose to do now. I want to show the relevance of the gospel on a day such as Remembrance Sunday [a remembrance of soldiers who had died in war] when instinctively almost, and certainly as the result of what is happening in the world in which we live, our minds are compelled to face and to think of the general situation in addition to our own particular situations. And, claiming as I do that the gospel deals with the whole of man and with the whole of his life in this world, it is important that we should see what it has to say about and to do with the position in which we find ourselves. You notice that the thing I am emphasizing is the all-importance of method. The many who do not think in a Christian and biblical manner believe that the business of the Christian church on a day such as this is to announce, for instance, a subject such as "The Geneva

119

Conference—Possibilities" and then go on to say what we think the states-men should do. That, it seems to me, is entirely false and contrary to the biblical method. The biblical method, rather, is to display God's truth and then to show the relevance of that to any given situation. You do not start with the situation—you end with the situation. The Bible invites us at the outset to stop looking on the horizontal level, as it were, to stop merely looking at the world and at men; it invites us at the very beginning to lift up our eyes and to look at God. In other words, the whole case presented in the Bible from beginning to end is that life and man and the world simply cannot be understood until we see everything in the light of the truth about God and in that context. Therefore we must start with the truth of God and only then go on to the immediate situation.

Let us proceed to show how that is done and how it is done in the very passage that we are considering. We have considered in detail these first three verses in this chapter, and we have been doing so in order that we might see what we ourselves are like by nature and what the world is like by nature. You cannot begin to solve the problems of mankind until you know the truth about man. How futile it is to attempt to do so apart from that. You must start with the character, the nature, the being of man. Instead of starting with international conferences and talk about contemporary events, we need to go much further back and ask, what sort of a creature is man? Obviously all our conclusions and all our proposals are going to be governed by the answer to that question. If man is really an essentially good creature who only needs a little more instruction and knowledge and information, obviously the treatment is going to be comparatively simple. But if what the apostle Paul says here about man as he is by nature and without Christ is true, then equally obviously, treatment along such lines is going to be entirely hopeless, and to attempt it is a sheer waste of time.

We must start with this doctrine. *What is true of man in sin?* What characterizes man as he is in sin without the grace of God? We have al-ready looked into this matter. Man is dead spiritually; he is governed by the devil, who operates through the mighty spiritual forces under his command, which in turn produce and control the mind and the outlook of the world. That is the position of man. And the result is that man, dominated by that evil power, lives a life of trespasses and sins; indeed, he has been born in such a way, as the result of his descent from Adam, that his very nature is fallen. He starts with a polluted nature. And finally, he is under the wrath of God. That is the apostle's statement in the first three verses.

What then is the relevance of all that to the present situation? What has it to say to us as we face the whole world situation at this present time? It is clear that a number of things can be very easily deduced from this teaching.

The first is that here we are given *the only real and adequate explanation of why there are such occurrences as wars*. Why do we have them? Why is man guilty of this madness? Why is it that men kill one another and have even gloried in war? What is the explanation of it all? There is only one answer; it is because man is as the apostle describes him. This is not only the teaching of the apostle Paul. You remember how James puts it in the fourth chapter of his epistle—"From whence come wars and fightings among you?"—and answers the question, "even of your lusts that war in your members" (James 4:1). That is the cause of war. It is man in his fallen condition. Now the realization of this truth and fact is absolutely vital for us as a starting point. This is true of nations, it is true of classes, it is true of individuals. There is surely nothing that is quite so illuminating and contradictory as the way in which people think along one line when they are thinking of nations and along a quite different line when they are thinking of individuals. There is little point in talking eloquently about the sanctity of international contracts while you are dealing with people who break their own marriage contracts and other personal contracts, for nations consist of individuals. The nation is not something abstract, and we are not entitled to expect conduct from a nation that we do not find in the individual. All these things have to be taken together.

This is a principle that operates throughout society from top to bottom, from the individual to the nation, to the continent, to the whole world itself. The explanation of the state of the world according to the Bible is that man is governed by desires of the flesh and of the mind. He is not so much interested in whether a thing is right or not—he is interested in the fact that he wants it, that he likes it, that he must have it. Of course we stand back aghast when a nation behaves like that. When Hitler walks in and annexes Austria we are horrified. Yes, people are horrified who do the very same thing in their personal lives. They do it in the matter of other men's wives; they do it in the matter of another man's position or business. It is the same thing exactly. There then is the principle. It is this lust that governs man-

121

kind. "Walk[ing] according to the course of this world," says the apostle, "we all had our conversation in times past in the lusts of our flesh, fulfilling the desires of the flesh and of the mind" (Eph. 2:2–3). The first deduction, therefore, is that here and here alone do we have an adequate explanation and understanding of why things are as they are.

The second deduction follows quite logically. It is that *while man continues to be thus governed, the world will continue to be as it is.* This is surely obvious. If it is the state of man in sin that has been responsible for the history of the past, obviously while man remains unchanged, the history of the future is going to be unchanged. Here we confront and come into collision with the optimism of the natural man who is always so sure and confident that somehow or another we in our generation can put things right. He feels that whereas all other generations who have gone before us have failed, we are in a different position, in a superior position. We are educated and cultured; we know whereas they did not know; we have advanced so much, we must succeed, and we are going to succeed. But if you believe this biblical doctrine of man in sin, you must see at once that is a fatal fallacy. If our troubles are due to the lusts that are in mankind in sin and that control men while they remain, there will be wars. We have specific teaching to that effect from our blessed Lord himself, who said, "Ye shall hear of wars and rumours of wars" (Matt. 24:6). He said also, "And as it was in the days of Noe [Noah], so shall it be also in the days of the Son of man," and "Likewise also as it was in the days of Lot"—in Sodom—"even thus shall it be" (Luke 17:26–30). That is our Lord's view of history.

If we grasp this teaching we shall be delivered at once from all the false enthusiasm and the false hopes of men who really believe that by bringing in some new organization you can outlaw war and banish it forever. The answer of the Bible is that you cannot do so while man remains unregenerate. Is this depressing? My reply is that whether it is depressing or not is not our concern; we should be concerned to know the truth. The modern man claims to be a realist. He has objected to Christianity because, according to him, it does not face the facts. It is not realistic, he says; it is always "pie in the sky," and you go into your chapels and you shut yourselves off and do not face the facts of life. Yet when we give him the facts, he objects on the grounds that they are depressing. It is the political and philosophical optimists who are not realists; it is the people who have never faced the facts about man in sin who are shutting their eyes and turning their backs upon reality. The Bible faces it all; it has a realistic view of life in this world, and it alone has it.

Now let us look at *the specific, direct teaching of the gospel*. What has the Christian message to say about this state and this condition, the explanation of which we have just been considering? The answer is that it says, "But God . . ." That is its message. What does that mean? The most convenient way of analyzing this matter is to put it first of all negatively and then positively. I regret that I have to start with a negative again. I must do so, because so many forget these negatives and thus deliver messages that cannot possibly be regarded as Christian at all. And yet they will be delivered in the name of Christianity and of the Christian church. I am profoundly convinced that what is keeping large numbers of people from Christ and from salvation and from the Christian church is this terrible confusion of which the church herself has been and is so guilty. There are many outside the church today because in the First World War the Christian church so frequently became a kind of recruiting office. Men were offended—and in a sense they were right to be offended. There are certain things that should never be confused. Let us note some of them.

What is this Christian message? We start by saying that *it is not a great appeal for patriotism*. That is not the Christian message. The Christian message does not denounce patriotism or say that there is anything wrong with it. The man is to be pitied who does not love his country and his nation. There is nothing in the Scriptures against that. It is God who has divided up the nations and defined their bounds and their habitations. It is God's will that there should be nations. But it is not God's will that there should be an aggressive nationalism. There is nothing wrong with a man honoring his own country and delighting in it, but it is utterly un-Christian to say "My country right or wrong." That is always wrong, that is fatally wrong; that is a complete denial of the teaching of Scripture. Take this great apostle who wrote this very epistle to the Ephesians. Here is a man who was a Jew, and if ever a man was proud of the fact of his nationality, it was the apostle Paul—"of the tribe of Benjamin, an Hebrew of the Hebrews" (Phil. 3:5). He was once a narrow nationalist who despised others. The Gentiles were dogs, outside the pale. But the thing in which he glories in this epistle, you remember, is this: "in whom ye also trusted" (1:13). The Gentiles have

123

come in, have been made "fellow heirs" with the Jews; the middle wall of partition has been broken down. "There is neither Jew nor Greek, there is neither bond nor free, there is neither male nor female: for ye are all one in Christ Jesus" (Gal. 3:28). That is the Christian position. "But God . . ." Here is the way to break down that nationalistic spirit that leads to war. To believe that we are always right and everybody else wrong is as wrong in nations as it is in individuals. It is always wrong. The Christian message is not just an appeal to patriotism. And if Christianity is portrayed in that form, it is a denial and a travesty of the message, and it is misleading in the eyes and the ears of those who listen to it.

But, second, *the Christian message is not just an appeal to courage or heroism* or to the manifestation of a great spirit of self-sacrifice. Let us be clear about this also. Christianity does not condemn courage; it does not condemn self-sacrifice or heroism. These qualities, these virtues are not specifically Christian. They are pagan virtues that were taught and inculcated, admired and praised before the Lord Jesus Christ ever came into this world. Courage was the supreme virtue according to the Greek pagan philosophers; it was the very essence of Stoicism. And that was why they regarded meekness, the meekness taught by the Christian faith, as weakness. There was no word for meekness in Greek pagan philosophy. Courage and strength and power—those were the things they believed in. That is why, you remember, Paul tells us that the preaching of the cross was "unto the Greeks foolishness." That someone who was crucified in weakness should be the Savior, and that that should be the way of salvation, to them was nonsense and rubbish. They placed no value on meekness and on humility; courage and power and heroism were the great virtues. So it is very important that we should realize that it is not part of the Christian message to exhort people to courage and heroism and to self-sacrifice. There is nothing specifically Christian in such ideas. Christianity does not condemn them, but that is not the Christian message. And the point I am emphasizing is this: when that has been presented as the Christian message, it has confused people and has led to the very division that the gospel itself was meant to heal.

But let us go on to the third matter. There are many people who seem to think that the Christian message is that we should just appeal to the world to put into practice the Christian principles. *This is the pacifist position, so-called.* They say, "You Christian people are always preaching about personal salvation and about doctrines and so on. Why do you not do something about wars?" Then, we say, "What do you want us to do?" They reply, "What you have to do is to tell the people to practice the Sermon on the Mount. Why do you not tell them to turn the other cheek and to love one another and so on? Then there would be an end of war. You have the solution; just get people to put into operation the principles of the teaching of Christ." What is the answer to that? The answer is the teaching of the first three verses in this second chapter of Paul's epistle to the Ephesians. You can preach the Sermon on the Mount to people who are "dead in trespasses and sins" until you have exhausted yourself and you will be none the wiser, and neither will they. They cannot practice it. They do not want to. They are enemies and aliens in their minds (see Col. 1:21). They are governed by "lusts." They fulfill "the desires of the flesh and of the mind" (Eph. 2:3). They are governed and ruled by this. How can they practice the Sermon on the Mount?

There is only one hope for man in sin, says Paul—"but God." Men need to be regenerated; they must be given a new nature before they can even understand the Sermon on the Mount, let alone begin to put it into practice. So it is but a travesty of the Christian message to speak of it as if it were but an appeal to men to rise up and to follow Christ in their own strength and to put into operation Christian principles of teaching. It is as much a travesty of the gospel as is the preaching of patriotism and imperialism. It is equally non-Christian. It is indeed dangerous heresy, the ancient Pelagian heresy, because it fails to realize that man, being what he is in sin, cannot possibly implement such teaching. To expect Christian conduct from people who are not yet Christians is dangerous heresy. You see how important our teaching is, and how essential it is that we should be clear about the true application of the Christian message to the modern world. That is why we do not spend our time talking about international conferences and politics and international relationships or industrial disputes or in preaching always on the question of pacifism and against physical warfare. To do so is simply to waste time, though it would probably attract publicity. What is needed is that we should start with this fundamental principle, the doctrine of man in sin, in his deadness, in his hopelessness, in his complete helplessness.

To sum up at this point, the negative principle is that the Christian faith, the Christian gospel, has no direct message for the world except to say that the world as it is is under the wrath of God, that it is under condemnation, and that all who die in that state will go to perdition. The only message of the Christian faith to an unbelieving world, in the first instance, is simply about judgment, a call to repentance, and an assurance that if they do repent and turn to Christ, they shall be delivered. The church, therefore, the Christian faith, has no message to the world apart from that.

But the Bible also teaches very plainly and clearly that while that is the message of God to the unbelieving world, God, nevertheless, has done something about that unbelieving world. What he has done in the first instance is this: *He has put a control upon the power of sin and of evil.* He has done so in the following way. As I have already reminded you, he has divided up the peoples of the world into nations. Not only so, he has ordained that there should be states and governments. "The powers that be," says Paul, in Romans 13:1, "are ordained of God." Whether it be a king or an emperor or a president of a republic, "the powers that be are ordained of God." It is God who has ordained magistrates and has given them the sword of power. Why? Simply to keep the manifestations of evil within bounds and under control. For if God had not done this, if the lusts that operate in us all by nature and by inheritance from Adam were allowed unlimited and uncontrolled manifestation, the world would be hell, and it would have hurtled itself to perdition long ago and would have destroyed itself. But God has put a limit upon it. He has put a bound even upon evil; he has held it in; he has restricted it. Indeed the apostle Paul in a most extraordinary statement in the epistle to the Romans (1:18ff.) proves the matter by saying that sometimes, for his own end and purposes, God withdraws that restraint partially. He says that God "gave them over to a reprobate mind" (v. 28). There are times and seasons when God seems to relax the restraint that he has put upon sin and evil in order that we may see it in all its horror. It may well be that we are living at such a time. But that is what the Bible tells us about what God does directly about man in sin. He controls the manifestations of his foul and evil and fallen nature. That is the *general* message.

But what is the *particular* message? This is the thing that the apostle is concerned to emphasize most of all in this immediate paragraph. *The message to individuals is that we can be delivered out of this present evil world,* that we can escape the condemnation that is coming for certain upon this world. That is the message the apostle preached. It is a message to individuals. It does not say that the world can be put right if we only implement Christian teaching; it is not an appeal to people to reform themselves and to do this or that. No; it is a message that says that as the result of what God has done in Christ Jesus, his Son, our Lord and Savior, we who were in the very warp and woof of that sinful, condemned world can be delivered out of it. He "gave himself for our sins," he says to the Galatians, "that he might deliver us from this present evil world." The world is doomed, the world is going to be destroyed and punished, the devil and all his forces are going to perdition, and all who belong to that realm will suffer the same punishment. But the message of the gospel to men and women individually is that they need not be participators in that. They can be taken out of it—out of "the kingdom of darkness"—and brought out from the power of Satan and unto God. That is its message to individual men and women. The world will remain as it is, but you can be delivered out of it, you can be taken out of it.

Not only that; we can also be introduced into and become citizens of a kingdom that is not of this world. As we go through this chapter we shall find Paul elaborating his own words. "The marvelous thing," he says in summary, "is that you Gentiles are in Christ and because of his blood have become fellow citizens with the saints; you have become citizens in the kingdom of God, the kingdom of Christ, the kingdom of light, the kingdom of heaven—a kingdom that is not of this world, a kingdom that cannot be shaken, a kingdom that cannot be moved." That is the kingdom into which we enter.

This is the most thrilling news a man can ever hear. Now we are all citizens of this country [England], our native land, and we are all involved in what happens to this country. If this country goes to war we shall be involved. We did not escape the bombs in the last war any more than anybody else simply because we were Christians. We are all involved in it; we are citizens of this world, and we share in the fate of this world. But thank God, here is something different. While remaining citizens of this world we become citizens of another kingdom, this other kingdom that has been opened to us by Christ—a spiritual kingdom, a kingdom that is not of this world, eternal in the heavens with God. That is the teaching of this message. "But God . . ."

The doctrine works itself out in practice like this: if I believe this message, from now on I am not going to pin my hopes, nor rest my affections finally on anything in this world. The natural man does so, of course; he pins his hopes on this world and its mind, its outlook, its statesmen, its mentality, its pleasures, its joys. He lives for it, and all his hopes are centered here, his affections are here. Not so the Christian. The Christian, having been given to see that this world is doomed, that it is under the wrath of God, has fled from "the wrath to come." He has believed the gospel, he has entered this other kingdom, and his hopes and affections are set there now, not here. The Christian is a man who, to use a scriptural phrase, knows that he is but "a stranger and a pilgrim" in this world. He is a mere sojourner; he does not any longer live for this world—he has seen through it, he sees beyond it. He is but a journeyman, a traveler, and, as James puts it (chapter 4), he is a man who has realized that his life is but "a vapour," a breath (v. 14). So he does not regard this world as permanent; he does not lay down his plans and say, "I am going to do this or that." Not at all! But rather, "If the Lord will . . ." It is all under God, and he realizes how contingent it is. He does not any longer pin his faith or set his affections on this world.

But still more marvelous, he is never taken by surprise over anything that happens in this world. That is why I said earlier that there is nothing that I know of that is so relevant to worldly circumstances as this gospel. The Christian is a man who is never surprised by what happens in the world. He is prepared for everything, prepared for anything. He is not at all surprised when a war breaks out. The non-Christian, and especially the idealist, of course, is greatly surprised. He really did believe at the end of the First World War that the League of Nations was going to abolish war forever. There were many who believed that the Locarno Pact of 1925 was finally going to do it, and they were very happy. They were confident that there would never be another war like that of 1914–1918. And when it came in 1939, they did not know how to explain it. But the true Christian, knowing that man is a creature who is governed by lusts, and that lust always produces war, knew perfectly well that no Locarno Pact or anything else could outlaw or abolish war. He knew that war might come at any time, and when it came he was not surprised. As Psalm 112 puts it in the seventh verse: "He shall not be afraid of evil tidings: his heart is fixed, trusting in the LORD."

Believing as we do this biblical doctrine of man in sin, we should never be surprised at what happens in the world. Are you surprised at all the murders, the thefts, the violence, the robbery, all the lying and the hatred, all the carnality, the sexuality? Does it surprise you as you look at your newspapers? It should not do so if you are a Christian. You should expect it. Man in sin of necessity behaves like that. He cannot help himself; he lives, he walks in trespasses and sins. He does it individually; he does it in groups. Therefore, there will be industrial strifes and misunderstandings and there will be wars. Oh, what pessimism! says someone. I say, no, what realism! Face it, be prepared for it, do not expect anything better from a world like this. It is a fallen, sinful, godless, evil world, and while man remains in sin, it will be like that. And it is as much like that today as it was in the days of Sodom and Gomorrah and in the time of the flood!

But, thank God, I have not finished. I go on to say that the Christian is a man who, realizing that he is living in such a world, and who, having no illusions at all about it, knows that he is linked to a power that enables him not only to bear whatever may come to him in such a world but indeed to be "more than conqueror" over it all. He does not just passively bear it; he does not merely put up with it and exercise courage. That is stoicism; that is paganism. The Christian, being in Christ, knowing something of what the apostle calls "the exceeding greatness of [God's] power to us-ward who believe" (Eph. 1:19) is strengthened, is enabled to endure. His heart does not quail, he is not defeated; indeed he can rejoice in tribulations. Let the world do its worst to him, let hell be let loose, he is sustained. "This is the victory that overcometh the world, even our faith" (1 John 5:4). So that if things really do become impossible, the Christian has resources, he still has comforts and consolations, he still has a strength of which all others are ignorant.

Finally, the Christian is absolutely certain and assured that whatever the world and men may do, he is safe in the hands of God. "We may boldly say," say the Scriptures, "The Lord is my helper, and I will not fear what man shall do unto me" (Heb. 13:6). Indeed, he knows that man in his malignity may insult him, may persecute him, may ravage him, may even destroy his body, but he also knows that nothing "shall be able to separate [him] from the love of God, which is in Christ Jesus our Lord" (Rom. 8:39). He knows that whatever may happen in this world of time, he is a son of God, an heir of glory. Indeed he knows that a day is coming when even this present sinful world shall be entirely redeemed, and there shall be "new heavens and a new earth, wherein dwelleth righteousness" (2 Pet. 3:13). The Christian can look forward to this. Some glorious day in the future, when his very body shall be renewed and glorified, when it shall no longer be weak, when it shall be no longer subject to sickness and old age and disease, when it will be a glorified body like that of the risen Christ, he knows that he in this glorified body shall walk the face of this very earth, out of which evil and sin and vileness shall have been burned by the fire of God. He will dwell in a perfect world, of which the Lamb, the Son of God, is the light and the sun, the brightness and the glory, and he shall enjoy it forever and ever. That is what the Christian message, the Christian faith, has to say to this wretched, distracted, unhappy, confused, frustrated, modern world. It is all the outcome of these essential doctrines that can be learned only in God's Word. There is the world—"But God . . ."

9

THE PURPOSE OF REVIVAL

(1959, 1980)
Joshua 4:21–24

From *Revival*

All his life Dr. Lloyd-Jones loved to hear about revivals, those great out-pourings of God's Holy Spirit in which unusual numbers are converted to Christian faith and during which the lives of many Christians themselves are renewed and transformed. Combined with his lifelong passion for history, one can say that there were few things that got him more excited than both reading accounts of the great revivals of the past and in the case of those contemporary to him (such as in East Africa or the Outer Hebrides) meeting the witnesses to such spiritually significant events.

It was his love of revival that determined his burial place in South Wales. Rather than being buried with his own family, he chose the cemetery in Newcastle Emlyn where so many of his wife's family were laid. This was not just evidence of his abiding love for Bethan. He valued this site because the chapel there had seen revival, not just once but twice, both in 1859 and in 1904–1905. It was one of those buried there, Evan Phillips, his wife's paternal grandfather, who had been so deeply involved in each event, as a young preacher in the first and as a senior statesman in the second. Bethan Phillips had herself, along with her older brother Ieuan, actually witnessed many of the extraordinary manifestations of the Holy Spirit in Wales in 1904–1905.

It is interesting, as Iain Murray notes, that Dr. Lloyd-Jones always gave a feeling of connection to great historical events, quoting a visiting Indian journalist on the powerful sense of the gospel and the reality of God that pervaded the Doctor's regular preaching at Westminster Chapel.

Zealous and long-standing though his love of history was, when it came to preaching sermons on revival in 1959—the centenary of the events not just in Britain but also in the United States—he chose to base what he said on Scripture and Bible exposition, not on history lessons.

So significant did he feel the lessons of revival to be that he interrupted his series on Ephesians to preach twenty-four sermons on what the Bible says about the subject.

The passage he selects from Joshua, with the children of Israel on the brink of a major decision as to which way to turn, with all around them looking hopeless, demonstrates very well the historical point that he was trying to make.

To him the church was, as he said, too comfortable, too happy with human methods, too certain that its own techniques could bring people in and persuade the unchurched to come back. Church leaders wished to entertain young people into becoming Christians, and they were using worldly insights to obtain spiritual outcomes.

What they needed was a sense of their own hopelessness, of their utter dependence upon God, of the futility of mere human endeavor, and a re-membrance of how God had rescued his people in times past and that only he could do so again. To see the stones that God had commanded Joshua to lay down would remind the children of Israel permanently that it was God who had rescued them—and as the Doctor went on to explain, this is what Scripture exists for today, to show us the mighty works of God in the lives of his people.

How often have we heard this before? Madison Avenue techniques and secular marketing methods are employed to persuade people to come into church. Nothing is new! History shows us again and again that human attempts to fill churches might last for a fleeting time, but fads always fail. Only the preaching of the gospel and the sovereign work of the Holy Spirit bring true revival, lasting Christian growth, and genuine inward change.

The sermon chosen was one he preached again in 1980. Significantly it was to be his last ever, with a quotation from the passage in Joshua: "What mean these stones?"

It was a fitting end!

And he spake unto the children of Israel, saying, When your children shall ask their fathers in time to come, saying, What mean these stones?

Then ye shall let your children know, saying, Israel came over this Jordan on dry land. For the LORD your God dried up the waters of Jordan from before you, until ye were passed over, as the LORD your God did to the Red sea, which he dried up from before us, until we were gone over: That all the people of the earth might know the hand of the LORD, that it is mighty: that ye might fear the LORD your God for ever. (Josh. 4:21–24)

We have, you remember, been looking at the story in the book of Joshua because it is a perfect illustration of why it is important for us to have monuments and reminders of the great things that God has done. We have seen that the principles on which God acts never vary. We are called upon to consider historical facts, significant and miraculous facts, and now we must move on to another aspect of this great subject of revival. What is the object and the purpose of it all? Here is this miraculous thing that happened. But why did it happen? Or, if I may put my question in a different way and ask with reverence, why does God do this from time to time? For we have been reminding ourselves that what happened one hundred years ago is but one in a series of similar events. From time to time in the long history of the church, there have been these visitations, these outpourings of God's Spirit. Nothing is clearer in the history of the church than that. Indeed, that does seem to be the history of the church. There was a great outpouring of the Spirit on the Day of Pentecost. That visitation persisted for some time, but then it began to wane and finally vanished. The church got into a powerless condition, so much so that some people thought the end had come. Then suddenly God poured out his Spirit again, and the church was raised up to the heights once more. For a time that persisted, but then it, too, gradually passed. So the history of the church is a sort of graph of ups and downs. That has been happening throughout the running centuries.

Now, the question we are concerned with at this point is, why does God do this from time to time? And the answer is given to us very perfectly in these verses that we are looking at now. The first reason given in verse 24 is this—"that all the people of the earth might know the hand of the LORD, that it is mighty." This then is the first reason that is given. God does this thing from time to time, God sends revival, blessing, upon the church in order that he may do something with respect to those who are outside. He is doing something that is going to arrest the attention of all the people of the earth. Here, we must always realize, is the chief reason for ever considering this matter at all. This is my main reason for calling attention to this whole subject of revival and for urging everybody to pray for revival, to look for it and to long for it. This is the reason—the glory of God. You see, Israel alone represented God and his glory. All the other nations of the world were pagan; they had their various gods, and they did not believe in or worship the God of Israel. But God had chosen Israel. He had made a nation for himself in order that through them and by means of them he might manifest his own glory and that they might bear this testimony to all the nations of the world. That was the real function of the children of Israel, and the other nations were watching them and were ready always to scoff at them and ridicule them. Whenever the nation of Israel was defeated or seemed to be helpless or was in any trouble, the other nations would always say, "Where is their God, the God of whom they have spoken so much and of whom they have boasted so much, where is he? Where is his power?"

And so the first reason for this miraculous act is that all these peoples and nations "might know the hand of the LORD, that it is mighty." God is vindicating himself; he is asserting his own glory and his own power. He is doing this in order that those on the outside, who scoff and speak in derision, may see something that will pull them up and arrest them and astound them. Now we must never lose sight of this. It is the main reason for being concerned about revival. We should not seek revival in order that we may have experiences. I have described experiences that do take place in revival, but we do not seek revival primarily for their sake. There are people who do. There are people who always rush to meetings where any kind of experience is promised, and they make the rounds from one meeting to another, people who are just itching and thirsting to have experiences, always thinking of themselves. But that is not the way in which it is put here, for the primary thing is the glory of God, the power and the name of God, the honor of God. So let us be perfectly clear about that.

There are people who are ready to jump at anything that will solve their problem or the problem of the church. Some years ago the main sections of the Christian church were not interested at all in evangelism. They despised it and dismissed it with derision. But today every section of the church is talking a great deal about evangelism. And the reason is that they are seeing the churches becoming empty, so they will take up anything that may help them to solve the problem of church attendance or even church finances.

And they would undoubtedly do likewise with respect to revival, but that is a terrible thing to do. Our overriding, controlling reason for having any interest at all in these matters should be the glory of God. Does it grieve you, my friends, that the name of God is being taken in vain and desecrated? Does it grieve you that we are living in a godless age—an age when men have sufficient arrogance to speak sarcastically in public and in private of the record of God's mighty deeds and actions?

But we are living in such an age, and the main reason we should be praying about revival is that we are anxious to see God's name vindicated and his glory manifested. We should be anxious to see something happening that will arrest the nations, all the peoples, and cause them to stop and to think again. So here is the first thing. You will find it constantly in the Scriptures. It is in many ways one of the leading themes, if not *the* leading theme, in the book of Psalms. Read the Psalms and see those men praying for a visitation of God's Spirit. Every time it is in order that the heathen who are scoffing may be silenced. The psalmists cry out to God that he should do something that will silence them. This is the end to which they are always looking, that God will do something and speak in such a way that will call everybody to "Be still, and know that I am God" (Ps. 46:10). That is the great theme of Psalm 46. The nations and their princes are all being addressed, these people who are arguing against God and querying whether there is such a God. "And listen" says the psalmist, "here is the God who makes wars cease; this is the God who arises and vindicates himself." Then, having displayed his case, he says, "Be still," give up, give in, admit "that I am God."

Now that is the thing of which we are reminded here. God himself told Joshua to tell the people his primary reason for setting up this memorial—that he might thus manifest his glory and silence the people who are outside. And that is what revival has invariably achieved. It has caused those who are outside the church and those who are inimical to Christianity to pay attention. For it is indeed a phenomenon. It is, as we have agreed, something miraculous. It is something that astounds them and causes them, of necessity, to stop and to look and to consider. Of course, their reason for stopping and considering may not be a good one. It may be sheer curiosity, but whatever it is, it does not matter, for it does make them stop and think. We have a classic example of this, of course, in Acts 2. It is the account of what happened on the Day of Pentecost when the Holy Spirit was

135

poured out, and we read that the people of Jerusalem and all the strangers who were gathered there were arrested, and they said, "What is this?" A phenomenon—something was happening, and they were forced to pay attention, and Peter had to get up and give his explanation, you remember. That is always what a revival does, and I maintain that there is nothing short of a revival that will have that effect. We have tried nearly everything else, but it does not succeed. The masses of the people even if they show a temporary interest show no more than that. Men can never do anything that will have this effect. This is always the action of God. If I may put it bluntly and clearly, what is needed is not a stunt but the action of God that will stun people. That is the difference. Man can produce stunts, and he is very clever at doing that. He can think of something fresh and new, and he will advertise it, but the people know the whole time that it is man's doing. "It's a stunt," they say. Stunts will never lead to this desired position. But when God arises and God acts, then something is happening that will force men's attention. They cannot understand it. Here psychologists are left without any explanation. They can explain stunts without difficulty, but they cannot explain this. That is the difference between man organizing something and God manifesting the right hand of his power and showing that it is mighty.

Now surely this is the crying need of the hour. We are aware of the position of the vast majority of the people of this country [England]; church attendance constitutes but 5 percent of the population. And though we may preach and fast and sweat and pray and do all we can, all our efforts seem to lead to nothing. What is needed is some mighty demonstration of the power of God, some enactment of the Almighty that will compel people to pay attention and to look and to listen. And the history of all the revivals of the past indicates so clearly that is invariably the effect of revival, without any exception at all. That is why I am calling attention to revival. That is why I am urging you to pray for this. When God acts, he can do more in a minute than man with his organizing can do in fifty years. Let us realize this tremendous possibility, therefore, and plead to God to make known his power and to manifest his glory in the midst of a crooked and perverse generation of people—people that even blaspheme his holy name and deny his very existence. For God's sake, for the glory of his name, let us intercede and pray for a visitation of God's Spirit.

There, then, is the first great reason—"that all the people of the earth might know the hand of the LORD, that it is mighty." The second reason is, "that ye might fear the LORD your God for ever." That is what I have been emphasizing, that revival is of great value to the church, as well as all it does for the world. "That [you] might know . . . that ye might fear the LORD your God for ever." So, what does it do for the church? Let me enumerate some of the things that are taught here quite plainly.

The first thing it does is to give the church an unusual consciousness of the presence of the power of God. "That ye [the children of Israel] might fear the LORD your God for ever." Now in the tenth verse of the previous chapter it is put much more explicitly and powerfully: "And Joshua said, Hereby ye shall know that the living God is among you." That is it. This is going to happen, said Joshua to the people, in order that you may know that the living God is among you. When you read this story of the children of Israel you see very clearly that they needed to be reminded of that. Though they were God's people, though he had done so many things for them and to them, though he had brought them out of Egypt, though he had brought them through the Red Sea, though he had led them in the wilderness where their feet did not swell and where they never lacked food because he fed them with manna, the bread from heaven, yet they were constantly fearful and grumbling, looking at the other nations and peoples and their gods, hesitant and doubtful. They behaved in a manner that makes us feel they were a people who did not realize their relationship to God. And God did this thing at the river of Jordan in order that they might know that the living God was among them.

Now this is the supreme need of the church today. In one way the main trouble with the Christian church as she is at this moment, the main trouble with every one of us in our daily life and living, is that we fail to realize that the living God is among us. What is the church? It is this institution, this body in which God dwells. He has promised, "I will be in you. I will dwell in you. I will walk among you." That is what he says. That is what he said to these children of Israel (see, for example, Exod. 29:45–46). That is what is transferred in exactly the same way to the Christian church. The Christian church is not a human organization and institution. She is, as the apostle Paul puts it at the end of Ephesians 2, a great building in which God dwells, a habitation of God.

This is an argument that is worked out in many places in the New

Testament epistles. But the church does not seem to realize that today. People persist in regarding the Christian church as just an institution, one institution among others, just a human organization. But that is not the church; the church is this body in which God himself dwells. And what he does in revival is to remind us of that. When God acts in revival, everybody present feels and knows that God is there. Of course, we believe this. We believe this by faith. Yes, but we should *know* it. We should have a realization of it. We should be conscious of his nearness. And that is what revival does for us. "I am going to do this thing," says God. "Then all of you will realize that I am among you, I am acting in your midst. I, the living God, have come down among you. I am in you. You are my people, and I dwell in you, and I walk in you." That is what the church needs to realize today.

But, of course, it is the very thing she does not realize. It is the thing we are always forgetting. But though I put that first, we must remember that God, at the same time, reminds us that the whole power that should be manifest in the church is his power, that everything the church does should be a manifestation of the power of God. What is the gospel? Well, you remember the answer of the apostle Paul: "It is the power of God unto salvation to every one that believeth" (Rom. 1:16). How easy it is to forget that. How easy to preach it as a system, to preach it as a collection of ideas, or just to preach it as a truth. Ah, but you can do that without power. There are people, says the apostle Paul, who have "a form of godliness, but deny the power thereof" (2 Tim. 3:5). Christianity is primarily a life. It is a power. It is a manifestation of energy. And as we realize that the living God is among us, we shall realize more and more this tremendous power.

That in turn will lead us to realize that the one thing that matters is that we should be rightly related to God and always reliant on his power. The apostle's great claim, you remember, in writing to the Corinthians is that when he came to them he did not preach to them with wisdom of men; it was "not with enticing words of man's wisdom" (1 Cor. 2.1–4). He could have done that. He was a very able man and one who was learned and very well read. But though he was going to a seat of learning—there was a university in Corinth—and he knew the mentality of the Greeks, he did not approach them along that line at all. He tells them later that he became a fool for Christ's sake, and many of them despised him because of that. But the apostle says he did not come in that way. In what way then? He says, "in demonstration of the Spirit and of power: that your faith should not stand in the wisdom of men, but in the power of God" (1 Cor. 2:4–5).

We all need to be reminded of this. Let me make a confession for all preachers. The outstanding temptation—the besetting sin—of every preacher, myself included, is that after you have prepared your sermons you feel that all is well. You have your two sermons ready for Sunday. Well, that is all right. You have your notes, and you can speak, and you can deliver your message. But that is not preaching! That can be utterly useless. Oh, it may be entertaining, there may be a certain amount of intellectual stimulus and profit in it, but that is not preaching. Preaching is a demonstration of the Spirit and of power. And a man has to realize, after he has prepared his sermons, that however perfectly he may have done so, that it is all waste and useless unless the power of the Spirit comes upon it and upon him. He must pray for that.

Yes, but not only he. Those who listen must also pray for that. How many people pray before they go to a service that the Spirit of God might come upon the preacher and use him and his message? The hearers as well as the preacher must pray for that; otherwise they are looking to him and to his message. All together must look to God and realize their utter dependence upon the power that he alone can give. And whenever there is a revival and God's power is manifested, you need not urge people to pray—they do. They want to see more and more of it. Revival, then, encourages us to pray, and that is why it is good for us to read these accounts and look back on what God has done, that we may realize that the living God is among us. And we must pray to him to manifest this power.

Negatively this means that revival delivers us from any and every form of self-reliance, which is the curse of the church. There is no difficulty at all in explaining the state of the Christian church today. It is so perfectly simple. I will tell you why the church is as she is today—it is because of self-reliance in the following forms.

First, reliance upon scholarship and learning. This came in about the middle of the nineteenth century. "Ah," people began to say, "we are now becoming more educated, and we have advanced. Of course we do not want the sort of thing they had in past centuries under Whitefield and Wesley and so on. We now want learned sermons." And so they began to have them. And great attention was paid to form and to style and to diction. Sermons were published, and it was obvious as the man was writing them that he had his eye on publication rather than on the service in which he was going to preach his sermon. Everything became learned and scholarly and philosophical, and great sermons were delivered. And that is one of the main causes and explanations of the state of the church today—reliance upon human learning and knowledge and wisdom.

Then, second, of course, the reliance upon organizing. In the last hundred years the church has multiplied her organizations and institutions in a way that she has never done before in all her long history. There have never been so many subsections of the Christian church as during the present century. Everything is being organized—age groups and everything else. And there are head offices that send you literature telling you how to do whatever your interest may be—how to handle children, how to handle young people, advice on this and that. All is perfectly organized, and yet look at the state of the church. They are relying on the organization.

Others rely on their own activities. As long as they are busy they think tremendous things are happening. And, of course, if you organize and if you are active, it will be reported in the papers—they must have something to report. And people say, "Tremendous things are happening. Look at it." But what is happening? Look at the church, that is the answer. No, my dear friends, we need to learn once more the difference between bustle and busyness and "the hand of the LORD, that it is mighty."

But when God acts and when people realize that the living God is among them, they are humbled, they are abased. Men do not count any longer. And the reports are not about what men have done but about what God has done and what happens to men as the result of God's action. A revival always humbles men, abases them, casts them to the floor, makes them feel they can do nothing, fills them with a sense of reverence and godly fear. Oh, how absent that is among us. How men are standing forward. But when revival comes, men push back, they are humbled to the ground, and the glory is given to God, because it is God's power that is in evidence.

Then my next point, of course, follows by logical necessity. When all this happens, the fear of men is taken away from us in every form. In Joshua 3:10 we read: "And Joshua said, Hereby ye shall know that the living God is among you, and that he will without fail drive out from before you the Canaanites, and the Hittites, and the Hivites, and the Perizzites, and the Girgashites, and the Amorites, and the Jebusites."

The children of Israel were about to enter the promised land, and they had been hearing about all these tribes. The spies had been sent forward, and they came back and said, "You know, there are giants in that land, and when we looked at them we felt that we were as grasshoppers." And they were trembling; they were afraid of these great powers that they had met when they entered the promised land. Here is the answer: when you know that the living God is among you, what are the Hittites, who are the Girgashites and the Jebusites, what are the whole lot of them put together? They become as nothing. The fear of men is taken away immediately when we realize that the living God is among us. And if ever the church needed this, it is now. The church is so afraid. She is afraid of organized sin, and her argument is, "We must do something because look at the world. It is attracting the young people; it gives them a happy pleasant Saturday night, entertains them, teaches them how to sing and do this and that. Now we must do the same thing. Bring your pop group or whatever into your Sunday night service. That is what they like, you see." The world is doing it, and the young people say, "I like it," and because the church is so afraid they are going to lose their young people they feel they must do the same. Oh, what a tragedy, what a departure from God's way!

The church has been afraid of the young people for a long time, and that is why she has multiplied these institutions to try to attract them. And she is afraid, too, of the lure of the modern world. People say, "What can we do? We are up against television nowadays. There was no television two hundred years ago. They had no radio, they had no cinema. There is our problem. We must do something," they say. They are afraid of these organizations and powers. And, too, they are terrified of learning and of knowledge. "Hear," they say, "what these experts are saying on the various radio and television programs, and our people hear these things. Is it intellectually respectable to be a Christian? Can you really talk about miracles still? And about dividing the Red Sea and the Jordan? Surely people will not believe all that!" So we trim and modify our gospel because we are afraid of learning and of knowledge and of science. That is what the church has been doing for a hundred years, and that is why she is as she is today. Then people say that Communism is spreading, and if it seems to succeed through using various methods, then we should use them too. They say that we must also

141

make our literature more effective. All right, go on doing these things, but if you rely upon them you are already defeated.

There is no need to be afraid of any of these powers—they have always been there. There is nothing new about all this. The Christian church always had to fight the world and the flesh and the devil. She had to fight the Roman Empire at the beginning. She had to fight the malignity of the Jews. She has always had enemies who are out to exterminate her. And the church has often quaked and feared, but never when there has been revival, because then they know that the living God is among them, and "he will without fail drive out from before you the Canaanites, and the Hittites, and the Hivites, and the Perizzites, and the Girgashites, and the Amorites, and the Jebusites" (Josh. 3:10). He names them one by one, you see, as I have been trying to do. What have we to fear from of all these things when the living God comes among us? Oh, for a touch of his power. Oh, that the church might realize that this is the answer, and then our fear of all our enemies and opponents would vanish like the morning mist. "Fear Him, ye saints, and you will then have nothing else to fear." That is how the writer of the hymn puts it, and how right he is. Revival does that for us.

And so, to sum it up, revival makes us look, and keeps us looking, to God and dependent upon him. Our supreme need, and our only need, is to know God, the living God, and the power of his might. We need nothing else. It is just that, the power of the living God, to know that the living God is among us and that nothing else matters. So we wait upon him. We look to him. We cry out to him, as Moses did when he was standing before the Red Sea, not knowing what to do, while the people were grumbling and complaining. God answered Moses and said, "Wherefore criest thou unto me? speak unto the children of Israel, that they go forward" (Ex. 14:15). And on they went.

> Stand then in His great might,
> With all His strength endued;
> And take, to arm you for the fight,
> The panoply of God.
>
> CHARLES WESLEY

That is what we need, my friends. And that is why I am urging you to pray for revival. We must look to him. God does this in order to give us encouragement, to show us that he is among us. And the reminder of what happened one hundred years ago should lead us to turn back to him. I say, forget everything else. We need to realize the presence of the living God among us. Let everything else be silent. This is no time for minor differences. We all need to know the touch of the power of the living God. May we continue and wait until we know it.

And then, of course, God does this in order to deliver us from our enemies—enemies without, enemies within. Yes, God did all these things to bring his people out of Egypt, out of the wilderness, into the blessed land of Canaan. He does it, I say, in order to lead us to the land of blessing—Canaan, a land flowing with milk and honey. What does this mean in the church? It means that there has never been a revival but that it has led to praise and to thanksgiving, to enjoyment of the riches of God's grace. The great characteristic of revival is ultimately praise, adoration, worship, full enjoyment, unmixed and evermore.

But in conclusion let me just direct your attention to one other thing. We have considered this great fact of what happens in revival. We have considered the nature of the fact, the miraculous, the almighty power of God. We have asked the question, why does God do this? I want to ask a last question: when does God do this? You want to know that, I hope. If you are longing and yearning, I am sure that you are asking the question, Oh, when is God going to do this? We have been praying, many of us for years. Nothing seems to happen. When does God send revival? Well, the answer is here in this story of Joshua, and it is confirmed by the history of the church.

There seem to me to be two main factors here. The first is this: God always seems to do this after a period of great trial and great discouragement. The text, we have seen, reminds us of two occasions—the crossing of the Red Sea and the crossing of the River Jordan. When does he do this marvelous thing? Oh, he does it after you have been in Egypt for a while, in the bondage, in the captivity, in the cruelty of Egypt, with the taskmasters and the lashes of their whips, trying to make bricks without sufficient straw. Bondage, aridity, cruelty, persecution, and trial. He does it after Egypt. He does it also after a period in the wilderness. Here are the children of Israel right before Jordan. Yes, but they had just been forty years in the wilderness, without a home, in the howling, barren wilderness with its storms and its trials, its testings and its provings—all that had happened to them there.

Read the story, and what a sad story it is. Yes, they had had a wilderness experience.

And on top of that they'd had another calamity, which to many of them must have seemed to be the end of all things. Moses, their great leader, had died. He had gone up onto a mountain, and he had never come back again. The man who had come to them originally with a message from God and had addressed them in their utter serfdom when they were brokenhearted, the man who had led them through so much, was gone. And a man called Joshua was left to lead them. Who was he and what was he? The position, you see, seemed to be utterly discouraging. Forty years in the wilderness, and now without a leader.

Ah, thank God for this. It is after such experiences that God sends revival. After Egypt, after the wilderness experience. God knows the Christian church has been in this wilderness many a long year. If you read the history of the church before about 1830 or 1840, you will find that in many countries there used to be regular revivals of religion almost every ten years or so. It has not been like that. There has only been one major revival since 1859. Oh, we have passed through a barren period, with that devastating higher criticism and the evil that it has done in pulpits and in pews everywhere. People have lost their belief in this living God and in the atonement and in reconciliation and have turned to wisdom, philosophy, and learning. We have passed through one of the most barren periods in the long history of the church. We have been like the prodigal son in that far country, spending our time in the fields with the swine and living on nothing but husks. Yes, we have been in bondage, we have been in fear, we have suffered persecution and derision, and it is still going on. We are still in the wilderness. Do not believe anything that suggests that we are out of it, for we are not. The church is in the wilderness. But thank God it is always after such a period that God acts and does his mighty deeds and shows forth his glory.

The second factor in this story is also most important. It is not only after Egypt or after the wilderness that God acts. The real moment, the moment of crisis, is when you are right up against the Red Sea, when you are actually on the border of Jordan. It is then he does it. You see, we can be forty years in the wilderness, but the mere fact of being in the wilderness does not produce it. No; it comes not in the wilderness but when we have actually arrived at this critical position. If I may use modern terminology,

God always seems to do this when we are right up against it and so much against it that we are hopeless and helpless. Do you remember the picture at the Red Sea? The children of Israel had been commanded to go on. Where were they to go? Well, they were taken to a point at which on one side was Pi-hahiroth and on the other side Baal-zephon, two mountains, one on each side of them. Behind them were Pharaoh and his hosts and the chariots, the army of Egypt. And there were the defenseless children of Israel with nothing to defend them at all—mountain here, mountain there, the enemy behind, and in front the Red Sea. It was a situation of complete and entire hopelessness and despair, with the people grumbling and complaining, asking Moses what it all meant, and Moses had nothing to do but to fall before God. And then the answer came, and the Red Sea was divided.

It was exactly the same here at Jordan. We are even given this interesting detail that the River Jordan was badly flooded for long months at that time of the year. They could not possibly cross it. There they were, facing a flood. How could they get through? It was then that God arose and manifested the right hand of his power and gave a display of his glory. I just put this to you in the form of a challenge. Read the histories and accounts of every revival that has ever taken place and you will invariably find that the one man or group, the little group of people, who have been used in this way by God to send revival have always known a state of utter desperation and final despair. Every single one of them. Read the journals of Whitefield and Wesley. Read the life history of all these men. They have always come to this place where they have realized their utter and absolute impotence, their final paralysis. There is the Red Sea. Here is the enemy. There are the mountains. They are shut in, they are shut down, they are crushed to their knees. It is always the prerequisite. That is always the moment at which God acts.

And that is what, I confess, troubles me and discourages me today. The Christian church is still so healthy, so confident in herself, so sure that she only needs to organize yet another effort, some further activity. She has not come up to the Red Sea. She has never been to Pi-hahiroth and Baal-zephon. She does not know that experience, and until she does I cannot see that we have much reason for anticipating a revival of religion and an outpouring of the Spirit of God. It may be, you see, that things infinitely worse than what we have already known will yet have to happen to us. You would have thought that two world wars would have done it, but they have not. You would have thought that the present position would have been enough, but it is not. God have mercy upon us. Until, I say, we arrive at Pi-hahiroth, Baal-zephon, Migdal, the enemy, the Red Sea, the utter hopelessness, Jordan in flood, the utter impossibility, and the final despair we will not have revival. May God bring us to that realization. May he so reveal his own glory and holiness to us. May he reveal unto us our utter impotence and hopelessness. May we see these things in such a way that we shall cease from men and look only unto the living God. And then there is no question but that he will hear us and will manifest his glory and his power.

10

THE SPIRIT HIMSELF BEARS WITNESS

(1955–1968)
Romans 8:16

From *Romans: Exposition of Chapter 8:5–17*

In his famous series on the epistle of Paul to the Romans, preached from 1955 to his retirement in 1968, Dr. Lloyd-Jones realized that several of the things that he would say were bound to be controversial. In the preface to the volume on Romans 8:5–17 (titled The Sons of God*) he actually states this in his preface to the book.*

Over the course of time, some of the Doctor's views have become profoundly controversial, and two of them in particular: church separation and the doctrine of the baptism and gifts of the Holy Spirit.

As we mentioned in the introduction to this whole volume, we have made a conscious decision to steer clear of these two major debates, both of which have generated much light and heat in the now more than three decades since his death in 1981. This book is aimed to reach those of all persuasions on both these topics. But on the other hand it would be strange to omit his views on the work of the Holy Spirit altogether, as they dominated much of his preaching in his final years at Westminster Chapel.

So we decided to adopt an irenic approach and chose a sermon that he preached in the early 1960s on a Friday evening. It is one that he edited himself in his own lifetime and that was published by the Banner of Truth in 1974 (and by Zondervan in the United States the next year). With this sermon there can be no dispute that he presented it to his publisher as it stands and that it was the Banner of Truth that brought out the book.

Rather than go over much disputed territory and distract from the main goal of our book, it might be better just to ask a few questions and then go on to a very important point, one that is often missed when considering the Doctor and his whole approach to Scripture and to doctrine.

So here are three quick questions:

1) *Does he advocate here that "the baptism of the Holy Spirit" is separate from conversion?*
2) *Does he show that it is a biblical term?*
3) *What does he say about any particular spiritual gifts that do or do not accompany such an event in a believer's life?*

Let the reader decide!

But rather than engage directly in what he himself says is a controversy, let us look at the wider issue of the Doctor and doctrine and his basis for what he believed and why.

As Protestants we all believe in the great Reformation teaching of sola scriptura. Dr. Lloyd-Jones believed in it passionately and practiced it all his life and ministry. Note in this sermon how he gets Scripture to validate other Scripture—that is always, surely, the Reformation method! He also brings in the witness of Christians in the history of the church, but this is evidence of what the Bible teaches rather than being our primary source of doctrinal inspiration.

Of course, one would argue, we are the same! But are we in practice? I rather wonder whether, if we were all totally honest with ourselves, we are in reality as influenced by tradition as the Roman Catholics. We would deny that, but subconsciously it is so often true. We are "Reformed," "Calvinist," "Baptist," and all sorts of other man-made and humanly constructed things.

We may not have a pope. But we do have people from history whom we follow and in whose light we so often interpret Scripture. Our shelves groan with commentaries from our heroes, and they are our guides as to what to think. We have contemporary heroes as well, mighty preachers whose sermons enthrall us and on whose every word we hang with delight.

So let us consider sola scriptura again. Is it really the Bible that determines our belief, or is it our denominational tradition or perhaps what our favorite preacher says on Sunday? For the Doctor, it really was the Bible alone, and surely that should be true for all of us as well.

> The Spirit itself beareth witness with our spirit, that we are the children
> of God. (Romans 8:16)

As we come to our positive exposition of this great statement I suggest that
we must do so in the light of two main considerations. First, we must follow
a rule that should always be observed in interpreting Scripture—namely,
that we should interpret Scripture by Scripture. We should always look for
parallel statements. That is a sound and cardinal principle of exegesis and
of exposition. If we are not quite clear as to the meaning of a statement,
we should look for parallel statements. In this case we find such a statement
in John's Gospel, chapter 7, verses 37 to 39, where we read: "In the last day,
that great day of the feast, Jesus stood and cried, saying, If any man thirst,
let him come unto me, and drink. He that believeth on me, as the scripture
hath said, out of his belly [his inward parts] shall flow rivers of living water.
(But this spake he of the Spirit, which they that believe on him should receive: for the Holy Ghost was not yet given; because that Jesus was not yet
glorified.)" Dealing as we are in this sixteenth verse with the work of the
Holy Spirit we go back to that statement in John chapter 7, where we find a
prophecy concerning the coming of the Spirit and his effect upon believers.
They will know complete satisfaction. Not only so, but they will become
the means of blessing to large numbers of other people.

Another important parallel statement is one that we have already met in
this very epistle in chapter 5, verse 5, where the apostle said, "because the
love of God is shed abroad in our hearts by the Holy Ghost which is given
unto us." When we dealt with that verse we were at pains to emphasize the
"shedding abroad." It is not a description of a man just managing to persuade himself that the love of God is in him. It does not mean our love to
God; it means God's love to us. In other words it is a description of a man
who is flooded with a consciousness of the love of God. The term "shed
abroad" suggests a profusion, an amplitude.

The same emphasis is found in the account of what happened on the
Day of Pentecost (Acts, chapter 2). The disciples had been fearful and apprehensive and uncertain after the death of our Lord and even his resurrection appearances. Though those events had brought them comfort and
a certain amount of understanding, they had not produced the vital trans-
forming effect that obviously took place on the Day of Pentecost. From
then on they were entirely different men; they were "baptized with [or by]

the Holy Ghost." The same thing is repeated in chapter 4 of Acts, where we are told that the place where they were assembled together was shaken, and "they were all filled with the Holy Ghost, and they spake the word of God with boldness" (v. 33). Another illustration is found in Acts 8 in the account of what happened to the Samaritans who had believed after Peter and John had gone down from Jerusalem and prayed for them and laid their hands upon them. And again in chapter 10 we find the case of Cornelius and his household. Finally, there is the case of the "disciples" at Ephesus on whom the apostle Paul laid hands, and they were filled and baptized with the Spirit (chapter 19).

All these, I suggest, are examples of what we are dealing with here in Romans 8:16. Take also what we find in the book of Revelation, chapter 2, verse 17: "He that hath an ear, let him hear what the Spirit saith unto the churches; To him that overcometh will I give to eat of the hidden manna, and will give him a white stone, and in the stone a new name written, which no man knoweth saving he that receiveth it." I maintain this is only another way of saying what the apostle says here in this sixteenth verse. The same idea is found in the twenty-eighth verse of Revelation, chapter 2: "And I will give him the morning star." We need not here be concerned with the exact meaning of the symbolism that is used in the book of Revelation. All I am indicating is that we are told in the verses I have quoted that the people who have obeyed and pleased the Lord will be given tokens of his good pleasure represented by "the hidden manna," "a white stone," and "the morning star." Then in the third chapter of the same book, in the message to the church at Philadelphia (v. 12), we find a similar idea: "Him that overcometh will I make a pillar in the temple of my God, and he shall go no more out: and I will write upon him the name of my God, and the name of the city of my God, which is new Jerusalem, which cometh down out of heaven from my God: and I will write upon him my new name." This further promise falls into the same category; it is given to believers, to members of the Christian church. They will be given something extra, something special, "the name of my God," "the name of the city of my God," "my new name." They will be quite certain that they belong to God and to the Lord Jesus Christ, that their eternal destiny is secure, and that they will be given some very special assurance and seal of their position and of their relationship to God.

Those passages help us understand Romans 8:16, and there are others. Is it not clear to anyone who reads the New Testament without prejudice that the early Christians, speaking generally, had a spiritual experience and insight and understanding that distinguishes them in a very striking manner from the vast majority of Christians at the present time? Take, for instance, what Peter, writing to ordinary members of the church, says in the first chapter of his first epistle: "Whom having not seen, ye love; in whom, though now ye see him not, yet believing, ye rejoice with joy unspeakable and full of glory" (v. 8). Those words were written to ordinary members of the Christian church, and they seem to have been characteristic of the life of the members of the early church. Such a background helps us to understand and interpret this verse: "The Spirit itself beareth witness with our spirit, that we are the children of God."

Our second consideration must be the light that is thrown on this text by the subsequent history of the Christian church. This again is a very valuable aid in interpreting a statement of Scripture. If we bring all Scripture down to the level of our own experience and understanding today we shall often rob it of some of its greatest glories. But if we look at the long history of the Christian church and pay attention to certain things that are to be seen in individuals and in groups of churches and perhaps in a whole country at times, we shall be given an insight into what we have in this verse. In other words, if you are in doubt about the meaning of such a verse as this, do not reduce it to something that may be true in your own experience and limit it to that. Read the lives of the saints, read the story of certain unusual people who have adorned the church of God, and listen to what they have to say. I propose to give several quotations in order to illustrate what I mean. Some have had experiences of which they do not hesitate to say, "At that moment the Spirit himself bore witness with my spirit that I am a child of God."

But in addition to individual experiences we have the phenomenon of great revivals. Revivals, and the history of revivals, are most important in this context. In such histories we read of people who have been members of churches, perhaps for years. They had believed on the Lord Jesus Christ, and they had a measure of assurance of salvation; but when the revival came, when the Spirit of God was poured down upon them, what happened to them was so marvelous that they began to think that up to that time they had never been Christians at all. They were suddenly given an absolute cer-

151

tainty and assurance of their relationship to God that they had never had before. That, it seems to me, is the very thing we have in the verse we are studying. So, in addition to the Scriptures that point directly to this particular operation of the Holy Spirit, we have this extraordinary confirmation in the lives of saints and in the whole history of the church at periods of revival, when the Spirit of God is poured out in an unusual manner and in great profusion and when numbers of people together suddenly come into this place of assurance and clarity of knowledge and of understanding.

So taking these two great canons of interpretation, at what conclusion do we arrive? The first conclusion is that this is obviously something that is done by the Holy Spirit himself. The apostle chose to put it in this way: "The Spirit itself [himself] beareth witness." Why did he not simply say, "The Spirit beareth witness," or "The Spirit also beareth witness with our spirit"? He deliberately said "The Spirit itself beareth witness," as if to safeguard us against the very errors we have considered and to make it clear to us that he is not concerned here with the witness of the *work* of the Spirit in us but with the *person* of the Spirit himself witnessing to us and with our spirits—which is a very different thing. We have already seen, in verse 14, what the work of the Spirit is, and that is to be a witness. We have seen in verse 15, still more strikingly, that it is when the Spirit comes into our hearts that we in our own spirits have the Spirit of adoption. That again is part of the work of the Spirit. But here Paul emphasizes that he is not dealing with such work of the Spirit but with what the Spirit himself does directly.

The witness and testimony of the Holy Spirit himself confirms the witness of our own spirits. Our own spirits cry, "Abba, Father," and they thereby witness to the fact that we are the children of God. We have a childlike spirit, a filial spirit within us. My own spirit tells me that I am a child of God, and I feel toward God as a child feels toward his father. But here the Spirit himself comes alongside the witness of my Spirit and himself bears his witness and his testimony. In other words the peculiar characteristic of what is described here is that it is a direct and an immediate witness of the Spirit himself.

I suggest that this is a part of "the baptism with the Holy Ghost," or if you prefer it, "the baptism *of* the Holy Spirit." That is why I referred to John 7:37–39 and Acts 2 and so on. Indeed I go further and say that what Paul is describing is the most essential aspect of "the baptism of the Holy Ghost."

We said, when dealing with verse 15, that "the Spirit of adoption" is a part of the baptism with the Holy Ghost, but that, as I have just been indicating, is really a preliminary part of that baptism. We cannot be baptized with the Holy Ghost without having the Spirit of adoption, but we can have the Spirit of adoption without knowing this further experience. That is why I say that the most vital and essential part, the essence, of being baptized with the Holy Ghost is that we have this particular form of assurance of our sonship of God.

I do not hesitate to say also that this is the same as the "sealing" of the Spirit. There are three references to the "sealing" of the Spirit in the New Testament. One is in the second epistle to the Corinthians, chapter 1, verse 22, where we are told: "[God] hath also sealed us, and given the earnest of the Spirit in our hearts." Another is found in Ephesians 1, verse 13, which reads: "In whom ye also trusted, after that ye heard the word of truth, the gospel of your salvation: in whom also after that ye believed"—or, a better translation, "in whom also having believed"—"ye were sealed with that holy Spirit of promise." The third reference is in Ephesians 4:30: "And grieve not the holy Spirit of God, whereby ye are sealed unto the day of redemption." These statements have a direct bearing upon the interpretation of this verse, and I suggest that they refer to exactly the same thing. In other words, the Spirit himself seals these promises to us and thereby testifies with our spirits as to our sonship.

There is obviously a difference between the sealing and the earnest, and the difference helps us understand our verse. Both the sealing and the earnest are concerned with the question of our inheritance, but they are interested in it in a different way. The sealing of the Spirit is that which assures me that I am a son of God and therefore an heir of God. The earnest of the Spirit gives me an installment of my inheritance, a first down payment of what I am later to receive in its fullness. If you buy a house, for example, and you do not have sufficient money to pay for it, you pay the seller an agreed lesser amount saying, "I give you this as an earnest that I will pay the remainder. I pay this on account, as a deposit." That is to say, you pay him an earnest. It can also be thought of as a foretaste or the firstfruits of a harvest, a portion of a fullness that is to come. The sealing and the earnest are both concerned with sonship, and especially with heirship, the earnest being that which is given to us "until [the time of] the redemption of the purchased possession" (Eph. 1:14). The sealing is more directly concerned with giving me assurance as to my sonship. So I assert that Romans 8:16 is just another way of stating the doctrine of the sealing of the Spirit. Verse 17 goes on to speak of the inheritance.

What are the characteristics of this action of the Spirit himself? The first is that the Spirit by a direct operation on our minds and hearts and spirits gives us an absolute certainty and assurance of our sonship. That is the great reality. It is not merely that he gives us a heightening of our understanding of the truth, neither is it merely that we are unusually conscious of being led in the direction of sanctification or that the Spirit promotes our sanctification. We have dealt with that in verse 14. This particular action of the Spirit himself must never be confused with sanctification. That, alas, was the error that was introduced by John Wesley and that has persisted ever since. This is not sanctification. It helps in and promotes our sanctification, but it is not sanctification itself. It is the Spirit telling us in this unusual way that we are the children of God. He lets us know in a way we have never known before that God loves us; as Romans 5:5 has stated it, "The love of God is shed abroad in our hearts." That is what the sealing means, and we must never confuse it with sanctification. Obviously a man who knows this has the greatest possible stimulus to become sanctified, but it is not sanctification itself. This leads us to greater efforts in connection with our sanctification.

Yet again this witness that the Spirit bears with our spirit is not only different from and additional to "the Spirit of adoption," it goes well beyond it. That is the real crux of the matter; it takes us into a realm entirely beyond the other. Let me use an illustration from the realm of human love. It is a wonderful thing to tell someone whom you love that you love him or her, but still more wonderful is the experience of being told by the other that he or she loves you. That is the greatest desire and yearning of every lover, and it is the exact difference here. In verse 15 we tell God that we love him. We have "the Spirit of adoption, whereby we cry, Abba, Father," the child's cry of love to the Father. Ah, but here it is God, through the Spirit, telling us that he loves us, and doing so in a most unmistakable manner. It is personal and secret. Our quotations from the book of Revelation emphasized the point that no one knows this but the one who receives it. It is a "hidden manna," it is "a white stone, and in the stone a new name written, which no man knoweth saving he that receiveth it." "I will give him the morning star" has the same message. It is a secret known only to those to whom it is given.

> The love of Jesus, what it is,
> None but His loved ones know.

BERNARD OF CLAIRVAUX
"JESUS, THE VERY THOUGHT OF THEE"

Furthermore, this is the highest form of assurance possible; there is nothing beyond it. It is the acme, the zenith of assurance and certainty of salvation! I emphasize my assertion by saying, negatively, that this is not a deduction. There is a form of assurance that is derived by deduction from the Scriptures. That is the form of assurance that most Christians seem to have, and many believe that it is the only form of assurance. They say, "Are you troubled about your salvation? You need not be; it is quite simple. Do you believe that the Bible is the Word of God?" "Yes, I do," you reply. "Very well, what does it say?" "It says, 'He that believeth is not condemned.'" "Do you believe that?" "Yes." "Well then, you are not condemned. The Word tells you so, and you have just to take God's Word for it." They then take you through a number of similar passages that tell you that if you believe, you are accepted and forgiven—you are "not condemned" and "have passed from death to life." They say, "There the Scripture tells you plainly to believe, and if you do, you can have full assurance." I am not concerned to criticize this method. As far as it goes, it is right. If we do not believe the Word of God, we make God a liar. We must not listen to the devil and his accusations when the Word of God tells us a thing quite plainly. It is right to have that assurance of salvation that is derived by deductions from plain, explicit statements of the Scripture. But this is only the first and the lowest form of assurance. Thank God for it. It will often hold your soul in times of satanic assaults. But you do not end there; that is only the beginning.

Second, what we have here in Romans 8:16 is also not what we deduce about ourselves when we apply to our lives and our experiences the various tests that are given us in the Scriptures. In our study of verse 14 we looked at ten such tests. They are summarized very clearly in the first epistle of John. "We know that we have passed from death unto life, because we love the brethren" (1 John 3:14). In other words, I would say that if you enjoy meetings of Christian people above all others you must be a Christian. That is one of the tests. The next time the devil tells you that you are not a Christian, face him with this question: "Explain to me how it is that I enjoy these things. Why do I prefer the society of Christian people to the best society I can find anywhere in the world that is not Christian? Why do I love the brethren? Why do I desire to keep God's commandments? Why do I desire to be holy? Where does it all come from?" You are deducing thereby from statements in the Scripture applied to your life and experience the fact that you are a child of God. That takes you a step further than the first one; it is better than the first one. The first was merely believing the bare Word of God. But now you have examined your life, and you are sure that you are not merely saying these things in a theoretical or intellectual manner; you are really living them. That is the second step.

But then there is a third step, which we found in verse 15. I remind you of this once more in order to show how the apostle is building up his argument. Having drawn these deductions, I now find in my own spirit something that makes me cry out, "Abba, Father." That is even better; it goes beyond the first two steps. But what we have in this sixteenth verse is still higher and is altogether in a class of its own. This is entirely the action of the Holy Spirit himself. I do nothing about this; it is entirely given. It is solely and exclusively what he does to me. The illustration we found in Thomas Goodwin about the father and the little boy brings this out perfectly. What the father did when he picked up the child and kissed him explains Romans 8:16. It does not change the relationship; it does not make that child a child. He already had an assurance of his sonship within himself. But he did not have it as he had it at the moment when he was enfolded in the arms of his father and the love was being poured out upon him. It is an extra assurance, and the child has done nothing; it has been done to him; it is all the action of the father. So is this! It is the Spirit himself who does it. We do no deducing here. It is not the result of a syllogism or of argumentation. It is the Spirit himself doing it to me.

To what does this lead? As I have said, this is obviously the highest and the greatest form of certainty and assurance that one can ever have of the fact that one is a child of God. At the same time, of course, it gives a better understanding of the whole plan of salvation; there is a kind of luminosity with respect to the truth. I have referred to that already in the individual experiences I have quoted, and we will consider more later on. In times of revival Christian people often say, "I have been reading my Bible and books about the Bible for years. I felt I understood, but in a flash I seemed to see everything with a clarity and a luminosity that I did not think possible to any man while yet in the body." Such a thing does happen, but that is not the essence of this experience. The essence is that he is telling you of his love for you—"God's love . . . poured into our hearts." He is making absolutely certain to you, more certain even than the fact that you are alive, that you are his child. Naturally that in turn leads you to love him—"We love him because he first loved us" (1 John 4:19). The more you know about his love to you, the greater will be your love to him. This and other results follow.

That, again, in turn leads to a great desire to please him in everything, to keep his commandments, never to offend him in anything, to honor his law. It also leads to that which is seen so clearly in the apostles after the Day of Pentecost—namely, a desire to witness to him, accompanied by the power and ability to do so. "We cannot but speak the things which we have seen and heard" (Acts 4:20). The apostles did so with great boldness and power, and their hearers were affected and convinced by it. They could not witness until they were absolutely certain of their position, until they were given this tremendous certainty. That is what happened on the Day of Pentecost. That is what happens always when one receives the baptism of the Spirit. We are given absolute assurance of God's love to us, that we are his children, and that he has loved us with an everlasting love.

Furthermore this experience may be accompanied by various gifts. It was so on the Day of Pentecost. I say "may be," however, for there are variations in this respect, and there is not an exact repetition each time. It is for this reason that those who say that if we have not spoken in tongues we have never been baptized with the Spirit are utterly unscriptural. The apostle asks in 1 Corinthians 12: "do all speak with tongues?" The answer obviously is no, just as all do not work miracles and so on. In the same way, when we look at the subsequent history of the Christian church in the times of great revival when the Spirit of God has been poured forth and thousands have been baptized with the Spirit, there is generally no mention of their working miracles, no suggestion that they spoke with tongues. Similarly this is true of individuals who have experienced this baptism. There may or may not be accompanying gifts. These, then, are variable factors. What is invariable, what is an absolute, is the certainty and assurance of God's love to his own, this knowledge beyond any doubt or question that they are his children. He tells us that himself: "The Spirit itself beareth witness with our spirit, that we are the children of God."

We move on to the last question. How is this experience given, how does it come to us, how does it happen? What stands out here so clearly is the absolute lordship of the Spirit. It is his action, and therefore he can do it in various ways. So any teaching that tells us that we have but to do this or that and it will happen to us is of necessity wrong. The Spirit deals with individual Christians in different ways. False experiences—those that are psychological or mechanical—can be duplicated exactly, but operations of the Spirit cannot be duplicated. He is the Lord, and he dispenses his gifts according to his own sovereign will. So he brings this certain knowledge of salvation to individual Christians in a variety of ways. The first answer to this question as to how it is given, therefore, is that we never know. It cannot be predicted; it cannot be controlled in any way or received at will. No one can promise to give us this blessing. Certain people claim that they can give the gift of the Spirit, but it is not so. It is the Spirit himself who does this, and we do not know how or when.

Another negative answer is that the blessing does not generally come through hearing an audible voice. There is no such indication in the Scripture nor in the subsequent history of men or churches. So when people claim to have heard an audible voice, we have a right to be suspicious. That is not generally the Spirit's way of working. But though it is not through an audible voice, the assurance is quite as definite and as unmistakable as an audible voice. Many can testify that "It was as if I had actually heard it with my very ears." It is the Spirit speaking to the inner man, to the inner ear. But thank God, it is not only as definite as the audible voice, it is even more sure because it happens in the highest part of our personality.

How does it come? Sometimes it comes when a Christian is alone, reading the Scriptures quietly, perhaps reading a passage that he has read many times before. Suddenly the passage seems to come out of the book and to speak to him directly in this particular way. It does not give him some general knowledge, but it stands out and meets him and impresses on his mind and heart and spirit in an unmistakable manner this personal message. It is as if it were written only for him that he is a child of God. That is the most common way in which it comes—through a word or a passage of Scripture.

Sometimes this experience happens to a man when he is not reading. Suddenly a word of Scripture that he has read before is brought into his mind. He is not thinking about it—he may actually be thinking about something quite different—but suddenly it is impressed upon his inner mind, and he becomes convinced that God loves him and that he is a child of God. The Spirit takes a word and brings it to him and impresses it upon him in an absolutely unmistakable manner. It may happen in a religious service, particularly in a preaching service. The preacher says something that means nothing to the vast majority of the people, but to one soul that had been unhappy, uncertain, doubting, and attacked by the devil it is the very voice of God speaking and telling him that he is a child of God and that God has loved him (or her) in particular. The soul never forgets what has thus happened.

But—and I must add this—the assurance does not always come through the Scripture. It has happened to many without any words at all; it is just an inner consciousness in the spirit given by the Spirit of God himself, apart from Scripture. I am much concerned to emphasize this, and for this reason: there are some who have disputed it. Some of the Puritans did so. They were so afraid of the Quakers who arose at the same time that they went so far as to say that you can never have this experience of assurance apart from the Word. In my view that is quite mistaken. The Quakers were undoubtedly wrong in much of their teaching. Some of them said that the Word did not matter at all and that what counted was the "inner light" and the work of the Spirit directly and immediately. That is clearly unscriptural because the Scripture has been given by the Spirit. But we also must not go to the extreme of saying that he can never deal with us immediately and directly and without the Word, for he has often done so. In any case take the case of the Romans to whom Paul was writing. They did not have the New Testament Scriptures, most of which had not even been written, and certainly not in the form in which we have them. They were dependent upon preaching and exhortation. How then could they have known that the Spirit was testifying with their spirits if it happens exclusively through the Word? We must be careful lest in our fear of a certain emphasis on the part of people who talk much about the Holy Spirit we may become guilty of "quenching the Spirit." Normally this testimony is given through the Word, but it can be given without the Word.

Let me quote a statement on this matter by Charles Haddon Spurgeon. In a sermon on full assurance, based upon Psalm 35:3, "say unto my soul, I am thy salvation," which he preached on April 28, 1861, he said:

> God has a way of speaking without the Word, and without the ministers, to our hearts. His Spirit can drop like the rain and distil like the dew, as the small rain upon the tender herb. We know not how it is, but sometimes there is a deep, sweet calm. Our conscience says, "I have been washed in the blood of Christ," and the Spirit of God saith, "Ay, 'tis true! 'tis true!" In such times we are so happy—so happy that we want to tell our joys—so blessed, that if we could but borrow angels' wings and fly away, we would scarce know the change when we passed through the pearly gates, for we have had heaven below, and there has been but little difference between that and heaven above. Oh, I wish my whole congregation without exception consisted of men and women who had heard the Spirit say, "I am *thy* salvation." What happy hymns! What happy prayers! You might go home to some poor single room; you might go to a scantily furnished house, and to a table that has barely bread upon it; but happy men! happy men! Better would be your dinner of herbs than a stalled ox without confidence in Christ; better your rich poverty than the poverty of the rich who have no faith in Jesus; better all the griefs you have to endure, when sanctified by assurance, than all the joys the worldling has, when unblessed by faith and unhallowed by love to God. I can say now,
>
> > Grant me the visits of thy face,
> > And I desire no more.
>
> Ah yes, the Spirit can do this apart from the Word, without the Word, apart from and without a preacher. He can make the direct statement, "I am thy salvation." 'Tis true! 'tis true! Thou hast been washed in the blood of Christ.[1]

I cannot but repeat the words of Spurgeon. Oh, that all Christians knew this and were able to use such words! It is meant for all; it is possible for all.

11

THE ONLY HOPE

(1963)
1 Corinthians 6:9–11

From *The Kingdom of God*

Martyn Lloyd-Jones always argued that God's truth was eternally relevant and that biblical exposition spoke to all peoples throughout time. Consequently he seldom preached topically, nor did he base sermons upon newspaper headlines.

This, as we have all seen by now, makes his sermons permanently contemporary, as applicable in, say, 2013 as in 1933. But the accusation that he never referred to events of the time is unfair, as this extract and the next one (preached in 1963) show us. In his lifetime when he edited his sermons for publication, he would cut out references to events at the time of his preaching the original. In essence his editors have followed the same principle.

However, we made two exceptions, of which this is the first. In 1963 there was a major sexual/political scandal in Britain, named after its worst offender, a man named John Profumo. He was Secretary of State for War (the politician in charge of the army) and was part of a very indecent and decadent social set, mainly based in London but also around the Astor family, the British cousins of their richer and better known-American relatives. One of his many liaisons was with a showgirl named Christine Keeler, who was also sleeping with the Russian military attaché in London, a Soviet spy.

As a young physician in London in the 1920s, Martyn Lloyd-Jones had been chief clinical assistant to Lord Horder, the royal doctor. He knew about the debauchery and decadence of London society in what we now call the Roaring Twenties. But all the antics of the great were hushed up and never revealed to the press, partly since newspaper owners were among those misbehaving. The Doctor was well aware of this as he was physician to one of them.

Nothing shocked him as a result, and with the Profumo scandal the real difference was that this time the press made it all vividly public, and the politicians were called to account for their decadence and immorality.

But for someone with a thoroughly biblical worldview such as Dr. Lloyd-Jones, all these scandals showed was that the scriptural account of humanity was exactly the right one—people really are that bad.

Indeed such had been the precise behavior of the Corinthians whom Paul was addressing in his epistle: "And such were some of you." Immorality is nothing new. One could certainly argue that in this and the previous century we are seeing a return to the total godlessness of Roman times. The veneer of Christian civilization that protected us is now increasingly a thing of the past, and the utter amorality of pre-Christian Roman society is becoming the norm once again.

However, this series of sermons, as with those on "The Cross" that followed later in 1963, were aimed primarily at non-Christians, who could see from the vice of the elite that everyone was truly rotten to the core. Nothing could be more relevant to an audience that year than what the Bible had to say.

And as always there was one answer—the message of Jesus Christ as Savior and Lord. Mere morality would always fail. Only spiritual rebirth in Jesus Christ could wash the sins away, as this sermon goes on so brilliantly to show.

> Know ye not that the unrighteous shall not inherit the kingdom of God? Be not deceived: neither fornicators, nor idolaters, nor adulterers, nor effeminate, nor abusers of themselves with mankind, nor thieves, nor covetous, nor drunkards, nor revilers, nor extortioners, shall inherit the kingdom of God. And such were some of you: but ye are washed, but ye are sanctified, but ye are justified in the name of the Lord Jesus, and by the Spirit of our God. (1 Cor. 6:9–11)

There is no more ridiculous charge brought against the Bible than the criticism that because it is an old book it has no longer anything to say; that because it is old it is out-of-date and not relevant to the present position. But there is nothing, if you really know your Bible, that you will find to be more remarkable about it than that it is always contemporary, always up-to-date, and always has the exact word to say at any particular juncture or stage in the long march and history of the human race. Take these three verses from 1 Corinthians 6. They might very well have been written for just this present hour; they have the very word that is needed at this particular moment.

Indeed, let me put it even further to emphasize this point of how contemporary the Bible always is. Those who meet here regularly on Sunday nights will know that since the last Sunday night of April we have been considering each week the teaching of the Bible concerning the kingdom of God, and those who attend here regularly must have observed that I have been preaching according to a plan and a purpose. Indeed I planned out this whole series of sermons and the ones that are to follow for the next four weeks. And according to my scheme and to my plan I was due to preach tonight on these verses that I have just read to you. I cannot regard that as an accident, my friends. Not only is the Word of God always contemporary, but there is such a thing as being led by the Spirit of God.

So if you can produce any statement from any literature or any speech or anything else anywhere in the world tonight that speaks so directly to this present moment as these verses that we are going to consider, I would be very interested to hear of them. But I know that you cannot do so. The Bible always has the word; it always has the last word. Why is this? It is because the Bible is what it says it is. It is the Word of God. It is not a human book, nor a book of human theories and ideas; it is a book written by different men who all agree in telling us that they were "moved" and carried along by the Spirit of God. They were not writing their own opinions; they were writing what God told them to write. So it is God's revelation with respect to man and his life in this world.

In other words, the business of the church is to preach the Bible, to unfold and expound the message of this Word of God. It has been given in order that we might be taught certain things. "Know ye not?" says Paul in these verses. He expects the Corinthians to know certain things, because he had been there preaching to them, and so had Apollos. And as a result these people had been given information and instruction. Now that is the business of the Bible. It is to give us knowledge that is absolutely vital to our life both in this world and in the world to come.

Or to put it another way, according to the Bible all our troubles as men and women in this world arise from one fundamental cause, and that is our ignorance of certain basic, fundamental truths. We need to be taught certain things plainly and clearly, and God has given us the Bible in order that this might happen. Jesus Christ, the Son of God, came into this world for exactly the same reason. "For this cause," he says, "came I into the world, that I should bear witness unto the truth" (John 18:37). He says also, "I am the light of the world" (John 8:12), and when he says that, he is saying, "I am the knowledge that the world needs. I am the only One who can enlighten men and women, the only One who can open their eyes and bring them out of darkness into knowledge." He came to teach—about God, about man, and about the way of salvation.

So the Bible gives us knowledge, and the way in which it does so is most remarkable. We have a perfect example and illustration of it in these words that we are considering. The Bible is not some kind of fairy tale, though people think it is. They say it is pie in the sky, that it is unrealistic. Unrealistic? It is the only book in the world I know that is absolutely real. It is a book of facts and of history, a book that tells us the plain, unvarnished truth about ourselves. Look at the first chapter of the epistle to the Romans—what a description of life as it is! It does not spare us anything. And this passage that we are looking at here is exactly the same.

In other words, the Bible does not paint some wonderful fairy story and give us a nice feeling inside and tell us we are all going to heaven and are all going to be happy. No, the Bible is a book that looks you in the face, examines you in the depths, and tells you the truth about yourself—unvarnished; it exposes it all.

And then it proceeds to deal with the two main questions. It says, "That is life!" The newspapers boast about making revelations. They claim to examine and to give true reports, but they do not, of course. They pick out certain facts now and again, but if you really want to know the truth about yourself, do not go to the newspapers. They are always praising us, always playing up to us; they would not sell if they did not. The newspapers are liars about the fundamental problems of life. They do not know them; indeed, they are partly the cause of the present muddle. They do not reveal the truth about man, about society, and about our nation. The Bible is the only book in the world that does that. It is the only honest and truthful book. And that is, let me emphasize again, because it is the Word of God.

Then, having put the facts before us in this unvarnished, almost violent manner, the Bible deals with two questions. It tells us, first of all, why things are like that. That is the first thing we want to know, is it not? It is not enough just to talk about the immorality around us. The question is, why are things as they are? So the Bible gives us the cause and the explanation of that. And second, thank God, it tells us about the only way in which these things can be put right. Now that is the message of the whole Bible from Genesis to Revelation. And that is what we find, in a most extraordinary summary form, in these three verses that we are now considering.

What is it that we need to be taught? "Know ye not?" says Paul. "Are you in ignorance of these matters?" Well, the first thing that we need to learn is the terrible danger of being deceived. "Know ye not that the unrighteous shall not inherit the kingdom of God? *Be not deceived. . . .*" The Bible warns us everywhere against this. Indeed, we can say that the case of the Bible is that man is in ignorance because he has been deceived. The whole story of the human race has gone wrong because man has been deceived by the devil.

We see this in Genesis 3. God made the world. He made it perfect; he made man perfect and put him in paradise. And man should have lived happily. He should have enjoyed the companionship of God, and he would have been given the gift of immortality, and that would have been the story. But that is not what has happened. The story has been one of unhappiness, jealousy, envy, murder, wars, all the horrors depicted in the Bible that we are familiar with in secular history.

So why has the history of the human race been as it has? The Bible says there is only one answer: the devil came in. We are told about the devil that he was "more subtil than any beast of the field" (Gen. 3:1), and it was in his subtlety and in his deceitfulness that he deceived Adam and Eve. That point is made in many places in the Holy Scriptures. Paul says in 2 Corinthians 11:2–3, "For I am jealous over you with godly jealousy: for I have espoused you to one husband, that I may present you as a chaste virgin to Christ. But I fear, lest by any means, as the serpent beguiled Eve through his subtilty, so your minds should be corrupted from the simplicity that is in Christ."

165

The same thing exactly is taught in the letter to the Hebrews where the writer warns his people in this way: "Exhort one another," he says, "daily, while it is called To day; lest any of you be hardened through the deceitfulness of sin" (Heb. 3:13). That is always the whole cause of the trouble. And the story has been what it has, from the very dawn of history, because men and women have been deceived by the devil and by the deceitfulness of sin.

That was the trouble in the time of the apostle Paul and in the time of our Lord himself, who taught about the danger even of those who have listened to the gospel being deceived by "the deceitfulness of riches" (Matt. 13:22). That is the "seed [sown] among the thorns"; people are deceived by this and are kept from understanding the real meaning of life. And our Lord prophesies that it will be like that even unto the very end of the age. He says, "As it was in the days of Noe [Noah], so shall it be . . . as it was in the days of Lot . . . even thus shall it be . . ." (Luke 17:26–30). There it is. Deceit is the central and the most essential trouble with the human race. "Be not deceived," says Paul, "do not be misled, do not be fooled," and the same thing needs to be said to this modern generation.

Now there are certain particular respects in which the human race at the present time is in danger of being deceived. Let me put some of them before you. The first, as we have already seen, is the claim that the Bible cannot speak to us now because it was written two thousand and more years ago. Some say, "We have learned so much since then and have advanced so much in our knowledge, so how can an old book like this speak to us any longer?" This is one of the master strokes of the devil, and so he prevents people from even reading the Bible. They will not listen to it; they put it out of court. So they are bereft of the one message that can help them.

We are told also that the Bible does not speak to us today because we are "different." Well, what are we like? This is what they were like two thousand years ago: "fornicators . . . idolaters . . . adulterers . . . effeminate . . . abusers of themselves with mankind . . . thieves . . . covetous . . . drunkards . . . revilers . . . extortioners." Are we no longer like that? There is no need to underline that, is there? The present crisis is because some of us are like that. So the Bible is speaking to men and women as they are today. They are the same as they always were. "Be not deceived"; this book is speaking to you—now! It is as up-to-date as it was in the days of Paul.

The second aspect of deceit is to say that moral ideas change. "We do

not think as our fathers used to think," people say. "We do not think as
they thought a hundred years ago, nor as they thought in the times of the
Bible—*we* have obtained knowledge. What they regarded as sin we can
explain biologically or medically or psychologically." They say, "Of course
people were very ignorant, and they used to condemn things, but with our
new understanding we no longer think like that."

In other words, they say that morality is something relative, that there
are no eternal principles and truths. What may be right for one generation
is wrong for another, and what was wrong for one is right for the next, men
say. So, for example, we are being told now that fornication is not always
wrong; sometimes it is right and a good thing. We are told adultery is not
always wrong either; sometimes it, too, may be right. Also homosexuality
is no longer wrong; it can be absolutely right for certain people. And to tell
a lie is not always wrong. If you want to show your love to your family and
shield them and protect them from harm, lying may be right in such circumstances. Everything is relative; there are no eternal standards of morality
and of righteousness and of truth. That is the modern teaching.

But according to the Bible, that is nothing but sheer deception. You have
no knowledge that entitles you to change moral canons and principles, none
at all. Psychology does not answer the problem. To which school of psychology do you belong? They are canceling one another out, and in a sense they
are all in the melting pot at the moment. There is no scientific knowledge
that in any way affects these moral canons. It is just man making his own
laws to please himself, to excuse himself, and to condone his evil. And so
you get the present muddle.

But there is a third form of deceit that is perhaps in many ways the most
serious one I have mentioned so far and the one that, in my opinion, has
been the cause of the trouble. Moral standards have been slipping and have
reached their present deplorable position for one main reason—namely,
that we have been taught that you can have morality without godliness.
People interpret that like this: "The moral teaching of the Bible is very
good," they say, "but we today cannot possibly accept its theology and its
doctrines."

Now there was a man who put this very clearly, a man who was highly
respected. He was a good man, I have no doubt, in a moral sense, but to
me he struck at the very foundations not only of Christianity but also of

the morality in which he was so interested. I am referring to the late Lord Birkett, the distinguished lawyer. He was being interviewed on television, and he was reminded that once upon a time he had been a local Methodist preacher. What had brought about the change? "Ah well," he said, "you know, one gets on, and one learns, and one finds things out . . . one does change. I no longer," he added, "believe the doctrines of Christianity. I hold on to the ethic of course. I no longer believe the doctrine, but the ethic of Jesus is the highest ethic the world has ever had."

That is the teaching that you can hold on to the ethic without the doctrines, that you can have morality without godliness. That has been the fatal teaching that has landed us in the present moral morass. People have fondly believed that you could hold on to these "good things" that are taught by Christianity while shedding the whole basis of Christianity. The modern position is demonstrating to us in a particularly painful, poignant manner that you cannot have morality without theology, that if you get rid of the doctrine you will soon lose your morality—and as a nation we have lost it.

The fourth way in which men and women deceive themselves is to say that death is the end and that there is nothing beyond it. That is the common belief today: when men and women die, they are finished; their life is gone, their bodies are put in a grave, and that is the end of them. But on what grounds do you say that? People say, "I no longer believe in life after death," but they cannot prove it; it is a mere assertion, a mere theory. Yet people believe it, and because they believe it, they cease to worship God. But it is pure deceit. "Be not deceived."

And then the last form of deceit is to say that God—if there is a God—is entirely love. Therefore, there is really no moral standard, no judgment, no punishment, and no hell. That is something that is being ridiculed, of course, this idea that God is a righteous Judge who will judge the whole world at the end of time and that some people will be punished in everlasting hell. "Out with such a suggestion!" they say. "It is impossible—it cannot be true." But they have not a vestige of proof for what they are saying. Again it is just sheer deceit; they are being deceived by the devil.

Now the answer to all these examples of modern deceit is given in our passage. These are the facts: "Know ye not that the unrighteous shall not inherit the kingdom of God? Be not deceived." In other words, the answer to all this is that God *is*—that God is our Maker and Creator and that what matters is what he says, not what we think, and not what we think he should say. God is what he is and not what we think he ought to be. We cannot conjure up a picture of him; we by philosophy cannot create a God. But that is what we are trying to do. Dignitaries in the church are doing this, and I hold them, too, responsible for the present moral collapse. I am not interested in the denunciation by bishops of what may be happening at the present time when they themselves deny the essence of the gospel.

You cannot separate godliness from morality, and the great statement of the Bible is that God is over all. He has made us and not we ourselves, and we are all in his hands. We say, "There are no moral standards; they are always changing." We say, "It does not matter—God is love, and all will be well." But the Bible says, "Be not deceived . . . the unrighteous shall not inherit the kingdom of God." That is what God says, that is what matters, and there is no excuse for our ignorance. God has revealed this to us from the very beginning of history.

There is no need to be uncertain as to what God expects and demands of us. He has made it perfectly plain. He started off even in the garden of Eden itself when he made this known to Adam and Eve. He said, "If you keep my commandments I will bless you; if you do not, I will turn you out." And out they went, and they have been out ever since. There is an eternal law of righteousness. God's law is an absolute law, and it is in all our consciences. He has written his law in the heart of every man and woman, as well as promulgating it in an external sense as he did in the Ten Commandments.

Not only has God make it clear that there is a moral standard that he demands from us—he made it equally clear that there is to be a judgment: "the unrighteous shall not inherit the kingdom of God."

Now this is just another way of saying that everybody in this world is in one of two positions: they are either in the kingdom of God or they are not. So the question is, have you inherited the kingdom of God? All of us will have to stand before God, and we will find ourselves either in the kingdom of God or outside it. That is judgment! And the message of the Bible is that this is the most important thing in the whole world.

It is so important because this is what determines our everlasting state and condition. That is why the apostle Paul was so anxious about these people. He says, "Do not let the devil deceive you into saying, 'I am in the

169

kingdom of God; therefore, I can drink and commit adultery and do everything I like, because God forgives me.'" "Oh," he says, "if you go on like that you are outside the kingdom, and you are going to hell." Judgment! Damnation!

This is what the modern world no longer believes. And that is why our country is as it is. Every man is his own god; every man does what he thinks is right. Why shouldn't he? And people explain and condone it. They may in a pharisaical manner all jump on a certain man, but they are guilty of the same things themselves in their thoughts. "There is no fear of God before their eyes" (Rom. 3:18). This is arrogant rebellion against God, but it also means facing a God who will judge the whole world in righteousness. The vital thing is that the judgment will send us either to heaven or to hell; it is either eternal bliss or eternal misery.

Everybody is concerned about the state of the country, but have you heard anybody talking about the state of the soul and eternal destiny? Yet that is what matters, and it matters to every one of us. Here, then, is one of the first things the Bible teaches us, this terrible, horrible danger of being deceived.

But second, it teaches us that nothing matters in the sight of God with respect to man but righteousness. "Know ye not that the unrighteous shall not inherit the kingdom of God?" It is not ability and cleverness that matters: this is the vogue and the cult of clever men and women today, is it not? "He is clever," they say; "she is brilliant." No, says the Bible, not ability, not knowledge, culture, or sophistication—the man about town, the clever people interested in art, interested in . . . Enjoyment and pleasure, money, wealth—those are the things that matter, we have been told, have we not? Plenty of money; "never had it so good!" And the country has never been so bad!

No, says the Bible. In the sight of God there is only one thing that matters, and that is righteousness! Which means, if you like, character. It is not whether I am clever or lacking in ability; it is not whether I am learned or ignorant; it is not my bank balance or lack of one. Rather, it is what I am; it is my character, my soul face-to-face with God. Righteousness, both in a nation and in an individual, is the only thing that matters with him. "Righteousness exalteth a nation" (Prov. 14:34). "Where there is no vision, the people perish" (Prov. 29:18), though they may have been great and though they sing the glories of the past. Where people live for sport and pleasure and money and getting on and cleverness, but "there is no vision . . . the people perish." Rome perished, and others have perished since.

So nothing matters in God's sight but this matter of righteousness. He revealed it in the garden of Eden and in the Ten Commandments. His own people have always realized this. The psalmist says, "Who shall ascend into the hill of the LORD? or who shall stand in his holy place? He that hath clean hands, and a pure heart" (Ps. 24:3–4). Not your clever fellow, not your brilliant men and women of affairs, not those who can speak cleverly, your sophisticated, modern people. No! "Clean hands"! "A pure heart"! That is what God wants.

David understood that. He said in another place, "Thou desirest truth in the inward parts" (Ps. 51:6). Yes, says our Lord, "Except your righteousness shall exceed the righteousness of the scribes and Pharisees, ye shall in no case enter into the kingdom of heaven" (Matt. 5:20). He says it again: "Ye are they which justify yourselves before men; but God knoweth your hearts: for that which is highly esteemed among men is abomination in the sight of God" (Luke 16:15). You get on, you are a cabinet minister, you are praised by men, but "highly esteemed among men is abomination in the sight of God." Righteousness!

Men and women were meant to live as God made them to live. They were meant to live to his glory and to keep his commandments. They were meant to be upright, to be pure and clean and honest and noble. They were put on their feet so that they might look into the face of God and enjoy his companionship. That is righteousness.

But the Bible goes on to tell us that we are all unrighteous by nature. "There is none righteous, no, not one" (Rom 3:10). In spite of all the divisions into class and education and money and all these other things, all are unrighteous. Unrighteousness takes different forms. We are not all guilty of these particular sins, but we are all sinners. There are many people in this land tonight who are guilty of these very sins that are mentioned in the list of our text. However, the fact that you may not be does not mean that you are righteous. To be righteous means that you love the Lord your God with all your heart and all your soul and all your mind and all your strength and that you love your neighbor as yourself. So are you righteous? Are you living to the glory of God and to his praise? That is righteousness! But none are righteous. "All," says the apostle Paul, "have sinned, and come short of the glory of God" (Rom. 3:23).

What is the cause of this? The Bible tells us, and this is the vital message, that each one of us born into this world is unrighteous because man fell from God. Adam was righteous until he listened to the devil, then he fell and became unrighteous. And man is unrighteous still because he has turned his back upon God. He is a rebel against him and has become the slave of the devil and of these lusts and passions. He becomes debased, depraved, and a miserable slave. So that is the second great thing that is taught to us in the Bible, and we have already considered this in our earlier studies: nothing matters in the presence of God but righteousness. And there we see ourselves all condemned, all sinners, and all unrighteous.

But, thank God, the gospel does not stop there. It tells us all this, and we need to know it. Let us look at these words again: "The unrighteous shall not inherit the kingdom of God. Be not deceived: neither fornicators, nor idolaters, nor adulterers, nor effeminate, nor abusers of themselves with mankind, nor thieves, nor covetous, nor drunkards, nor revilers, nor extortioners, shall inherit the kingdom of God. And such were some of you: but . . ."—and here is the essential message of the gospel—"but ye are washed, but ye are sanctified, but ye are justified in the name of the Lord Jesus, and by the Spirit of our God."

What, then, does the gospel have to say about this deplorable state in which we find ourselves as a nation at this moment? And it is not only true of this nation, it is true of all the nations. What is the message? Well, it is not a mere message of denunciation of sin and of the sinner. You do not need to be a Christian to do that. Moral men and women are holding up their hands in horror tonight. They are not Christians, but they are moral people, and they are denouncing it.

Neither is the message of the church merely one of exhortation or appeal. I read the other day of a church dignitary saying that we must "clean up the stables," and all the leaders are expressing their opinions upon "this moral degeneracy" and so on. But that is nothing but pharisaism! Our Lord has dealt with that once and forever in the incident that is described to us at the beginning of the eighth chapter of John's Gospel. They brought a woman to him who had been caught in the very act of adultery. They rushed her into his presence and wanted to know what his verdict was on the case.

And he, instead of answering them, began to write on the ground. But they were pressing him, so he looked at them and said, "He that is without sin among you, let him first cast a stone at her" (v. 7). And they all slunk out as quietly and as quickly as they could, leaving the woman and her blessed Lord together alone.

Be careful what you are doing, my friend. It is a very simple thing to point a finger of scorn at a man and to condemn him. But what about you? Is your heart clean? Are your hands clean? Be careful! Examine yourself! It is an easy thing to make scapegoats. I am not defending any wrongdoing; there is no defense of sin. But I would emphasize that the gospel does not merely denounce it, nor does it merely make a moral appeal. We shall hear a lot of that in the future. We shall hear great appeals to the nation to pull together, and we are going to put up a show of being Christian again. It is of no value; it is a sham.

Nor is the gospel just an appeal for more moral education or any other form of education. Many people believe that education is the solution to all our problems. A political leader said recently, "The strength of a nation depends upon its education. Education is the key to unlock the storehouse of the future." But education, though it is a good thing, is not enough. It is often the best educated people who are some of the ringleaders in vice and evil and who sink to such deplorable levels.

Nor does the gospel message merely tell men and women to believe in Christ and to say, "Lord, Lord!" and then say that everything is all right. That is the very thing against which Paul is warning the Corinthians. Here were these members of the church at Corinth, and yet some of them were guilty of foul and terrible sins, which he has mentioned in the fifth chapter. And they thought they were all right because they believed in Christ. And there are many such people today, too many by far in our churches. They say, "I made my decision for Christ; I gave myself to him," and they think that puts them right, that they can live as they like. But that is antinomianism—living in sin, living in dishonesty, living carelessly even while saying, "Lord, Lord!" It does not work. "The unrighteous shall not inherit the kingdom of God." Merely to say that you believe is not enough; that is not the gospel.

I am afraid, however, that we shall see a good deal of this. We shall have some kind of moral cleansing, and people will attend services and will be told in the press that cabinet ministers are attending services and people are showing an interest in religion. But if it is not a change in heart, it is a lie, it is deceit again. Even attendance at the house of God is not enough, though it is a good and an excellent thing in itself.

What is the message of the gospel then? Well, thank God it is here in this passage. It is a message of salvation. We do not denounce sinners—we save them. We do not point a finger of scorn at them like a Pharisee. We go to them and say, "You can be delivered out of this. You can be washed, you can be cleansed and renewed, you can be justified in the name of the Lord Jesus." It is a message of hope, a message of salvation. But let us make sure that we have the message of the New Testament, the old, old, gospel, this plain, unvarnished Word! It gives hope for the vilest because it does not merely appeal to men and women to pull themselves together; it tells them that God will take hold of them. "It is the power of God unto salvation to every one that believeth" (Rom. 1:16). It is a message that comes to men and women in the depths of degradation and sin and evil and tells them that they can be converted, that they can be saved, that they can be renewed. Look again at that list of sins in our passage. "That is what you were!" says Paul. "But you are no longer that. Why? Oh, because you have been washed, you have been sanctified, you have been justified in the name of the Lord Jesus and by the power of our God."

I am privileged to preach a gospel that can wash us from the filth of sin, a gospel that can cleanse us and purify us from the pollution of sin, a gospel that can absolve us from its guilt and give us a robe of righteousness to stand in the presence of our holy God. This is a gospel that not only preaches forgiveness, it preaches renewal, rebirth, regeneration. It preaches that a new man or woman can rise out of the ashes of failure and walk as a saint before God.

How does it happen? Paul answers the question—"in the name of the Lord Jesus, and by the Spirit of our God." The Christian message is that the Son of God, the Lord Jesus Christ, came out of heaven into this world in order to save us. He did not come merely to teach us and to exhort us, to condemn our sin and to say, "This is how to live, follow me." He knew we could not. Here we are, guilty of lusts and passions—slaves! And we are all slaves to something. Is there not something that gets you down? Do you not feel ashamed as we consider these things? What about that sin that you keep repeating? Why do you not stop it? You are a slave to it, that is why. It might not be adultery, but it might be jealousy or envy or malice or spite or hatred or an inordinate ambition and pride in the things of this world. And it is the power of God alone that can save us.

So Jesus Christ came to reconcile us to God. We are guilty before God, and how can we have communion with him and how can we be blessed when we are guilty? I cannot undo my past, I cannot live the law, so what can I do? Christ came, and he has done it for me! He became man, he put himself under the law, he has kept it, he has borne my sins in his own body on the tree, he has been smitten for me! And in him God forgives me, and he takes his righteousness and puts it on me. ". . . justified in the name of the Lord Jesus!"

Adulterers or fornicators or liars or murderers or even perverts of the worst type when they believe in the Lord Jesus Christ are delivered, are washed, are justified, are sanctified! The Christ of God has come to deliver them, to lift them out, and to set them upon their feet and establish their goings. I am not here to denounce a poor man who is a sinner like I am! I am here to tell him—if he could hear my words, and God grant that he may—that he can be delivered, he can be pardoned, he can be renewed, he can start a new life in Jesus Christ.

That is the Christian message! Not pharisaism, not decency and pretense and playacting at religion, but entirely new men and women, with righteousness in their hearts and the righteousness of Christ upon them, living to the glory of God—born again. And it is all possible because the Lord Jesus Christ, the Son of God, came from heaven and died on the cross. Here is the gospel! Thank God it is! We do not merely point fingers and condemn. We do condemn, but we wound in order to heal, we knock down in order to lift up. We show men their guilt and their helplessness and their hopelessness and their woe that they may submit to the power of God unto salvation through Jesus Christ our Lord, by the Spirit of our God.

And so, what of you? Are you righteous? Are you ready to stand in the presence of God at the bar of eternal judgment? Are you living a righteous and a holy life? Are you clean? Are your hands and your heart clean? Is your mind or your imagination clean? Forget everybody else—start with yourself and realize that you, too, need to be washed and sanctified. Can you use the words that were written by William Cowper?

The dying thief rejoiced to see
That fountain in his day;
And there have I, though vile as he,
Washed all my sins away.

Have you? Have you seen this message, and are you ready to say:

I hear Thy welcome voice
That calls me, Lord, to Thee,
For cleansing in Thy precious blood
That flowed on Calvary.

LEWIS HARTSOUGH

If you have not realized your own need of cleansing, you are in no position to point a finger at somebody else. If you have not seen that nothing but the blood of Christ can cleanse you from the guilt and power of sin, then you are not a Christian, you are a miserable self-righteous Pharisee. See your own blackness and pollution, turn to him, and say:

I am coming, Lord,
Coming now to Thee!
Wash me, cleanse me in the blood
That flowed on Calvary.

And, you know, when you are washed and when you are cleansed, you will have some sympathy with fallen men and women. You will not make a sensation of such cases and talk self-righteously; you will be sorry for them, you will pray for them, you will want to tell them the message, so they can be delivered. Why do they live this filthy life? It is because they do not know of a better one. It is because they are ignorant of the gospel. It is because they are being deceived by the devil and by modern learning, often preached by the Christian church herself.

The only people who can help moral failures in this world and be of any value in society at this moment are men and women who, having realized their own impurity and their own utter hopelessness, have turned to him and have said:

Rock of ages, cleft for me,
Let me hide myself in Thee;

Let the water and the blood,
From Thy riven side which flowed,
Be of sin the double cure,
Save from wrath and make me pure.

AUGUSTUS TOPLADY

And when Jesus Christ has washed and cleansed them, they can tell others that they have but to do the same thing and they will know the moral, spiritual cleansing that the Son of God alone can give and the new walk and the new life that the Holy Spirit of God alone can enable one to walk. "But ye are washed, but ye are sanctified, but ye are justified in the name of the Lord Jesus, and by the Spirit of our God."

Thank God, in spite of our present position there is a hope tonight! It is the only hope. It is the gospel of Jesus Christ and him crucified! Do you know him? Are you resting upon him? Have you been washed and cleansed and renewed by him?

12

HE IS OUR PEACE

(1963)
Galatians 6:14

From *The Cross*

Bethan Lloyd-Jones always maintained that her husband was a true evangelist. Seldom has a sermon proved this quite so dramatically as the one you are about to read, since it is the one that he delivered the Sunday evening after the death of President John F. Kennedy in Dallas in November 1963.

The JFK assassination is the kind of iconic event that no one forgets. Just as everyone over the age of eighteen can probably remember where they were and how they reacted on September 11, 2001, those of us in our midfifties and over can remember exactly what we were doing when the news broke of Kennedy's shocking and unexpected tragic death. November 22, 1963—also the day upon which C. S. Lewis and Aldous Huxley died—joins 9/11 as one of those rare dates in history that sears its way into global consciousness.

As with the chapter from The Kingdom of God *at the time of the Profumo scandal, the family decided to leave in the Kennedy reference in the relevant sermon when* The Cross *was published, and for the same reason.*

"Put not your trust in princes," says the Bible in Psalm 146:3, and how true that verse remains. But equally how many people, not just in the United States, had put their earthly trust in the young, dynamic JFK, a man about whom we now know rather a lot, but who at that time embodied the hopes, fears, and aspirations of a whole generation around the world.

Yet now those dreams were shattered.

However, he was not the only young man to have died a violent death, and as Martyn Lloyd-Jones goes on to demonstrate, Jesus not only suf-

fered a premature and cruel end but rose again from the dead, our Lord and Savior.

It was not just the hope in Kennedy himself that was so wrong but the entire worldview that went with it. As the Doctor pointed out, the whole history of the twentieth century demonstrated the futility of such a belief, let alone the death of one individual, however tragic.

Only Jesus on the cross, taking the punishment for our sins to reconcile us to God, could ever provide the true answer. As the Doctor goes on to show us, the problems of this world are spiritual, not political or economic or social.

As his text puts it: "But God forbid that I should glory, save in the cross of our Lord Jesus Christ. . . ." There was, the Doctor argued, no hope for the world apart from the gospel, and the cross of Jesus Christ was at the center of that gospel message. It was, as the Doctor realized, evangelism, not politics, that was the only hope, as it had always been.

We live in an era in which evangelicals are making exactly the same mistakes as theological liberals made in the nineteenth century. The view is that political outcomes can change the face of a nation, everything rides upon who wins the presidential election, and it is a chosen politician who can save America, even someone who does not profess any kind of biblical Christian faith.

This sermon shows the sheer futility of such an approach. In the 1960s it was liberals who put their trust in princes; now it is often evangelicals. But the Bible's answer is the same—we should glory in Jesus Christ, crucified and risen.

In the Cross of Christ I glory,
Towering o'er the wrecks of time.

JOHN BOWRING

Thank God that the Christian can sing words like that in a world like this. Let us now try to find some further reasons why we can do so and why it is possible for all to do so if they but believe the gospel of our Lord and Savior, Jesus Christ. So let us return to Galatians 6:14: "But God forbid that I should glory, save in the cross of our Lord Jesus Christ, by whom the world is crucified unto me, and I unto the world." There is no hope for this world apart from the gospel, and the essence of the gospel, as we have seen, is this message about the cross.

Now the author of the hymn that we have just quoted tells us all that he found in the cross. Whatever his mood or state or condition, the cross sanctified it all—pain or pleasure, whatever was happening to him. The cross always speaks. That is the apostle's position. He glories in this because he has discovered that whatever is happening to him, this is the message that is always with him, and that turns everything to his advantage, and so he makes his boast in the cross.

Now we have been examining the various things that the apostle here and in other places in his writings tells us about the cross. But still we have not finished. "God forbid that I should glory," says the apostle, "save in the cross." There is no end to it. It is such a tremendous thing, and so I move forward now to give one further reason that the apostle has for glorying in the cross of the Lord Jesus Christ. This is that the cross of our Lord Jesus Christ alone can produce true unity and real peace among men. Now it is to that I want to call your attention, and what a time it is to consider this, because everybody's mind is engaged on the whole question of how to produce unity in the world. The assassination of the late President Kennedy pinpoints that in a very acute manner for us.

Now I am not going to preach on President Kennedy, but it would be madness not to see what that terrible event, that awful event, should make us all think about. He was a man who was struggling and striving in various ways to bring men and women together. There are those who would say that he met his death because he was trying to solve the problem of integration in the United States. Black and white—how to bring them together—how to bring an end to segregation and how to produce integration. It was certainly one of the problems with which he was struggling. He went to Texas because he was concerned about that. Then he faced the problem of the two groupings of the nations of the world, the Iron Curtain between them. He was striving, he was struggling with this problem of how to bring together these two warring factions of human nature and of humankind. Here was a man who gave his life and his activity to that very question, to that very matter. And I have no doubt that it is true to say that in many ways he met his death because of these things. We are concerned, then, with this problem. We are in a world that is full of tension, full of divisions, full of strife, full of the danger of war. We are in a world that is divided up hopelessly, a world of unhappiness and pain.

The Bible has always said that this world is an evil world. Nothing else says that. The newspapers do not say it; the newspapers regard an event such as President Kennedy's assassination as exceptional. It is only exceptional in the one sense that it happens to be unusually dramatic. But the world is full of that kind of thing. That is the sort of world in which we are living. The world seems shocked because of the unexpected. It is not unexpected. It is not unusual. This is "this present evil world" as the Bible calls it. I am not exaggerating this particular thing. I have my own views with regard to whoever may have committed this dastardly crime, but I do maintain that this is but one of the manifestations of a strife, a warfare, an antagonism, a bitterness, and a hatred. It is just a particularly ugly manifestation of it. But the thing itself belongs to a whole category that is, alas, the cause of our greatest troubles in this world today. And that is why I am calling attention to it.

Now I want to look at it not only in terms of the world situation but also in terms of our individual lives. One of the greatest fallacies today is that we draw too sharp a distinction between the individual and the mass, between nations and persons or individuals. A nation is nothing after all but a collection of individuals, or you might say that it is nothing but the individual writ large. The world is a sort of macrocosm of which man is a microcosm, and what is true of the nations of the world is true of individuals. There are groupings and divisions within all the nations, and divisions and groupings and antagonisms and tensions in yet smaller units, even in families—divisions, strife, disagreement, misunderstanding. But we can take it even further. How many of you know perfect rest? How many know real peace and quiet? Is there not a warfare going on in you? Is there not a strife and a tension, is there not a conflict? We have to say there is—we are all born like that. We are born creatures of conflict, within and without, in every realm and department of life. And what I want to try to demonstrate is that there is only one thing in the whole world at this moment that can deal with this warfare and tension and strife. It is the cross of our Lord and Savior, Jesus Christ.

If you read the second chapter of Paul's epistle to the Ephesians, you will notice what the apostle had to say there. It was not surprising that he gloried in the cross, because the cross of the Lord Jesus Christ had done what he regarded as the most wonderful and amazing thing that he had ever known—it had produced the Christian church. Why is this so wonderful? It is wonderful for the reason that together, side by side in the Christian church, there were Jews and Gentiles. Now that was the thing that never failed to amaze the apostle. You remember that the ancient world was divided up into Jews and all the rest, the Gentiles. The Jews despised the Gentiles and would refer to them as dogs. The Gentiles, too, had their own view of the Jews, and it appeared to be an utter impossibility that they could ever come together. There was, as the apostle says in that very chapter, a "middle wall of partition" between them.

The wall in Berlin, you see, is not the first wall that has been built in this world to separate people from one another. The world has always had its iron curtains. We change the terminology, but the fact has always been there: "the middle wall of partition," Jews on one side, Gentiles on the other side, and between them a bitter hatred and animosity that we can scarcely even imagine. The apostle Paul, before his conversion, was one of the most bitter Jews the world has ever known. He was a Jew who reveled in it and prided himself in it, and he despised the Gentiles. But the extraordinary thing he finds is that in the Christian church Jews and Gentiles are found together, and "the middle wall of partition," as he says, has been "broken down." He keeps on repeating that in the epistle to the Ephesians. He says in Ephesians 1:11, 13: "In whom also we have obtained an inheritance, being predestinated according to the purpose of him who worketh all things after the counsel of his own will. . . . In whom ye also trusted"—"we," being the Jews, "ye also," the Gentiles—"after that ye heard the word of truth."

And then, as we saw in the second chapter, let me remind you, he said, "Wherefore remember, that ye being in time past Gentiles in the flesh, who are called Uncircumcision by that which is called the Circumcision in the flesh made by hands; that at that time ye were without Christ, being aliens from the commonwealth of Israel, and strangers from the covenants of promise, having no hope, and without God in the world: But now in Christ Jesus ye who sometimes [at one time] were far off are made nigh by the blood of Christ. For he is our peace, who hath made both one, and hath broken down the middle wall of partition between us; having abolished in his flesh the enmity, even the law of commandments contained in ordinances; for to make in himself of twain one new man, so making peace" (2:11–15).

To the apostle this was the most amazing and astounding thing conceivable. The impossible had happened: Jew and Gentile had been brought together, and there was one new man in the Christian church worshipping the same God and glorying in the same Savior.

That is therefore one of the chief reasons why Paul gloried in the cross of Christ. And it is that which I want to expound to you. Let me do it like this. What is the cause of the divisions and the enmities that characterize the life of this world? Is that not the big question that comes up at this time? I am not going to talk politics to you or even pay tribute to the late President Kennedy; that is not what I am called upon to do. Others do that kind of thing. The Christian preacher must deal with causes, and thank God, in the light of Scripture we can do so in a manner that the statesman cannot do, because (and I say this to the glory of God) here is the only explanation.

What is the cause of the division? What is the cause of the unhappiness that is in the world today? Why is the world as it is? Why have we had these wars? Why are the nations preparing for a further war? Why is there tragedy and trouble and discord? And there is only one answer to all the questions. It is the pride of the natural, unregenerate human heart. Pride, nothing else. Let me show you how it works. The Bible is full of this teaching. Way back at the very beginning it gives us the story of how one brother murdered another brother. Cain murdered Abel. Why did he do it? He did it because of jealousy, and jealousy is the child of pride. There it is right away back at the very beginning, and it has gone on ever since. This old book is full of accounts of that kind of thing. There are foolish people today who say that you should not give the Old Testament to a child to read because of the terrible things you find there, the sins of David and stories like that. That is just the point. The Bible is an honest book, a realistic one that tells you the truth. It shows human nature as it is, and it conceals nothing. Pride shows itself in all kinds of ways. Take the prophet Jeremiah. He has a great statement about all this. He was given clear insight by God to see the cause of trouble, and he puts it like this: "Thus saith the LORD, Let not the wise man glory in his wisdom, neither let the mighty man glory in his might, let not the rich man glory in his riches." "Glory" means "boast." "But let him that glorieth glory in this, that he understandeth and knoweth me, that I am the LORD which exercise lovingkindness, judgment, and righteousness, in the earth: for in these things I delight, saith the LORD" (Jer. 9:23–24).

Then you come to the New Testament, and you get exactly the same thing. The apostle Paul, in writing to the Corinthians, shows how the world in his time was divided up not only into Jew and Gentile, but it was divided up into Greeks and barbarians, wise and unwise, too. The world has always been like this. You will find it again in Ephesians 2, and then you have an extraordinary statement of the same thing by the apostle in Philippians 3. Read this little bit of autobiography that he gives us. He says, "For we are the circumcision, which worship God in the spirit, and rejoice in Christ Jesus, and have no confidence in the flesh. Though," he says, "I might also have confidence in the flesh. If any other man thinketh that he hath whereof he might trust in the flesh, I more: Circumcised the eighth day, of the stock of Israel, of the tribe of Benjamin, an Hebrew of the Hebrews; as touching the law, a Pharisee; concerning zeal, persecuting the church; touching the righteousness which is in the law, blameless" (3:3–6). There he was, proud of it all.

Now these are but some of the texts that we have in the Scriptures, and there are many more that show us that the essential cause of all the strife and the unhappiness and the tension in the world, and ultimately all the tragedy, both in individuals and in the life of nations and groups within the nations, is the result of pride. How does it work? Well, let me take you through the sorry catalog, and if we do not use a time such as this to do that, then I say we have failed, and failed completely. What do men and women take pride in, and what is it that causes this pride of theirs to lead to divisions?

Well, as we are told, they take pride in their *birth* and in their race. You remember how Kipling spoke about "the lesser breeds without the law." Pride of birth, pride of race, pride of nationality, pride of color—black and white. This is the tension in the world today; this is part of the trouble. It may not be the only cause of the tragedy that has taken place, but men are standing apart because of these things. Human beings, souls in the sight of God, but divided by color, black and white; and remember, there are these elements on both sides. You get this trouble with respect to nationality, with respect to race, with respect to the accident of birth, and all these things—all those matters that the apostle enumerates in Ephesians 2 and

185

in Philippians 3. Now the apostle himself, before he became an apostle and before he became a Christian, delighted in these things. He was proud of them and of the fact that he was "an Hebrew of the Hebrews." He looked down upon everybody who was not. He was born into a particular tribe, the tribe of Benjamin, and he was filled with pride in all this.

Another cause of strife is *power*—pride in one's power. How much tension is there in the world today between the "haves" and the "have nots"? Those who have want to hold on to what they have. Those who have not, want it. Each one is consumed with an equal passion, and inevitably you get strife and tension, with people wanting something and wanting to hold on to something. Now this is true of nations. It has been one of the most prolific causes of wars, particularly in the present century, but it has been a cause of wars long before that. Greed, the desire to have, to have power, to be great, to be wonderful. Wealth and the power of wealth. It is the cause of so much industrial strife. Employer and employed—the employed want a greater share of that which has hitherto been the possession of the employers, and each side becomes rigid. So you get tension and strife, you get division, and ultimately you get war. But it is all the result of pride. Power is a wonderful thing. Nations get drunk on power. Individuals get drunk on it too, and once they have it, they want to hold it. "Uneasy lies the head that wears the crown." Lust for power and for domination. The whole of human history is redolent of this kind of thing, and pride of power does it.

And pride of *intellect* does exactly the same thing. We have seen how the ancient world was divided up into Greeks and barbarians, the wise and the unwise. The Greeks were a very intellectual people, as well as a people of great military prowess. They had produced a succession of mighty philosophers, the greatest philosophers the world has ever known, and they were proud of it. So they looked at all the other nations of the world, and they said, "What do they know? What do they understand? What philosophy do they have? Some of them are good at fighting, some of them are good at business, some of them are good at navigation, but they do not understand." So they divided up the whole world into Greeks and barbarians, the wise and the unwise.

But again here was rivalry and tension, stress and strain, and it is as common in the world today as it was then. These subtle divisions and distinctions permeate the whole of life. I have come across many cases in this world where this very thing has caused grave agony, even within families. It happens that one member of the family, being a bit brighter than the rest, goes on with his education. He goes to a university, and the others do not. I have known that leads to heartache, and almost heartbreak, in certain families. The man who has intellect and is given an opportunity has sinful pride, and the others feel a certain amount of jealousy and envy. "Who is he?" they say, "Because he has a little knowledge, does he think he is better?" You must be aware of all this. It is one of the many social problems that are worrying the minds of the authorities in this country at the present time.

Those, then, are the three main ways in which this pride that is in man, because he is a sinner, has manifested itself throughout the running centuries. The next step in the argument is that there is nothing known to the world today that can deal with that situation. Now that is a very strong statement to make, is it not? But I make it. The state of the world at this moment is an absolute proof of that. The world can never make peace. All the world can do is to put an end, or at least put a stop for the time being, to actual war. The world at its best has never produced anything beyond a temporary cessation of hostilities. It can produce nothing but a kind of armed interval, in which we are not actually fighting.

But you see the whole fallacy behind what the world is doing is that it does not realize that merely not to fight is not peace. Peace is positive, not negative. Peace means love, sympathy, understanding, a true unity, and the world knows nothing about that, and it cannot produce it. Now this is to me a most vital and important thing, for it shows that the world must inevitably fail. But the world fools itself, because it regards the cessation of hostilities as positive peace. Let me give you an illustration of this. In the First World War they used poison gas in fighting one another. But did you realize that in the Second World War they did not use it? Some of us remember receiving instructions in 1938 about what to do if mustard gas, etc., were used, but it was never used. Why not? Was it because the world has advanced? Was it because man at last has love in his heart toward his fellow man? No. There was only one answer. Both sides had mustard gas, and each side knew that if they used it, the other would retaliate. Therefore neither side used it. That was not peace; that was just the avoidance of doing something that was going to do you harm. There is no advance, there is no development, and I think there is a real case for saying that what has given us what we call peace since the end of World War II in 1945 is not that the nations of the world are any more intelligent than they were, or any more loving than they were, or that they have come any nearer to one another than they were. There is only one thing that has done it, and that is the possession of the atom bombs on the two sides. Was that not what solved the Cuban missile crisis? The two sides knew that if one used it, the other would retaliate and they would both suffer, so they did not use it.

But that is not peace—that is fear. That is not what we really mean by peace. Peace, I say, is something positive. Peace means a new attitude, a new understanding. Peace means a love. But the world, even at its best, is incapable of producing it. Or take another argument. There are certain people in this country who say "better Red [Communist] than dead." Let this country go in for unilateral disarmament—anything is better than war, they say. And they are prepared to do that. But you see that again is no solution, because if you did that, what would happen is that one section of the world would be dominated by another. That is not peace. When a bullet keeps everybody else down, there is no fighting, but it is not peace. The weakling is just dominated by the bully, and if you go in for unilateral disarmament that is the inevitable result. You will be governed by the Reds, or, if the Red gives in, he will be governed by the rest. That is not peace—that is domination. That is the peace that comes from the death of everything that is most glorious in human nature; that is serfdom. You do not get wars in places where there is serfdom; you do not even get strikes. But that is not peace, because it is entirely negative.

Not only that, take all the efforts that are being made in the world, and as you look at them and as you examine them, you see behind them a spirit of hatred and enmity, a spirit of strife. Let us be realistic and face the facts. The late President Kennedy was hated and reviled by many of his own fellow countrymen—not only by the man who performed this murderous act, but by many others, by good and respectable people who hated him because of his policies—and there is animosity and hatred on both sides.

So when you look at the world, even at its best and at its highest, you see at once that it does not produce any peace. I have to say, in order to be honest and to be plain, that some of the most bitter men I have ever met in my life have been pacifists. I have never seen such bitter hatred in the hearts of men as in some pacifists I have known. They have been impossible to get along with, impossible to work with. They have been animated by a spirit of hatred against militarism. But that is not peace. While there is bitterness in your heart, you do not have peace. The world cannot produce peace. The world can never bring down the middle walls of partition. It can produce a kind of gentlemanly appearance of peace; it can succeed in having a cessation of hostilities, but only because it is wise and politically advantageous and utilitarian to do so. But it is always waiting for the opportunity to show its true nature, and one only has to produce some invention before anyone else for the antagonism to appear. Can you believe the words of nations, can you believe the solemn pledges and vows? The history of the world gives the lie to any claim to peace.

If this century has done nothing else, it has proved absolutely and beyond any controversy that man cannot be taught by education to live in a peaceable manner and to love his friends and his enemies. Now there was a great argument that this could be done. The late H. G. Wells was the outstanding proponent of this theory. War, he and others taught, can be banished if only you educate people. It is ignorant people who fight, they said, and the more ignorant they are, the more they fight. It is ignorance that causes people to fight. Educate them, show them the folly of war, show them the monstrosity and the evil of it, show them that nothing ever comes of war but harm and suffering, maiming and bitterness and all the rest. Show them that, and they will burn all their arms, and they will all embrace one another, and there will never be another war. Poor man! The last war convinced him otherwise, so he wrote his last book and called it *Mind at the End of Its Tether*. It was the end of the tether and beyond it. This [twentieth] century, the most educated of all the centuries, has been the most bloody, and never has the world been so full of war and tension and strife and dispute as it is at this very time. Man cannot produce peace. Man cannot bring the opposites together, because, as I have been trying to show you, the trouble is in the heart of man—not in his mind but in his heart. It is his passion, lust, desire, pride. Man's pride is greater than his understanding, and in order to please his own pride and to pamper it, he will do things that in his inner man he knows to be wrong. Pride is the biggest power in the world, and nothing that is known to man can deal with the problem of pride. That is why I assert again that there is only one thing in the world at this moment that can give peace and unity, that can bring men and women together and give us any hope of real true peace, and that is the cross of Christ. That is why the apostle gloried in it.

How does the cross do this? It is really perfectly simple. The gospel is simple because it always gets to the root of the problem, and having come to the root of the problem, it does not waste its time trying various expedients. It knows there is only one way of peace, and it comes straight to it. The first thing the cross does is to show us to ourselves. Of course, we always defend ourselves, do we not? It isn't my fault, we say, it is his. If only he understood. Or take husbands and wives, when they separate from one another. You listen to the story of the husband: "This woman is impossible!" Then you listen to the woman: "That man of mine, I could not live with him, he is an impossible man!" It is always somebody else, is it not? We are never wrong; we are very wonderful, if only we could be understood. The trouble is, people do not understand us. We are all people of peace. None of us wants to quarrel with anybody, we are not jealous or envious, we are not quarrelsome. It is always somebody else, always that other person. Do you know what the gospel does, what the cross does? It shows you to yourself. And nothing in the whole world does that but the cross. There is nothing that will ever humble a man or a nation but the cross of Christ. I have tried to show you that everything else inevitably fails. But the cross tells us the simple plain truth about ourselves.

Think of it like this. Why did the Son of God ever come into this world? Why did he leave the courts of glory? Why was he born as a little babe? Why did he take unto him human nature? There is only one answer. He came because man could not save himself. He said that. "The Son of man," he says, "is come to seek and to save that which was lost" (Luke 19:10). And when I look at that cross and see him dying there, what he tells me is this: "You have nothing whereof to boast." The cross tells me that I am a complete failure and that I am such a failure that he had to come from heaven, not merely to teach and preach in this world, but to die on the cross. Nothing else could save us. I could not keep his teaching. How could I obey the teaching of the Lord Jesus Christ in the Sermon on the Mount, I who cannot live up to my own code, who cannot please other people? It is impossible. We cannot keep ordinary rules, we cannot keep the law of the land, let alone imitate Christ in his perfection. He condemns us completely and absolutely.

Look at this man, the apostle Paul, look at him as Saul of Tarsus. There he was, proud and boastful, "circumcised the eighth day, of the stock of Israel, of the tribe of Benjamin, an Hebrew of the Hebrews; as touching the law, a Pharisee; concerning zeal, persecuting the church; touching the righteousness which is in the law, blameless"; the perfect man, absolutely moral, absolutely religious, a most learned man, chief of the Pharisees. And then he met Christ. One glimpse of that blessed face humbled him to the dust, and the light that Christ by the Spirit cast upon the very law that he thought he knew so well convinced him immediately that he had not kept it. He had missed one little word in the law, the word "covet." "Thou shalt not covet"—he had never seen it.

Here was the great expert on the law, who had studied it all his life, who was on top in the examinations always, in every test that was given concerning knowledge of the law, and he had never seen it. He says, "I had not known sin, but by the law: for I had not known lust, except the law had said, Thou shalt not covet" (Rom. 7:7). But the moment he saw that, he was finished. "For I was alive without the law once"—he thought he was perfect. He thought he was satisfactory before God. ". . . but when the commandment came, sin revived, and I died" (v. 9). And the man who had thought he was perfect is heard crying out, "O wretched man that I am! who shall deliver me from the body of this death?" (v. 24). He is in a muddle, in utter confusion. "The good that I would I do not: but the evil which I would not, that I do. Now if I do that I would not, it is no more I that do it, but sin that dwelleth in me. I find then a law, that, when I would do good, evil is present with me. For I delight in the law of God after the inward man: But I see another law in my members, warring against the law of my mind, and bringing me into captivity to the law of sin which is in my members. O wretched man that I am! who shall deliver me from the body of this death?" (vv. 19–24). That is what the cross of Christ showed him. It showed him that he was a complete, utter, absolute failure in word, thought, and deed. He had nothing of which to be proud. He was a wretched, abominable failure. The cross had humbled him and crushed him to the ground. Once you see yourself like that, you forget other people.

But there is more. The cross also reveals to us the truth about others. It makes of twain one new man. It deals with both of us, which is why it is so wonderful. I myself have to be put down first. It is no use until I am humbled, until I stop saying, "I am all right, it is the other man." I am put down, but then it helps me see the other man also. The cross shows me that these other people also are souls, that it does not matter what the color of their skin is, or whether they are wealthy or poor, whether they are very learned or very ignorant. It does not matter whether they are very powerful or very weak, they are souls. They are men and women, like me, made originally in the image of God and standing before God in all the dignity of human nature. But why do they behave as they do? That is the question, and before I myself was humbled, I never went beyond that. I said, "It is because they are wrong. I am right, and they are wrong." I have now seen that I am wrong, altogether wrong, but what of them? Ah, now I am enabled to see them in a new way. They are the victims of the devil even as I was. The devil is controlling them, and as I see this I begin to pity them. In other words, what the cross does is to make us both see ourselves exactly as we are, and the moment that happens we see that there is no difference at all between us and other people.

Remember how we used to hear, during the last war, of the wonderful things that were happening here in London, how the Duchess and Mrs. Mops were talking together in a very friendly manner, in the same air raid shelter. When you are within half a centimeter of death, it does not matter very much who you are, does it? Nor what you are by birth. You may both be dead the next moment. So differences were forgotten. The cross does that; it shows us that we are all exactly the same. We are one in sin. We are one in failure. We are one in misery. We are one in helplessness and hopelessness. What is the point of boasting that you are a Jew when you are as much a failure as the Gentile? What is the point of boasting that you have the law if you cannot keep it? What is the point of boasting about your great brain if you do not know how to live? What is the point of boasting about your money and your wealth if you are miserable in your own heart and soul and filled with jealousy and envy and malice and spite? What is the use of anything? What is the value of anything? What is the point of everything? The cross humbles us.

> My richest gain I count but loss,
> And pour contempt on all my pride.

It is the cross of Christ that brings us all down to the same place. All have sinned and come short of the glory of God. The differences between nations (and groups within them) and individuals are nothing when you look at the cross of Christ. We are all miserable, helpless, hopeless sinners. There is nothing in which we can boast. As the apostle puts it in Philippians 3:7–9, "But what things were gain to me, those I counted loss for Christ. Yea doubtless, and I count all things but loss for the excellency of the knowledge of Christ Jesus my Lord: for whom," he says, "I have suffered the loss of all things, and do count them but dung, that I may win Christ, and be found in him, not having mine own righteousness, which is of the law, but that which is through the faith of Christ, the righteousness which is of God by faith."

Once you really see this message of the cross, you see yourself groveling on the dust and the floor, a miserable failure, a hopeless sinner. You can do nothing, neither can your neighbor; you are together in your complete helplessness and hopelessness. But thank God it does not leave you there. You both look up together into the face of the one and only Savior, the Savior of the world, "the Lamb of God, which taketh away the sin of the world." He is not only the Savior of the western world, he is also the Savior of the people on the other side of the Iron Curtain, which is why I never preach against Communism or against anything else. I am not called to preach against; I am called to hold a Savior forth. He can save Communists as well as he can save capitalists. He can save blacks as well as whites. He has come to save souls; he is the Savior of the world. "For there is none other name under heaven given among men, whereby we must be saved" (Acts 4:12). Here is the only one who can encompass the whole world, the whole universe, and all in utter helplessness can look to him. And this is what is so wonderful about it—it is he who saves. It is not we but he who saves. It is not even our believing in him that saves us; it is he who saves us. His going to that cross and submitting himself as the Lamb of God and having our sins put upon him by his Father and bearing the stroke, the punishment, for us—that is what saves us. He does it all.

There is nothing for anybody to boast in. "For by grace are ye saved through faith; and that not of yourselves: it is the gift of God: not of works, lest any man should boast" (Eph. 2:8–9). We are all paupers, and as "he is our peace," we are all given exactly the same gift. Nobody has anything to boast about. We have done nothing; we could do nothing. He has done it all. So Paul, writing to the Romans, asks, "Where is boasting then? It is excluded" (Rom. 3:27). "He that glorieth, let him glory in the Lord" (1 Cor.

1:31). "What hast thou," says the Scripture, "that thou didst not receive?" (1 Cor. 4:7). You see, the cross makes us one in every respect. We are one in sin, we are one in failure, we are one in helplessness and in hopelessness. We believe in the one and only Savior together. We receive the same forgiveness; we are equally the children of God. By grace we share the same divine life, we have the same hope of glory, and we all look with admiration and praise and rejoicing and glory into the face of the same Savior.

That is the only way that you will ever get peace in this world. That is how "the middle wall of partition" was broken down between the Jew and the Gentile. What is the point of being a Jew if you cannot keep the law about which you talk so much? None at all. There is no difference. "All have sinned, and come short of the glory of God" (Rom. 3:23). Here is the hope in this world today, and there is none other. While men and nations stand up in their arrogance and self-confidence, there will be nothing but spite and malice and hatred and war and bitterness and horror. But the moment any man or any woman sees the truth as it is in Jesus Christ and him crucified, all that is banished, it becomes dung and loss.

> My richest gain I count but loss,
> And pour contempt on all my pride.

What fools we all are. What have you to boast in? Who are you? How do you live? You tell me you are a great intellectual, and I ask you, how do you live? What if everybody knew the things you do? What if everybody knew the things you think or the things you play with in your imagination? Where do you stand? You who are self-satisfied, are you ready to come up and to be cross-examined and to be honest and admit how you live and all the jealous, envious, rapacious thoughts and how you commit murder in your mind? You have not done what that wretched assassin did in Dallas, Texas, the other day, but you have done it in your spirit. You have murdered people. You hate them with a bitter hatred, and that is the thing that is damnable and causes the division and builds walls of partition. But it is only the cross that tells us that. There is nothing that will humble the pride of men and of nations except to see the truth as it is revealed by the cross of our Lord Jesus Christ.

But once you have seen it, it will grind you to the dust. You will have nothing to pride yourself in, nothing to boast of; you will lose your jealousy and your envy. You are one with all sinners, but thank God the cross will show you the way out, and it will lift you up. And it will lift others with you. It will make peace, and it will make of twain one new man, so making peace. Together you will be able to go to God with your petitions and your praise and your thanksgiving. All the divisions will be gone, and you will be one with all who believe the same message, rejoicing in him and enjoying this new life that he has purchased for you at the cost and the price of his own precious blood.

I wish in many ways that I could believe that the assassination of John F. Kennedy is going to bring the nations of the world together. I know it will not. It cannot. It will probably produce more strife and bitter hatred. But there is a death, there is a murder that once took place that can reconcile because it reconciles men to God. It also reconciles them to one another. Stop thinking in terms of nations; think of yourself first. Is that old pride there, is this the thing that governs you? I pray that God may show us to ourselves in the light of the cross of Christ, that all our ugly pride may go, and that we may see our utter hopelessness and helplessness. I pray that we may look up unto him who loved us so dearly that he even gave his life voluntarily in order that we might be rescued and saved, reconciled to God, and reconciled to our fellow men and women. God forbid that I should glory in anything save in the death on the cross of our Lord Jesus Christ.

13

WHERE ART THOU?

(1948)
Genesis 3:9

From *The Gospel in Genesis*

In the New Testament the gift of pastor-teacher is listed separately from that of evangelist. In today's Christian world we too often divide the two roles: there are professional evangelists and people whose full-time job it is to pastor a church.

But while there is biblical justification for this split, need it always be the case? If we consider the life and career of Martyn Lloyd-Jones we can observe that he possessed both gifts in abundance. The sermon chosen here is a classic example and one of those where it is easiest to hear the Doctor's voice as one reads it. He was never theatrical, but to be a non-Christian in the congregation when this was preached would surely have been a profoundly uncomfortable experience.

As mentioned in the main introduction, he made it his pattern especially to address non-Christians in his evening sermons at Westminster Chapel. What is interesting to reflect upon is that the 6:30 service was often packed despite the fact that he did none of the things felt necessary at the time to win audiences and gain the attention of non-Christians. There was no choir, no drama, nor were there testimonies, or indeed any of the paraphernalia deemed necessary then or since. What we had is what you read here—straight biblical exposition.

Furthermore he used a text from the Old Testament. This shows that we can use any part of the Bible for evangelism, since God's call to Adam has remained unaltered since the beginning of time.

Not only that, but while the Doctor firmly rejected the whole decision-based theology of Finney and his successors, the sermon does not end with a suggestion of reading a booklet or of coming to a course. There is nothing wrong with such methodology, since countless numbers have become

Christians at home, in their room at the university, and in all sorts of other places. But it is evident that Dr. Lloyd-Jones was preaching with a view to his sermon being a complete message, and one to which his listeners should respond.

Having a firmly Pauline doctrine of salvation, he never feared that people had to make an instant choice in case they never heard the gospel again. His confidence in the convicting power of the Holy Spirit was absolute. He believed that preaching the good news could bring his hearers to see their plight as sinners and their only hope in salvation through Jesus Christ there and then. Just because he knew that emotional manipulation and human technique were both profoundly wrong and utterly unbiblical did not mean that people could not be converted as they sat.

We do not need to be legalistic and follow all the Doctor's practice to the letter. Maybe mornings can now be a better time to bring non-Christian friends? Maybe they might prefer to come to weeknight meetings?

But surely his methodology and the firm biblical principles upon which his evangelistic preaching was based apply as much in the twenty-first century as in the mid-twentieth. Contrary to what many Arminians believe, his passionately held belief in the doctrines of grace made his evangelism and its firmly scriptural base all the more powerful. Humans, as we see from this sermon, are unaltered since the human race began. God's message of salvation never changes, nor do his methods. What you are about to read shows us why.

And the LORD God called unto Adam, and said unto him, Where art thou? (Gen. 3:9)

Before we can possibly understand the meaning of that statement in verse 9, we must look again at the great context. Genesis 3, let me remind you, is one of the most important chapters in the whole Bible because here we have a history of the world and at the same time all the main outlines of salvation. This one chapter summarizes it all for us.

There is a pathetic and ridiculous attitude on the part of so many—an attitude based on nothing but sheer ignorance—that somehow or other the Bible, while a very interesting old book, has nothing to do with the modern world. But it is the very essence of preaching to deal with modern life because the Bible really is concerned about that. It is a timeless book because it is a book about life, a book about the soul. It is a book from God, giving us a view of ourselves and of all others, revealing the causes of our troubles and showing us the sheer waste of energy, apart from anything else, that is involved in trying to solve our problems in any way except that which is offered to us so freely in our Lord and Savior, Jesus Christ.

So here is the history without which we cannot understand why the whole world, and each one of us in particular, is as it is at this moment. There is no other explanation. Many other answers are being offered, of course, and we are familiar with them. But our position is that having looked at them all, and having perhaps tried many of them and having found them all to fail—as the Bible tells us from the beginning that they must and will—we come back to this. The biblical message authenticates itself in experience. It has done so throughout the centuries, and its claim is that it is as true today as it has ever been and is as relevant to men and women in their predicament today as it was a thousand or two thousand or even three thousand years ago.

Now that is the general position. And I have been anxious to emphasize that this chapter is not only a record of actual history but in addition is a full explanation of what each one of us does in our lives. That is the remarkable thing about the Bible. That is why it gives us so much history. Each of us in our turn repeats what was done at the beginning, and we go on repeating it. That is why there is, as the author of Ecclesiastes tells us, "no new thing under the sun" (1:9). And there really is not, as far as men and women are concerned.

If you think that we are all so different today, just make a list of the things that people are doing in London or wherever at this moment—you will find that these were all being done in Old Testament times. Not in exactly the same form perhaps, but still the same things. There is no difference. You will find it all here. For all their cleverness and brilliant advances and inventions, men and women seem to be quite incapable of inventing a new sin. Have you ever thought of that? The sins we commit have all been thought of before, and they have all been practiced before. According to the Bible—and I suggest to you that our own experiences and the history of the world to this moment confirm this teaching—man as a being does not

199

change at all. So what we find in the third chapter of Genesis is true today of every human individual in this world.

We have seen that there is one real cause of all our troubles, and that is our wrong attitude toward God—everything stems from that. So we have been spending our time, in particular, tracing and analyzing that wrong attitude. We considered it first from the aspect of the intellect, and then we went on to think about some of the consequences—the persistent sense of loss and incompleteness, the guilt and shame, the fear of life and the fear of death. Finally, we have seen how even when God comes to us, we run away from him because of our totally wrong idea concerning him. Our final tragedy is that we refuse the one thing that can put us right.

Now we go on from there because the story goes on. We have seen what man did that produced the fall, and we have seen what he is like as a result of the fall. So you might have thought that the story would end there. But it does not. It goes on, and it must go on. And that is a central message of the Bible.

Why does the story go on? Well, according to this record it is because, whether we like it or not, this is God's world. And you cannot stop God from coming to his world, his own property, his own possession. We never like that, of course. That is the whole essence of our modern objection to God, the objection of people as they are by nature. We think we have got rid of him and have finished with him. We are now going to carry on without God. And we constantly decide to do that. But remember the eighth verse of Genesis 3: "And they heard the voice of the LORD God walking in the garden in the cool of the day: and Adam and his wife hid themselves from the presence of the LORD God amongst the trees of the garden," as if to say, "If we only get behind there and hide, he'll just walk straight on, and then we'll be able to come out again, and all will be well. And if we hear him again, we'll go hide again."

But the backs of the trees belong to God quite as much as the fronts of the trees. The whole garden belongs to God. The universe is God's. So the story has to go on. And this is the first principle, surely, that we all need to learn and to grasp. We are not independent creatures in this world. We do not own it, and we cannot order it and decide what happens in it. That is the first great lesson here. It is God from beginning to end. It is God making his world. He owns it. It is his possession. He controls it. He sustains it.

He guides it. He interferes with it. He comes into it. He erupts into it. It is always God's. That is the lesson—God coming into the garden when Adam and Eve thought that they had finished with him.

And what God does, as we are reminded here, is this: he continues to speak. That is the thing. We see this here from beginning to end. God made man in his own image, and he spoke to him. And man listened and replied. That was perfection. That was paradise. That was man as he was meant to be. God speaking—man listening to God. The greatest thing man can ever know is to be spoken to by God. But man decided to stop that. He did not want that anymore. He did not believe in that any longer. And he thought it ended there. But God went on speaking.

Adam and Eve hid at the back of the trees, but this is what happened: "And the LORD God called unto Adam, and said unto him, Where art thou?" (v. 9). And they heard God, and they could not avoid him, and they had to come out of hiding.

"Where art thou?"

It was God speaking. Oh, yes, God speaks to men and women! That is the great message of the Bible. God addresses us in many different ways—he speaks in the conscience, he speaks in history, he speaks in events. You cannot understand history apart from that. We find a great deal of this—and certainly the only adequate explanation of it—in God's Book. Even in secular history God speaks in an endless number of ways. But we are all deaf as the result of sin and do not hear him.

God does not always speak with an audible voice as he spoke to Adam and Eve hiding there behind the trees. In the book of Job we are told that sometimes, when man has become impervious, God speaks by dreams and visions in the night (4:13; 7:14). He speaks through accidents, through illnesses, through death. Supremely he speaks in this Word of his, which is his word addressed to us. And then, beyond it all, God speaks to us in his Son: "God, who at sundry times and in divers manners spake in time past unto the fathers by the prophets, hath in these last days spoken unto us by his Son" (Heb. 1:1–2).

So let us now concentrate on how God speaks, because it is all suggested to us, it seems to me, in this ninth verse of Genesis 3 and in some of the following verses.

The first thing I notice is that God addresses us personally. "And

201

the LORD God called unto Adam, and said unto him, Where art thou?" "Where art thou?" It was a personal address to Adam. Here is one of the truths that we must grasp at the very outset. We all know by experience that there is nothing we are so slow to understand as this fact. Do you see what happened? Before we come to this verse, we find a good deal of conversation by other people, and they have been talking about God. "Yea," said the devil, "hath God said . . . ?" And Eve replied, "Yes, God has said . . ." Adam and Eve and the devil were, as it were, having a conversation about God, and they were expressing their opinions about him. But suddenly, in this ninth verse, the whole situation changed. Now God was addressing Adam and Eve as they were hiding behind the trees. The positions were reversed. And that is the first thing that happens to a man or woman who is on the way to becoming a Christian. The first thing we become conscious of is that we are being addressed. To put it another way, Adam suddenly found that far from being the investigator, he was the one being investigated.

"Adam, where art thou?"

The Lord God had come down, and he was looking, he was searching. Adam and his position and condition were under investigation. Before that Adam had been walking around the garden. He had listened to the devil's suggestion and had thought he was in a position of supremacy. He was looking on, and he was expressing his opinions. But now he found himself being addressed, under examination, investigated.

Surely my meaning is perfectly clear. If you have a discussion with people about religion and about Christianity, you will always find that they talk as the investigators. Ha! With their great brains they are going to look into this question of the Bible. They are going to investigate God. They have the ability. And God? Well, God is a kind of specimen, as it were, to be put on the table, to be dissected, to be analyzed, to be considered. Modern man is investigating the universe, investigating religion, investigating God. Man is on the throne; he is the judge on the bench. Ah, yes, he has considered Buddhism and Confucianism and Hinduism. Now he will try Christianity. "Well now, what about Christ?"

I am not caricaturing this, am I? Have we not all done this? We imagine that we are in a position to investigate. But suddenly we are brought to the realization that we are the ones who are being examined, that we have been betraying ourselves without realizing it. And the more we talk, the more we betray ourselves and the more we are examined.

I want to ask a question. Have you realized, my friend, that in this life you are on trial? You are not doing the trying. You are being tried. Shall I sum this up by putting it in terms of what a great man once said? Referring to a man who had remarked that he saw absolutely nothing in the novels of Sir Walter Scott, this great man commented that such a person was not telling us anything about Scott but was telling us a very great deal about himself! How true that is. And it is exactly the same with regard to this whole matter of investigating God. We fondly imagine that we are in the position of examiners, but suddenly something happens to us, and we are conscious of the fact that we are being looked at, that we are being addressed, that we are being spoken to, that a word has come to us.

Have you reached that stage, my friend? Have you realized that in this world we are workers and travelers and are not simply spectators sitting in a gallery looking on at some game that is being played by other people in the arena? Do you not realize that you are involved and that every second you live judgments are being formed about you and that by what you do here you are determining not only what happens to you in this world but also in eternity?

But let me put that in a slightly different form. Adam was suddenly made to realize that he was not only being addressed but that it was he himself as a person who was being considered. What was under investigation was not merely his ideas and his thoughts and his position in a philosophical sense but he himself. And this is absolutely true about us all. Christianity is not a matter of opinions. When God addresses us in the various ways that I have indicated, he is not talking to us about our opinions. He is not a bit interested in them. He is interested in us. "Where art thou? I am speaking to you. Adam, where are *you*?" That is what God says.

But how cleverly we avoid all this. We are ready to express our opinions and to have our arguments. We think that Christianity is a matter for discussion. What do you start with? Well, you may start, if you like, with the being of God. Then, having dealt with that, we say, "Of course, there's the question of miracles. Are miracles possible? Can they happen?" So we may spend another evening discussing miracles. This is all *discussing* Christianity, is it not? We think that is what Christianity is about.

And then we come to Jesus of Nazareth and the Christian claim that he was God and man, that there were two natures in that one person. Well, we must spend at least a night on this. Let's have this out. Is that possible? Is it conceivable?

Then there is this question of Jesus's death on a cross on Calvary's hill, the great doctrine about something called "atonement"—that one died for others, that he made himself a substitute, and so on. So we take this up. Is this even moral? Is it conceivable? Can it happen? We spend a whole night arguing about that.

And the whole time we think we have been discussing Christianity. There is a sense, of course, in which we have, but there is another sense in which we have not, because, my friend, you can not only go to your grave but you can even go to hell just doing that. Christianity, primarily, is not a discussion about ideas. It is a discussion about *you*.

"Adam, where art thou? I am looking for you. I am interested in you, the individual person."

And that is the first thing men and women realize when they are on their way to becoming Christians. Throughout their lives they have never faced themselves at all. They have been protecting themselves. They have been putting up camouflage to conceal themselves. That is the meaning of all the arguments and disputations about these various questions. "Something is coming that's going to be a little bit personal and may be difficult. Very well, let's hide behind the trees." And we hide behind the trees of philosophies and ideas and comparative religions and abstruse questions, and as long as we are there, it is all outside us. But God penetrates through it all.

It is about you, my friend, you as an individual at this moment. It is all about you and your life and what you are doing with it and where you are going. Has this come personally to you yet?

May I ask another question? Do you resent this personal emphasis? Lord Melbourne, one of the Victorian prime ministers, spoke for many a modern man when he said, "Things have come to a very pretty pass if religion's going to start being personal."

"Adam, where art thou?"

Have you realized that this is a personal matter? A personal decision? A personal coming face-to-face with God? You are confronted by God. God is addressing you. God is speaking to you—to you! He is not interested primarily in your ideas but in you yourself as you pass through this life and through this world once and once only.

What next? Well, the next step is that God forces us to face where we are and what we are. "Adam, *where* art thou? Where exactly are you, and what are you doing there?" In other words, this whole business of preaching and of the gospel brings me face-to-face with the fact of where I am and of where I ought to be. Before, when God, as it were, came into that garden called paradise, Adam was always there to meet him. He looked forward to his coming, rejoiced in his coming, ran to meet him with a smile on his face. But now, for the first time, he did not do that; he was hiding behind some trees. And God said, "Where are you? You have never been there before. What are you doing there? Come out. That is not the place for you. You ought not to be there; you ought to be here."

And that is precisely what God is asking every one of us at this moment. "Where are you? Where are you in life and in this world?" Let me subdivide this. Where are you intellectually? Where are you in your thinking? Have you really faced all the facts? May I put it as simply and as bluntly and as plainly as this? You may say to me that you have long since rejected Christianity. Well, I only want to ask one question: have you ever read the Bible through? I have found that all of us tend to dismiss Christianity without really knowing what it is. We have never really taken the trouble to find out. We have dismissed it as a prejudice. We have not read the Bible, we have not even read the New Testament, we know nothing about the history of the church, and yet we dismiss it all.

I say that is intellectually dishonest. Where are we, I repeat, in the matter of the mind and the whole process of thought and the complete view of life? Have we really brought in all the factors? Have we included life itself in our conduct and our behavior? Have we listened to the voice of conscience? Have we looked into the face of death? Have we looked beyond? Have we considered the testimony of some of the best and the greatest people that the world has ever known? Have we read the history of revivals? Where are we intellectually? Have we really brought all this in?

That is the challenge of the Word of God. God knows perfectly well that we hide behind these intellectual trees. I have already mentioned a number of them. But as long as you are there, you are not seeing things clearly. You must come out into the open, says the Bible, and really face the truth.

"Ah," you say, "but I've always thought that Christianity is sob stuff."

That is because you have dismissed it without considering it. Christianity is reasonable. It is valid argument. It has a case. It comes to you as a fully orbed revelation of the truth of God. You will find this discussed in many books. For example, you cannot dispute the brainpower of C. S. Lewis, can you? Read his book *Surprised by Joy*, in which he tells you something of his history in these matters. But he is only one of many. My friends, it is intellectually dishonest to say that Christianity is not intellectually respectable. That is hiding behind trees. That is a refusal to come out into the open and really face it all and really try it. So I say that the Bible asks where we are intellectually.

In the same way, and perhaps with much more insistence, the Bible comes to us and asks us where we are morally. Oh, how much easier it is to argue about philosophy and theology than to face ourselves in a moral sense. Where are we in the matter of chastity? In the matter of purity? In the matter of honesty? In the matter of soul cleanliness? In the whole matter of our life and living? That is the first thing, surely, that we all ought to be considering. Before you try to understand miracles, let me commend to you that you start trying to understand yourself.

Why do we go on doing things that we know to be wrong? Why do we get pleasure from that? Why do we continue though we know that we will have pain later on? Why do we do such things? That is the problem. That is the real issue facing men and women—not their grand opinions about abstractions, but they themselves.

"Adam, where are you?"

Where are you morally? What of the credit, the moral credit, with which you began? What is the account like at this moment? What if the books were opened in public? What if your life and your story could be flashed onto a screen? That is what the Bible is interested in. That is what it is talking about. It is personal, and it is direct, and it is about our own lives.

Let me give you the supreme example of this. It is to be found in the Scriptures, in the fourth chapter of the Gospel according to John, where we read of our Lord's dealings with a woman of Samaria. Our Lord was tired, so he sat down by the side of the well, and the woman came along to draw water. At once they began to converse. They talked about Jews and Samaritans, and they talked about the well and the depth of the well and about

Jacob who had dug the well. And the woman was enjoying the conversation and was arguing very cleverly. They talked about God and about worship.

But in the middle of all this our Lord suddenly said, "Go, call thy husband, and come hither." The woman had to reply honestly and say, "I have no husband." And our Lord looked at her and said, "Thou hast well said, I have no husband: For thou hast had five husbands; and he whom thou now hast is not thy husband: in that saidst thou truly" (John 4:16–18).

That is the Lord Jesus Christ's method. He puts an end to all the argument and disputation about a thousand and one questions. He brings it right home to the woman herself. Here is a woman who would talk about God and about worship, and yet she was living in adultery, and our Lord made her face it. "Come out," he said in essence, "from behind that tree. Come out into the open. I know all about you."

"Adam, *where* art thou?"

And that is the thing that God is saying to all of us. My dear friend, face yourself and your own life—what you are actually doing, what you actually are, the thoughts that you fondle, the imaginations that you delight in, the things you do, the things that you know perfectly well are in your mind and you are ashamed of them. You would not publicly confess that you are guilty of them all. That is what God is talking about. That is Christianity. "Adam, come out from that hiding place." Is this clear, my friends?

Let me give you just one other illustration of this, from the Old Testament, the famous story of David. We are told that David was suddenly tempted, and his lust got the better of him. He committed adultery, and then, to cover it over, he committed murder. And he thought all was well, but God had seen it, and God was displeased. So God sent his servant Nathan to talk to David.

Nathan put a conundrum to David. "O king," he said, "something has happened." And he painted a picture of a man who, though he had many sheep, stole the only sheep belonging to another man. Hearing this, David was filled with wrath and indignation and said that man had to be punished. Nothing was too severe for him.

Then Nathan paused, looked at David, and said, "Thou art the man." He said in essence, "I'm speaking about you, David. You thought that I was putting a question of inequity to you and discussing a moral problem in general. But, King David, I have been speaking about *you*" (2 Sam. 12:1–7).

"Adam, where art thou?"

It is you, your life, your moral behavior, your total personality that is under investigation.

The next point that I must emphasize is this: when God comes to us and speaks to us personally, he makes us realize the true nature and character of what we have just been doing. He puts it like this: "Who told thee that thou wast naked? Hast thou eaten of the tree, whereof I commanded thee that thou shouldest not eat?" (Gen. 3:11). God made Adam and Eve face the exact nature of what they had done. It was not just a question of eating fruit. They had broken his commandment; they had violated his holy law. They had raised themselves up in rebellion against him. God brought it right home to them.

And, you know, the gospel does that. It fixes and establishes sin. How does it do that? Well, it teaches the true nature of sin. I have just been discussing the case of David. Let me come back to it again. David, after he had seen the truth and after he had repented, sat down and wrote Psalm 51, and in that psalm, in which he dealt with this very sin that he had committed, he put it like this: "Against thee, thee only, have I sinned, and done this evil in thy sight" (v. 4). David meant that the terrible thing about his sin, the thing that makes sin sin, was not so much that he had been guilty of adultery and of murder, though that was bad enough, but that he had sinned against God. He had violated the law of God. He was a rebel against God. That is the reality that we do not see. We are prepared, perhaps, to admit the category of sin, of wrongdoing, but we regard it as merely some transgression of a moral code, the breaking of a law, and we say there is no more to it than that. But, my dear friend, there is.

You and I, as human beings, were made in the image of God. And we were meant to live a life that such persons should live. We were meant to be in correspondence with God and to live in enjoyment of him. We were meant to be righteous and holy and true and upright. And what is sin? It is a departure from that. The trouble, is it not, is that we all tend to think of sin only in terms of particular actions. But the terrible thing about sin is that it is a violation of God's creation. It is robbing God. It is spitting into the face of God. Any life today that is not lived to the glory of God is in the depth of sin. God made Adam see all this, and Eve saw it, and anyone who comes under conviction of sin must of necessity see it.

So the final question for all of us is just this: where are you at this moment? Do you know God? Do you love him? Do you delight in him? Is it your greatest concern to please him and to live to his glory and to his honor? God would have you see that unless that is your purpose, you are a vile sinner. He brings that home to you. You have departed from where he put you. You are hiding somewhere. You are out of the pathway. You are someplace where you should not be. And you are transgressing the law of God and who you were meant to be. God brings us to see that.

Is that not what is so lacking in the modern world? Many people believe in respectability, but they do not believe in God. And they are terrible sinners—as terrible as the people who are living in the gutters of London at this moment. Sin is against God. "I have sinned," says the prodigal son to his father. "I have sinned against heaven, and in thy sight" (Luke 15:21). That is the nature of sin, and it is always true of us.

But that brings me to my last point, which is that God, when he thus comes to us and speaks to us, not only gives us a personal address, but in order to bring us to repentance, he then proceeds to tell us about judgment. You remember how he did it there in the garden at the beginning. God came to Adam and Eve and, having drawn them out of their hiding place and having shown them themselves and their sin, he pronounced judgment.

I am sorry, my friend, if you do not like the idea of judgment. No natural person has ever liked judgment. But whether we like it or not, it is a fact. God himself revealed his judgment at the very beginning. He came after man. You cannot get away from God. Of course, you can walk away from church and say you will never come back again, but that is not walking out of God's universe, that is not walking out of God's sight. You can hide yourself, get away, rush into the thickets and imagine that he will not see you. But he will call you out just as he has always called man out of hiding. God's judgment is being repeated in the history of the world and of every human individual at this very moment.

And what is God's judgment? Well, you can subdivide it into the present and the future. There is an immediate judgment that always comes as a result of sin. What is that? Well, God pronounced in Genesis 3 that there would be a perpetual conflict between the Serpent and the woman and between the seed of the Serpent and the seed of the woman. And is that not absolutely true? Are we not all in this conflict, and do we not know all about it? Consider temptation—evil drawing us, enticing us, battling against that which is best and noblest and most upright in us. Do you not see this everywhere—in the newspapers, on the billboards, in all places of amusement, on the streets? This struggle between the seed of the Serpent and the seed of the woman is the whole problem of life and of existence. The moment we enter into this life we are already in the fight. The battle of morality. The battle of purity. The battle of chastity. The battle of honesty. And what a fight it is! The current is dragging us down. How difficult it is to fight against it and to battle upstream. This is a verification of God's judgment.

But the blindness that sin produces in us prevents us from seeing that all this is nothing but part of God's judgment on sin. Man thought that by listening to the devil and eating that forbidden fruit he was going to have an easy time, that there would be an end of conformity to law, that he would be a god, that he would be absolutely free. But he put himself into shackles and into chains, and he has been struggling in them ever since. The seed of the Serpent and the seed of the woman are locked in this endless fight between the hell that life can be and God's plan for us. We have all known it, and not only that, but the sorrow and the suffering too. "In sorrow thou shalt bring forth children" (Gen. 3:16), in pain and suffering. This is history. These are facts.

That, my friend, is part of God's judgment. It is all part of God's pronouncement on rebellion and sin. What greater joy is there than the coming of a child into a family? But think of the accompanying strain, the struggle, the suffering, the oft-repeated sorrow. It is sin that produces all that. It is the wrong attitude toward God. It is man's rebellion against God. It is man taking the law unto himself. That is why there is all this suffering and sorrow and illness and disease and pain and all the problems.

But not only that, there is the very struggle for existence—the toil of earning one's livelihood, getting one's daily bread, the hardness, the thorns and the thistles, the competition and the troubles. Why is it that thorns and thistles grow so abundantly? Why is it so difficult to get a crop of wheat or corn out of the ground? Why this endless fighting, with everything against us? All we get we have to work for with the very sweat of our brow. Again, this is just part of God's judgment on sin. And men and women have been trying to deal with it and to cope with it ever since, but they cannot. They would like to get back to that paradise, but they have been driven out. God drove Adam and Eve out, and he put at the entrance the cherubim and the flaming sword turning in every direction. And though man in civilization has been rushing against that gate and trying to burst through, the flaming sword keeps him back. The whole story of civilization, in a sense, is a story of futility, a history of failure.

Even some great historians who are not Christians at all talk of the cyclical theory of history. We ever seem to be advancing. We are on the point of getting there. But we just go around the other side of the circle, and we are back where we were. Civilization goes around and around in cycles. There is no forward advance. There is no end. There is no reaching the ultimate objective. Life is simply a futile procedure. Around and around we go. We rise. We succeed. We fail. We fall. Down they go—dynasties, empires, individuals. That is always true. It is because of the flaming sword and the cherubim at the east end of the garden of Eden. Man will never get back there by his own efforts; he is incapable of it. He is not allowed to; he has been driven out—that is the judgment upon sin. But that is only the present; there is something beyond.

"And unto dust shalt thou return" (Gen. 3:19). Death, physical death, came in as part of the punishment of sin. Tennyson tells us:

[Man] thinks he was not made to die.

"IN MEMORIAM A. H. H."

That is just part of man's recollection of what he once was. But as he is now, he has the seeds of mortality within him. The moment he is born, he is beginning to die. A little baby was born a second ago. You say that there at any rate is someone who is beginning to live. I can say with equal accuracy that there is someone who has started dying. The first breath is but the first of a series that is leading to the last. That is not being morbid; that is being factual. We are born to die. Death, the inevitable end, comes to pass, and beyond it we face God.

My dear friends, you know you have to face all that. And you do not come to the garden until you have. This is no sob story. This is not a patent remedy. This is not one of your optimistic philosophies. This is not a kind of spiritual outlook that says, "Come along, let's be bright and cheerful and happy and walk with a new step; it's all right." It is terribly wrong. And God would have us see how terribly wrong it is.

211

Do you realize where you are? Where are you at this moment? How long have you lived in this world? How much longer do you think you are going to be here? What have you done with your life? What have you made of it? What is your record? Are you proud of it? What are your achievements? What is your secret life? What is the history of your mind and your thought and your imagination and your heart?

"Adam, where are you?"

In every respect, where are you, man? Where are you, woman? Come out of that hiding place and face the truth, for you have to. You are in God's world. You are God's creature, and you cannot avoid him. You cannot evade him. You have to deal with him. And if you do not listen to him in life, you will have to listen to him in death. When your name is called out at the great judgment throne in eternity, you will have to step forward and listen to the verdict.

But I must not stop there. I know that nobody will really listen to what I am about to say who does not believe what I have just been saying. It is only the desperate who come to Christ. It is only those who know they are sick who see their need of the physician. But thank God there is the physician.

I told you about the judgment, but God went on. There is to be this struggle between the seed of the Serpent and the seed of the woman, but the seed of the woman shall bruise the Serpent's head (Gen. 3:15). The God who calls you to come out of your hiding place calls you out not only to condemn you but to tell you that he has made a way to bring you back to paradise, if you believe and acknowledge the condemnation. He tells you that he has sent his only Son, the seed of the woman, into this world to do something that makes the cherubim and the flaming sword fall back and allow us in. Jesus of Nazareth, the Son of God, has borne the judgment of the sin of all who believe in him and who look to him. And if you trust in him, he will take you through the gate into the joy of the Lord. And if you enter in with him now, you will be able to say:

Today thy mercy calls us to wash away our sin;
However great our trespass, whatever we have been;
However long from mercy we may have turned away,
Thy blood, O Christ, can cleanse us, and make us white today.

Thank God for this gospel because:

When all things seem against us, to drive us to despair,
We know one gate is open, one ear will hear our prayer.

OSWALD ALLEN
"TODAY THY MERCY CALLS US"

If you have heard God speaking to you, cry out to him for mercy, and he will not refuse you. Jesus said, "Him that cometh to me I will in no wise cast out" (John 6:37). So from your hiding place of failure and shame and misery and unhappiness, come out and cry to him, and he will deliver you.

14

SEEKING THE FACE OF GOD

(1967)
Psalm 27

From *Seeking the Face of God*

How practical is expository preaching?

One of the great myths of today is that preaching from Scripture is somehow theoretical and abstract and of no use to the everyday, real-life concerns of ordinary people.

Dr. Lloyd-Jones preached on a number of Psalms, and those sermons later became a book entitled Seeking the Face of God. *The title sermon shows that the view summarized in the previous paragraph is not merely simplistic but is in fact utter nonsense! He demonstrates here that there is nothing more practical and useful for life than the Psalms written by David and others thousands of years ago. Millennia may have passed, but King David's inspired poetry is as vital for survival today as it was then.*

Dr. Lloyd-Jones was a great enthusiast for the Puritans. One of the aspects of their life and thinking is how practical they were—"experimental" or "experiential" as was the expression at the time. They were people who lived normal lives, and if one thinks of those who survived the English Civil War of the sixteenth century, they went through some of the most savage kind of fighting imaginable and came out the other side of it only to be persecuted by King Charles II (as happened to John Bunyan).

Doctrine, in other words, is profoundly down-to-earth. And as the Doctor shows us from Psalm 27, that is precisely because it starts not with us but with God and who he is. Today's therapeutic culture, and its touchy-feely Christian imitators, always starts with us and with our felt needs. The whole point of David in the Psalms and of the Puritans hundreds of years later is that they do what Scripture does and begin with God.

This helps us survive whatever happens to us. David was someone who lived through unimaginable trauma, as we see from the accounts of his life in the Old Testament. In his writings in the Psalms, he is wonderfully and refreshingly honest about how truly dreadful life can be. God's people do not pretend that suffering does not happen to them or that they are indifferent to it. But the key thing that Dr. Lloyd-Jones brings out so well here is that they have a totally God-centered, not man-centered approach, not just to life's problems but to absolutely everything. This conditions our whole worldview, and as doctrine and Scripture are at the heart of that worldview, biblical exposition, far from being impractical or academic, is actually the most practical and down-to-earth thing that there is, as this sermon now shows us!

The LORD is my light and my salvation; whom shall I fear? the LORD is the strength of my life; of whom shall I be afraid? . . . Though an host should encamp against me, my heart shall not fear: though war should rise against me, in this will I be confident. (Psalm 27:1, 3)

Psalm 27 is a psalm we must always remember. It is a song and should be taken as a whole because generally the psalmist has one great message to give us in each psalm. That is particularly true of this Twenty-seventh Psalm, but we can perhaps look at one verse in particular, verse 4:

One thing have I desired of the LORD, that will I seek after; that I may dwell in the house of the LORD all the days of my life, to behold the beauty of the LORD, and to enquire in his temple.

Now, as in most of the psalms, the psalmist here is giving us his experience, because he is anxious to praise God. He is also anxious to help others. That is the whole purpose of sharing a personal experience—not to call attention to oneself but to call attention to the Lord who is the giver of all and who alone is worthy to be praised. As we look at the experience of this man, we can learn many lessons from him. He is teaching us here how to face the battle of life and of living.

That is the great value of the book of Psalms. They are always so practical because they are experimental or experiential. They have this additional value: each psalmist is not a man writing theoretically about life. It is generally someone who, having passed through some experience that tried and tested him, has again discovered the way of success and of triumph. So he wants to celebrate that and to pass on the information to others. Another great value, of course, of the psalms is that they are always so honest. The psalmist does not pretend he is better than he is. He opens his heart; he exposes himself to us, as it were, exactly as he is. He tells us about his fears and his forebodings; he never conceals any of his own weaknesses. So we feel that he speaks to our condition.

As far as this psalm is concerned, no one can decide for certain whether the psalmist wrote it immediately after a great trying experience or whether he wrote it while he was actually facing some such trial. It is probably a psalm of David, and therefore we can assume that as David was constantly suffering troubles and tribulations, he is telling us of some very recent experience in this psalm.

The value of all this to us is obvious because, after all, each of us is involved in struggle in our daily lives. Nothing is so wrong, and indeed dishonest, as to pretend that the moment you become a Christian all your problems are left behind and you will never have any difficulties from then on. That is just not true. The Christian is not promised an easy time in this world; indeed, the reverse is much nearer the truth. We are told in many places in the New Testament that as Christians we can expect unusual trials precisely because we are followers of the Lord.

Look at his life. There he was, the Son of God in this world; yet he was tried, he was tempted, he was tested, he had to suffer the contradiction of sinners against himself. His life was full of battle and conflict. And if that was true of him, as he himself pointed out in John 15, how much more likely is it to be true of his followers. Because we are Christians, the devil and all his forces will be particularly concerned to try us and to test us; to bring us down, if not into sin, at any rate into a condition of defeat and of unhappiness, filled with a sense of insecurity and a spirit of fear.

So the New Testament, as well as the Old, prepares us for all that. God's people have had great trials and tribulations and fights while they were in this world. We are not promised an easy time, but what we are assured is that in spite of it all we can be "more than conquerors" (Rom. 8:37). That is the Christian position. Scripture does not minimize the problems, nor does it tell us that there will be none; rather, it faces them as they are. Indeed, I have often claimed that the Bible is the most honest book in the world. It is the politicians, philosophers, and poets who are always promising us that our troubles will be abolished. These are dangerous optimists, these idealists who are always saying they are going to make a perfect world.

The Bible never says that. The Bible tells us the precise opposite. It says that because men and women are in rebellion against God and are sinners, the world will be full of problems and difficulties. There will be "wars and rumours of wars" (Mark 13:7). The Bible has always said that. It is other people, those who do not believe the Bible, who promise that by some human organization we will banish war. But the Bible is realistic and tells us that enemies and powers are set against us, but that in spite of that we can be "more than conquerors through him that loved us" (Rom. 8:37).

How are you getting on in this battle? Are you triumphant, are you assured? That is what we are meant to be as God's people. How are you facing the stresses and the trials, the troubles and the tribulations of life? Well, in this psalm we turn to the right way of facing these problems because here the psalmist tells us, out of his own experience, the only way whereby we can indeed truly do so in a world like this.

Here, then, is a psalm of fourteen verses that can be divided up simply into three sections. In the first section, verses 1–6, the psalmist expresses his confidence, his assurance. Then in the second section, verses 7–12, he comes to petition, to prayer, out of the midst of the struggle and conflict and agony. And then in verses 13–14 he arrives at his final conclusion with regard to this whole matter. Or, to put it in another way, in the first section the psalmist is in heaven, in the second section he is very much down to earth, and in the third section he gives us his decision with regard to the whole of his future and to how life is to be faced.

So what we have here in this psalm is what we may well call a strategy for living, how to face the battle and the conflict of life. As you know, you must always start with strategy, not with tactics, because if you do not you will soon find yourself defeated. You may think you are getting a little victory in one place, but you have forgotten something else. So you must start with a grand strategy of life, and that is stated to perfection in this psalm. Here it is: we must always start in heaven, with God. Then having done that, we come to earth and face the problems of life and of living as we find them in the light of what we have already seen in heaven with God.

That, then, is the great principle, and we all get into trouble because we forget this essential strategy. Never start with your problems. Never! Never start with earth; never start with men. Always start in heaven; always start with God. That is really the one great message of this psalm, but the psalmist puts it, of course, in different ways. He puts it in experiential form so that he is very much with us and one of us. But this is the essential principle, and if we do not grasp it, there is no point in continuing. The one thing with which we must always start is our relationship with God. The whole trouble in the world today is due to the fact that this has been forgotten. People always start with themselves, with the world, with life, with their problems. This is true of all who are not Christians, and that is why they never truly succeed. They have already started in a wrong way, and that must inevitably lead to failure.

So having established the strategy in our minds, let us follow the psalmist as he works this out for us. Pay attention to him, and ask God to give you understanding through his Spirit, so that you may grasp this most precious truth that can revolutionize your whole life and your outlook upon it. Do you feel defeated, frightened, fearful of life? My dear friend, here is the very thing you need. Take heed for all you are worth, for all your life, and this man will show you how to be more than a conqueror.

We start, therefore, with the psalmist's confidence:

> The Lord is my light and my salvation; whom shall I fear? the Lord is the strength of my life; of whom shall I be afraid? When the wicked, even mine enemies and my foes, came upon me to eat up my flesh, they stumbled and fell. (vv. 1–2)

And notice this:

> Though an host should encamp against me, my heart shall not fear: though war should rise against me, in this will I be confident. (v. 3)

Then he goes on in the fifth and sixth verses:

> For in the time of trouble he shall hide me in his pavilion: in the secret of his tabernacle shall he hide me; he shall set me up upon a rock. And now shall mine head be lifted up above mine enemies round about me.

And he ends this section by saying, "I will sing, yea, I will sing praises unto the Lord."

Now this is tremendous confidence. He says in effect, "I am not afraid, nor is there any need to be afraid. Even though my enemies all gather and conspire together and come upon me all at the same time, it does not matter. Even if war rises against me, I am not going to be afraid. Nothing can ever defeat me, whatever it may be." This is overwhelming assurance, and it is, of course, typical of the attitude of these men of God that we read of in the Bible from the very beginning to the very end.

If you want a corresponding statement in the New Testament, consider the end of that great eighth chapter of Paul's epistle to the Romans, where the apostle, having given a list of his trials and troubles and tribulations, saying that we are led every day as "sheep for the slaughter," comes to this conclusion: "For I am persuaded"—I am certain—"that neither death, nor life, nor angels, nor principalities, nor powers, nor things present, nor things to come, nor height, nor depth, nor any other creature, shall be able to separate us from the love of God, which is in Christ Jesus our Lord" (vv. 38–39).

"I know! I am certain!" There is the great Christian note: facing life at its very worst, yet there is no fear, no uncertainty. There is no shrinking or trembling as you look at the unknown future. Not at all! "Whatever it may be, I am confident! I am persuaded! I am certain! I am sure!"

Now, these things are not theoretical. You and I are men and women living in the midst of life. Do you have this confidence? Are you facing life like that? Are you able to face the future, whatever it may be, and say, "I know, I am certain, I shall not fear, whatever may happen; in this I am confident"?

But then we must ask a question: what is the source of this man's confidence? Or is it just foolhardiness, some kind of braggadocio? Or is he a man we can listen to? He is, of course, because he is so honest; he is not merely making wild statements. We have known people who are confident beyond their ability, have we not? We remember the apostle Peter telling our Lord that even if all men deserted him, he would never do so, yet in a few hours Peter was denying him in base cowardice.

But this is very different. On what does the psalmist base his confidence? What is the source of his great assurance? Well, he tells us quite plainly that it is nothing in himself, nothing at all. That is the meaning of the extraordinary thirteenth verse: "I had fainted, unless I had believed to see the goodness of the LORD in the land of the living." The words "I had fainted" are not in the original Hebrew. They have been supplied, and rightly so, by the translator. The psalmist is writing under the stress of deep emotion. He remembers the terrible predicament that he was in, the forces that were against him, and his consciousness of his own weakness. So he just blurts out, "Unless I had believed to see the goodness of the LORD . . ." "Unless I had believed, I would have been completely undone; I would have been filled with despair; I would have fainted."

Here, you see, is the starting point, and we must not forget it. This man is not a mere boaster, a braggart. He is not just a foolish man who has confidence in himself and who says that he does not care what life may bring against him because he is so sure and certain of himself. He does not write like the poet at the end of the last century:

> It matters not how strait the gate,
> How charged with punishments the scroll.
> I am the master of my fate:
> I am the captain of my soul.
>
> W. E. HENLEY, "INVICTUS"

It is not that sort of nonsense at all. A person who speaks like that in self-confidence is someone who always fails, and there are many ways in which we can do that. To become a cynic is failure. Just to resign yourself to life and its attendant circumstances is failure. And there are many like that. They do not solve the problem, they never get over the difficulties, nor do they ever know what it is to sing and to rejoice and to be filled with the spirit of exultation. There is no true victory there. At their best, self-confident people merely put up with things; they keep a stiff upper lip and brace their shoulders and go on with some philosophy of courage. But that is not what we have here. And others, of course, do not even do that. They just become complete failures, obviously defeated by the various temptations and trials of life.

But the thing about the psalmist is that he is filled with this spirit of assurance, of rejoicing and praising, all of which is due to the fact that his confidence is not in himself. So the first thing we must always learn in this world, the first great characteristic of us as Christian people, is that we are no longer self-confident. We know the truth about ourselves. Like the apostle Paul, we realize that "we wrestle not against flesh and blood, but

221

against principalities, against powers, against the rulers of the darkness of this world, against spiritual wickedness in high [or heavenly] places" (Eph. 6:12). We know what we are up against, and we realize our own utter weakness and helplessness: "I had fainted, unless I had believed to see the goodness of the LORD in the land of the living."

That, then, is the first point, which is a negative but an all-important one. If you feel that you are competent to stand up to life and that you can deal with all these things that are set against you, you are the simplest novice, an ignoramus. You do not really understand the problems, and you do not understand yourself. This man's confidence is not based upon himself, and he makes it quite plain as to what the source of his confidence is: It is "the LORD."

This is always a distinguishing mark of a Christian. Our confidence is entirely and altogether in the Lord. The psalmist brings this out in a tremendous manner: "The LORD is my light and my salvation." He starts with the Lord. And how does he end? "Wait, I say, on the LORD." He begins with him, and he ends with him. Altogether, in this psalm of fourteen verses, he mentions the name of the Lord thirteen times—six times in the first section, four times in the second section, and three times in the third.

But not only that, he starts the first section with him: "The LORD is my light and my salvation" and ends it by saying, "I will sing, yea, I will sing praises unto the LORD." Then he starts the second section with "Hear, O LORD, when I cry with my voice." And on he goes: "Thy face, LORD, will I seek"; "the LORD will take me up"; "the goodness of the LORD," right down to his final exhortation to us, which he repeats: "Wait on the LORD . . . wait, I say, on the LORD."

Here is the whole secret: it is the Lord. It is not man himself; it is not the believer. It is his confidence in the Lord. On what does he base this confidence? What is the Lord to him? Well, he gives us the answer: "The LORD is my light." And we do not need much imagination to know what he means by that. Light is the opposite of darkness, the opposite of despair. The gospel itself, in a sense, is introduced to us in that way: "The people which sat in darkness saw great light" (Matt. 4:16).

What happens to us all as the result of troubles and tribulations in life is that we are in darkness. We do not understand, and so we say, "Why should these things be happening? Why should I have to endure all this? I've tried to do this and that—I've tried to be godly and religious, but this is what is happening to me." So we are in trouble and in darkness. Not only that, we do not see what we can do about it. We seek solutions, and this is the whole story of civilization. The world has been seeking light, answers to all our problems. This is the whole meaning of philosophy and all the efforts of statesmen and governments, trying to find some light to illumine the darkness, to find a way out and a way of deliverance. But there is none.

And so the whole world is in darkness, and the people of today have given up. The characteristic of our age is cynicism. We see this in public entertainment ("What's the use of anything? Distrust everybody"), and people think it is so funny and amusing. This is a terrible commentary on life, and it is tragic. Such people do not believe in anybody or anything any longer. That is darkness, and that is humanity when left to itself. The problems are obviously gigantic and immense, and people cannot begin to understand them. So they sit down, finally, in utter hopelessness and despair. "There is nothing to be done," they say.

But "The LORD is my light." Of course he is! That is the only light that is in the world today. Look at the light that these children of Israel had; they had more than anybody else. In spite of all their grumbling and all their disobedience, they knew certain things that nobody else did, and that is why they stand out as the greatest people under the old dispensation. That is why their civilization was a purer one and a better one, compared with the life of paganism as you can read about it in the history of the Greeks and the Romans and all the others. The Lord had given them light through the law that he gave to Moses. Then you come to the New Testament, and suddenly everything changes, and one appears who could say, "I am the light of the world: he that followeth me shall not walk in darkness, but shall have the light of life" (John 8:12); "I am the way, the truth, and the life: no man cometh unto the Father, but by me" (John 14:6).

Light and understanding—the whole thing is explained to us, and those who believe this revelation given by the Lord are not surprised that the world is as it is. We do not believe in something foolish like evolution and hold that the world is getting better and better, because we can see it getting worse and worse. We observe the futility and everything else, but we understand; we know that it is all due to man's rebellion against God. We do not expect anything different. We have light on the situation. We are no longer defeated because we see another way, another kind of life, the way out. "The LORD is my light." It does not matter what problem confronts the Christian. We can always find light on it in the Bible—it never fails. "The LORD is my light and"—therefore—"my salvation," my deliverer. He is the One who guarantees my welfare, the One who shows me the way to escape. Again, to quote Paul, we can be made "more than conquerors" with the resources, the power, and all the things that God gives.

So the Lord is light, and he is salvation. He is our deliverance. He is an emancipator, and he delivers us from the thralldom of this world. We are translated from the kingdom of darkness into the kingdom of God's dear Son. We belong to a different realm; though we are still in this world, our citizenship is in heaven. And this means salvation: there is a translation, a deliverance, a movement, and we are taken out of it all. It is not that we do not have to suffer, but we are taken out of it in understanding and in spirit and are put into this position of peace and rest and safety.

Then, third, the psalmist goes on to say, "The LORD is the strength of my life." This, again, is a theme that runs right through the Bible. He is referring here, of course, to the power of the Lord. David sees the enemies; he is no fool. He can assess their strength. He knows the number of their battalions and of their dispositions: "though war should rise against me." He is fully aware of all this and of his own weakness. But he has a power behind him, a reserve; he has one who understands and who is illimitable in all his resources and all his power. When God rises, all this man's enemies are scattered. "The LORD is the strength of my life; of whom shall I be afraid?" As the old hymn puts it:

A Sovereign Protector I have,
Unseen, yet forever at hand,
Unchangeably faithful to save,
Almighty to rule and command.
He smiles, and my comforts abound;
His grace as the dew shall descend;
And walls of salvation surround
The soul He delights to defend.

AUGUSTUS TOPLADY (1740–1778),
"A SOVEREIGN PROTECTOR I HAVE"

Or as Martin Luther (1483–1546) put it:

A safe stronghold our God is still,
A trusty shield and weapon;
He'll help us clear from all the ill
That hath us now o'ertaken.

TRANSLATOR, THOMAS CARLYLE (1795–1881),
"A SAFE STRONGHOLD OUR GOD IS STILL"

This, you see, is the source of the psalmist's confidence. He knows that this is true about God. "God is light, and in him is no darkness at all" (1 John 1:5). God is wisdom. God is knowledge. God is all these to perfection. And add to that his might and his power and the strength of his arm—the irresistible God!

But the psalmist also knows other things about God lest we be frightened by his glory and greatness. This man knows about God's concern for us. He says in the eighth verse, "When thou saidst, Seek ye my face; my heart said unto thee, Thy face, LORD, will I seek." Though he is so great and high and though he does not need us, we are his people. He is concerned for us, and he invites us to come to him. When we are in trouble, he in various ways comes to us and says, "Seek my face"—"turn to me—roll your burdens onto me." God comes to us even when we are overwhelmed by troubles and are beginning to turn to human expediency and do not know what to do. When we are utterly bewildered and frustrated, suddenly something says within us, "Why not turn to God?" It is God himself who is doing this by the Spirit. He prompts us: "Seek my face. You see, you've forgotten me."

And this is the great word of the whole Bible: "Come unto me, all ye that labour and are heavy laden, and I will give you rest" (Matt. 11:28). Or as we find Peter putting it in 1 Peter 5:8–9, "Your adversary the devil, as a roaring lion, walketh about, seeking whom he may devour: Whom resist stedfast in the faith." How can we do this? Well, there is only one way to do it, says Peter: "casting all your care upon him" (v. 7). Why should you do so? Because "he careth for you." He knows all about you; he is interested in your welfare. "The very hairs of your head are all numbered," said Jesus Christ (Matt. 10:30). Nothing can happen to you apart from his knowing and working.

Not only that, this One who is seated at the right hand of the Father has been in this world and knows all about it. He suffered all that we suffer. He suffered the contradiction of sinners against himself. He resisted unto blood. He understands all about the travail and the agony and the weakness of the flesh. He knows it all because he came in the likeness of sinful flesh. And so, with his great care and concern, God says, "Seek ye my face." He encourages us to come to him. He is not only ready and willing and waiting to help us, he even prompts us to come to him in prayer. The hymn writer Toplady knew this so well from experience. God is not merely the hearer of prayer, he is the inspirer of prayer also.

> Inspirer and Hearer of prayer,
> Thou Shepherd and Guardian of Thine,
> My all to Thy covenant care,
> I, sleeping or waking, resign.

AUGUSTUS TOPLADY,
"INSPIRER AND HEARER OF PRAYER"

This is the basis of the psalmist's confidence.

And then in verse 10 he says, "When my father and my mother forsake me, then the LORD will take me up." This is a blessed phrase because we struggle, we stumble, and we fall, do we not? There we are, lying on the ground, unable to pick ourselves up, and nobody else can do so either. But this everlasting and eternal God is ever ready to take us up. He takes hold of us; he gets us onto our feet and establishes our goings. He is always ready to stoop to our weakness, mighty as he is.

In the same verse we find our final confidence—his unchangeableness. "When my father and my mother forsake me, then the LORD will take me up." Thank God for fathers and mothers, but they are fallible. They are only human, they are sinful, and they have often forsaken us. Indeed, many people have been forsaken by their father and mother simply because they have become Christians. The love of a father and a mother is a wonderful thing, but one of the great tragedies of life is that there are points at which it fails. We are all changeable; we cannot be relied upon in an ultimate sense. There is only One who can be relied upon, and that is God. As one of our hymns puts it:

> "Can a woman's tender care
> Cease towards the child she bare?

Yes, she may forgetful be,
Yet will I remember Thee."

Then God speaks:

"Mine is an unchanging love,
Higher than the heights above,
Deeper than the depths beneath,
Free and faithful, strong as death."

WILLIAM COWPER (1731–1800),
"LOVEST THOU ME?"

You see, even if human love does not turn its back upon us, there is a point beyond which it cannot go, even when it wants to. There are certain secret problems, agonies of the soul, with which a father and a mother cannot help. But God still can! And even in the agony of death, when all human aid has failed, God is still with us. There, then, is the basis and source of this psalmist's confidence. He knows that these things are true of God, and because these things are true, he is afraid of nothing. He can challenge the whole universe. With such a God, it matters not what rises against him.

So I ask the question again: do you face life like this? Are you "more than conqueror"? If not, are you asking, "How can I get this confidence? How can I attain to the position of the psalmist? How can I not only get it but maintain it and continue with it?" But he has anticipated you and wrote his psalm in order to help you. And here are his answers.

The first great thing is: *believe in the Lord.* "I had fainted, unless I had believed" (Ps. 27:13). This is always the beginning. You cannot have anything without belief. The author of the epistle to the Hebrews says, "He that cometh to God must believe that he is, and that he is a rewarder of them that diligently seek him" (11:6). I have nothing to offer you if you do not believe in God. I leave you to the utter despair and horror, the final bankruptcy, of some of those clever people who vaunt their unbelief and their emptiness on television programs. There is nothing, nothing at all, apart from belief in God. Accept this revelation, humble yourself, become like a little child, and believe the truth.

But even that is not enough. Some people believe the truth about God as it is revealed in the Bible and yet remain in trouble and defeated. Why?

227

Because they have not gone on to do the other things that this man tells us. Belief is the starting point, but only the starting point. You can be a Christian and yet be miserable and unhappy because you fail to go on to the second point, which he emphasizes in verse 4: "One thing have I desired of the LORD, that will I seek after; that I may dwell in the house of the LORD all the days of my life, to behold the beauty of the LORD, and to enquire in his temple."

This "one thing," this total concentration upon God, is essential. You may say, "I've always believed in God. Isn't that enough?" People have often told me, "I've always believed in God. I've always said my prayers." And yet they are full of troubles and problems and defeat because mere belief in God is of no value. "The devils also believe, and tremble," says James 2:19. God must become the supreme focus of your life. He must be the one object of your desire and of your ambition.

This, too, is found throughout the Scriptures. The apostle Paul, at the height of his great experience, says that this is his desire, the one thing that he wants: "that I may know him, and the power of his resurrection, and the fellowship of his sufferings" (Phil. 3:10). "This one thing I do, forgetting those things which are behind . . . I press toward the mark" (Phil. 3:13–14). It is the realization that nothing really matters ultimately in life except my relationship to God: "that I may dwell in the house of the LORD all the days of my life."

This does not refer to a physical building, nor does it mean that you want to spend the whole of your time in a chapel or a church—that is only a part of it. What he really means is this: "that I might belong to the household of God; that I am ever in communion with God, in fellowship with God, in touch with him." In effect the psalmist is saying, "What I want above everything else in this world is always to be in an intimate relationship with God, so that whatever happens, I am with him and he is with me." This is the one thing he wants. This is the first thing in his life and the secret of his whole position.

Then what does he desire and what does he dwell on? Here again I want you to notice the order of these things. This man's supreme desire is to worship God and to adore him, so that is what he starts with: "One thing have I desired of the LORD, that will I seek after; that I may dwell in the house of the LORD all the days of my life." What for? "*To behold the beauty of the*

LORD." He repeats this in the thirteenth verse: "I had fainted, unless I had believed to see the goodness of the LORD."

A much better translation of the word rendered "behold" in verse 4 would have been "gaze upon, meditate upon, consider": "to gaze upon the beauty of the LORD." It means to see the desirableness of God, to see his goodness, to consider and to meditate upon and to contemplate his excellencies. This is what this man wants above everything else.

He does not start with answers to prayers and deliverance or this and that particular blessing. Not at all! He wants to know God and to gaze upon him. This is adoration; this is worship! He is talking about the being of God and about God's dealings with us. His supreme ambition is to gaze upon the glory of the being of God. Let a poet express it for us:

> My God, how wonderful Thou art,
> Thy majesty, how bright;
> How beautiful Thy mercy seat
> In depths of burning light!
>
> How dread are Thy eternal years,
> O Everlasting Lord,
> By prostrate spirits day and night
> Incessantly adored.
>
> How wonderful, how beautiful,
> The sight of Thee must be;
> Thy endless wisdom, boundless power,
> And glorious purity!

FREDERICK W. FABER (1814–1863),
"MY GOD, HOW WONDERFUL THOU ART"

The psalmist wanted to gaze upon the glory of God, the beauty of the Lord in his very being, the consideration of his attributes. Do you do this? Is this your supreme ambition? Is this your greatest desire? My dear friend, this is the whole secret of life! If you want to be "more than [a] conqueror" like this man, you must spend your time as he did. This must be your supreme desire.

Then he considers God's dealings with us: "the goodness of the LORD in the land of the living" (Ps. 27:13). Let another poet express this:

When all Thy mercies, O my God,
My rising soul surveys,
Transported with the view, I'm lost
In wonder, love and praise.

JOSEPH ADDISON (1672–1719),
"WHEN ALL THY MERCIES, O MY GOD"

Do you know anything about that? Does your soul rise as you contemplate these things? Do you know something of these transports of delight? Do you spend your time gazing upon him? The psalmist starts with worship and adoration, and we also see this in the New Testament. "We all, with open face," says Paul, "beholding as in a glass the glory of the Lord . . ." (2 Cor. 3:18). That is it; you "set your affection on things above, not on things on the earth" (Col. 3:2).

Having begun in this way, the psalmist moves on to praise: "I will sing, yea, I will sing praises unto the LORD" (Ps. 27:6). You see, that is the secret of this man. You say your prayers, do you not? And when you are in trouble, you go to God and ask for this blessing or that. But you do not get it, do you? Then you say, "What's the point of praying if my prayers are not answered?" Of course they are not—you do not know how to pray. You should never start with yourself and your petitions. You must start with God and gaze upon his glory—the glory of his person and of his works—and then praise him.

Praise the Lord, God's glories show, Alleluia!
Saints within God's courts below, Alleluia!
Angels round the throne above, Alleluia!
All that see and share God's love, Alleluia!

Praise the Lord, great mercies trace, Alleluia!
Praise His providence and grace, Alleluia!
All that God for us has done, Alleluia!
All God sends us through the Son, Alleluia!

HENRY FRANCIS LYTE (1793–1847),
"PRAISE THE LORD, GOD'S GLORIES SHOW"

Do you praise God? When you are on your knees alone, do you just say your prayers mechanically, or do you truly praise him? Do you trace his providence and grace? Do you "count your blessings and name them one by one"? And does your heart well up within you and pour itself out in praise and thanksgiving? Only after he has done all that does the psalmist take his petitions to God: "Hear, O LORD, when I cry with my voice: have mercy also upon me, and answer me. . . . Hide not thy face far from me; put not thy servant away in anger: thou hast been my help; leave me not, neither forsake me, O God of my salvation. . . . Deliver me not over unto the will of mine enemies: for false witnesses are risen up against me, and such as breathe out cruelty" (vv. 7, 9, 12).

Once more, have you understood this strategy of prayer? This is the way to pray. The apostle Paul has said it all, as we have seen, in Philippians 4:6: "Be careful [anxious] for nothing; but in every thing"—or in all circumstances—"by prayer and supplication with thanksgiving let your requests be made known unto God." There it is: you start with adoration, wonder, and amazement. You gaze upon the Lord and all his glorious attributes—what he has been, what he has done for us, and all the wonders of his work. You trace them out, you praise him, and then, knowing him, you bring your petitions to him, whatever they may be.

Then the psalmist says, having done all that, wait for the answer. Everything does not finish the moment you have uttered your petition. "*Wait* on the LORD" (v. 14). He has heard you; he will do what you have asked, and he will do it in his own way.

Then, finally, this man comes to his inevitable conclusion: "[You know, if I hadn't] believed to see the goodness of the LORD in the land of the living, [if I didn't know that God is ready and waiting to bless his people in this world as well as in that which is to come], I [would have] fainted."

So he says to himself, "Wait on the LORD: be of good courage, and he shall strengthen thine heart: wait, I say, on the LORD." Start like that, and keep on like that. Make it the central thing of your life to gaze upon God, to arrive at a knowledge of him that will be intimate and personal, a communion with him that will ravish your heart and cause your soul to rise up to him. Seek his face (v. 8), and go on seeking it. Wait upon him. Let us praise him and put ourselves entirely and completely in his hands.

And if you do this, you will find that he will be your light, your salvation, your strength and power, your never-failing refuge.

No earthly father loves like Thee,
No mother, e'er so mild,

Bears and forebears as Thou hast done,
With me, Thy sinful child.

Father of Jesus, love's reward!
What rapture will it be
Prostrate before Thy throne to lie,
And gaze, and gaze on Thee.

FREDERICK WILLIAM FABER (1814–1863),
"MY GOD, HOW WONDERFUL THOU ART"

How wonderful is this beatific vision—the end at which all the true people of God who wait upon him shall ultimately arrive!

15

WHY CHRIST HAD TO SUFFER

(1968)
Acts 8:30

From *Acts: Chapters 1–8*

It is God who determines the path that our lives take, and we are not, as the Doctor used to like to remind us, "the master of our fate" as the humanist arrogance of a Victorian poem preferred to put it.

So when he ascended the pulpit in Westminster Chapel to preach what you are about to read, Dr. Lloyd-Jones had no idea that this would be his last sermon as that church's minister and that a unique thirty-year incumbency was coming to an end. He was diagnosed with cancer, and his survival was not one that could be taken for granted. In the end we know that God spared him for another momentous thirteen years of what was to be worldwide ministry. Not only did he continue to preach but also edited many sermons that were to be read by millions of people all over the world.

How significant it was, therefore, that his last sermon at "the Chapel" should be an evangelistic one, and from Philip's conversation in the desert with the Ethiopian eunuch, a proselyte but someone completely outside the normal frame of the Jewish faith. Now everyone can hear the gospel, as the account from the book of Acts makes clear.

On his graveside in Llangeitho Martyn Lloyd-Jones had the simple words, "For I determined not to know any thing among you, save Jesus Christ, and him crucified" (from 1 Corinthians 2:2). And this is precisely what he did in his last Westminster Chapel sermon on why Christ had to suffer. His final words as minister were: "Have you seen and understood that it is by dying for you on the cross that the Lord Jesus Christ saves you and reconciles you to God?"

This is the very heart of the gospel. But how often is it actually preached just like this today? Why do we think that people in the West in the early years of the twenty-first century are any different from those living in 1968 or indeed in AD 68? Humanity and the urgent need for salvation in Jesus Christ have never changed. God has not changed either, nor has the power of the Holy Spirit to work in people to bring them to realize their sins and their need to be saved.

Martyn Lloyd-Jones had such confidence in who God is and what he can accomplish that he could preach this message boldly and unadorned, just as the apostles had proclaimed it back in the first century. Let us pray that we can all have the same confidence in God, in his message, and in the Bible that so distinguished the thirty years that Dr. Lloyd-Jones spent preaching from the pulpit of Westminster Chapel.

And Philip ran thither to him, and heard him read the prophet Esaias, and said, Understandest thou what thou readest? (Acts 8:30)

We have been considering together the difficulties that people get into about our Lord's death on the cross. We have seen that they do not understand it because they do not face it, they do not look at it, they are always idealizing it. They are doing the very thing that the apostle Paul says must not be done: "For Christ sent me . . . to preach the gospel: not with wisdom of words, lest the cross of Christ should be made of none effect" (1 Cor. 1:17). People make it into something beautiful and wonderful. But it is not. The cross is offensive, and that is what comes out in that prophecy of Isaiah that we have been looking at together—the terrible suffering. "His visage was . . . marred" (Isa. 52:14). The cross is ugly. It is foul. We notice the way in which our Lord's death on the cross was prophesied there in Isaiah and the way in which, when you read the latter chapters of the Gospels, you see that prophecy fulfilled in detail—the agony of our Lord, the agony in the garden, the agony on the cross, the intense suffering.

All this surely shows us at once that no superficial explanation of the cross is adequate—there is a great mystery here. Why did he have to suffer such terrible things? Why, I ask again, the cry of abandonment on the cross—"My God, my God, why hast thou forsaken me?" (Mark 15:34)? That is a part of the suffering; it is a part of the message of the cross. There is something profound here, something desperate, something that demands that cry. What is it?

That is the truth that we will address. Obviously the cross happened because it had to happen. God would never have allowed it if the salvation of humanity could have been procured or effected in any other way. So the great question is, why did that death on the cross have to happen?

It is because people do not understand the answer to this question that they are in trouble, but it is all here in Isaiah 53. The Ethiopian eunuch was already reading the explanation, though he did not understand it. Do you understand it? Do you know why the Son of God had to die in that terrible way? He was not your "pale Galilean,"[1] not your aesthete. No! Throughout his life he was "a man of sorrows, and acquainted with grief," but why? The answer is in Isaiah 53.

Or to put it another way, the answer is in the cross itself. But the trouble is that we talk about the cross instead of looking at it, instead of listening to it. The cross speaks. You remember that the author of the epistle to the Hebrews says that we are interested in a blood "that speaketh better things than that of Abel" (12:24). There is a message coming from the cross, and we would hear it if we would but listen to it and not just turn it into something beautiful that we can all admire and seek to emulate. We must realize that it is unique, that it stands alone. So what is the meaning of the cross? Why did our Lord have to die in that way?

The first explanation of why our Lord had to endure and suffer all that he did is the state and the condition of man by nature. Here is the way we begin to understand it. He was innocent, but he suffered because of us: "He was wounded for our transgressions, he was bruised for our iniquities: the chastisement of our peace was upon him" (Isa. 53:5). If you do not understand the meaning of the death of Christ upon the cross—why it had to happen and why that death in particular was the means of salvation—the main explanation of your lack of understanding is that you have never understood yourself, you have never realized the truth about yourself, you have never realized the condition in which you are by nature. This is always the first difficulty.

Now there are many different ways in which I could show you your true condition. It is, if you like, the whole tendency of modern man to start with the New Testament and not to be interested in the Old, and the moment you do that you are already wrong. The Old Testament is an introduction to the New. There is a sense in which you cannot understand the life and death of our Lord except in the light of the Old Testament. This was undoubtedly the very thing that Philip said to this Ethiopian eunuch. He said in effect, "This great message is all one. Eight hundred years before these events took place in Jerusalem, a man was given a preview of them—they are a part of God's great plan of salvation. Ever since the fall of man God had been promising that he would send a great deliverer who would deliver in a particular way, and this was the way." Then he "preached unto him Jesus."

The Old Testament will tell you why Jesus had to come and why, especially, he had to suffer. I am not surprised that people do not like this aspect of the message. It is what the apostle Paul calls "the offence of the cross" (Gal. 5:11). The cross is offensive. If you let its message really come out, it will offend people. It did so at the time. Why did they jeer at our Lord as he was dying? It was because they caught something of this message. Paul says that the cross is "unto the Jews a stumblingblock, and unto the Greeks foolishness" (1 Cor. 1:23).

What is the offense of the cross? The death of a martyr is not offensive. Indeed, we tend to admire it. Some try to imitate and emulate martyrs. The world applauds them and admires them. Self-sacrifice—a man passively giving himself, not resisting—this is a message that people like. But they are taking away from the message of the cross because the cross is always an offense. And the reason for the offense is found in the answer to the question, why did our Lord have to endure all this? That answer is in a little word that is so vital in the biblical message—the word *sin*. It is all due to sin. It is all due to our state and condition.

What is the condition of the human race? Why did the Son of God have to come into the world, and why, especially, did he die on that cross? The first answer is that men and women are guilty before God. Here is the beginning; here is the law, if you like. But people do not like the law. They want love; they want a positive message. But you cannot understand the positive message unless you have first accepted the negative. Look at the words used in Isaiah 53:5, "He was wounded for our *transgressions*, he was bruised for our *iniquities*." These two words, "transgressions" and "iniquities," are vital words; they are key biblical words. And this is because they bring home to us the truth about ourselves. You will not understand the cross unless you understand these words, and you will not understand yourself either or the state of your world today.

Griefs! Sorrows! That is the world we are in, is it not? But why are there griefs and sorrows? Why are there wars? Is there anything more superficial than men and women making protests about war? The thing we ought to be concerned about is what causes it. Can this be explained in terms of a president or prime minister or certain men? Of course it cannot. The problem is much deeper than that. To ask about the cause is to ask a profound question—it is the whole question of humanity in sin. Griefs and sorrows are the result of "transgressions" and "iniquities." We need to consider the message found in Isaiah 53 and not merely make vapid antiwar protestations. These are not Christianity. They miss the whole point. They depict Jesus as a passive resister, as a pacifist, and they take the whole glory out of the cross as well as the horror and the terror and the ugliness of this visage "marred more than any man." That is too superficial.

Here is the real explanation. You can only understand the meaning of the terms "transgressions" and "iniquities" if you understand something about the biblical teaching concerning the law of God. God made us in his own image and placed us in this world. But having made us, and God being God, he told us that we must live in a certain way. God is the King; he is the ruler of the universe. It is his. Whether you like it or not, it is a fact that the world belongs to God. And he has given us laws and has told us quite plainly that we will only be happy and will only enjoy life in this world as long as we are obedient to and conform to his holy laws. And we can know what this law is because he has put it within every one of us; it is in our consciences. You can try to explain away the conscience in terms of psychology, but you cannot silence it. God's law is written in our heart, says Paul (see Rom. 2:15).

But in addition to that, God has stated his law in an external, objective manner through Moses and the children of Israel. That is where the Old Testament comes in. God made a nation for himself to witness to him. The world had gone wrong and was in all the kinds of trouble that you find in the modern world. Read the account of civilization before the flood, and you might very well be reading about modern centuries. All the horrors of the world before the flood are upon us today. Man, you see, has ceased to listen to his conscience. "Every imagination of the thoughts of his heart was only evil continually," says Genesis 6:5. So punishment came.

After that God took hold of a man named Abraham, called him out of paganism, and turned this man into a nation. What for? Largely in order to speak to humanity. He formed this nation so that he might teach. He gave them, as Paul reminds the Romans, "the oracles of God" (3:2). We have already come across that in the seventh chapter of Acts. Stephen, in his great self-defense before the Sanhedrin, works that point out. Refresh your memories by reading chapter 7 of the book of Acts. God did this in order that his laws might be perfectly plain and clear. So if we do not listen to our consciences, we have the Ten Commandments—the two tables of the law: man in his relationship to God and man in his relationship to his fellow man. The Ten Commandments are an explicit statement, under ten headings, of how God intends human beings to live.

You only begin to understand the meaning of the cross when you start with the law, because the moment you look at that you see at once that humanity is guilty before God. We see this verdict, again, in Romans 3: "There is none righteous, no, not one" (v. 10); "that every mouth may be stopped, and all the world may become guilty before God" (v. 19). It does not matter what political party you belong to, it does not matter what social class you belong to, it does not matter whether you are wealthy or poor—the whole world is guilty before God. This is what matters, not our superficial divisions and distinctions.

Why is the whole world guilty before God? Because it has not kept God's law. The epistle to the Romans is the great exposition of human sin and guilt, and I am certain that Philip, in his own way, was giving the eunuch this same great doctrine that Paul works out there. The Jews thought that possessing the law put them right with God, but Paul says, "For not the hearers of the law are just before God, but the doers of the law shall be justified" (Rom. 2:13). The fact that you know the law does not help you if you do not keep it, and the trouble is that the whole world has not kept the law of God. Thus sin is sometimes defined in the Bible as missing the mark, not coming up to the standard, falling short of the position in which we ought to be. That is a part of the guilt.

But it is not the only part. We have not only failed to live up to the standards and the dictates of God's law, we have actually and deliberately broken it. That is the meaning of "transgressions"—deliberately flouting or breaking the law, deliberately acting in an unrighteous manner. The law states that we have deliberately broken it. This is another source of guilt. But the most terrible cause of guilt is that in doing all this we have been manifesting our rebellion against God.

Here is the reason why the world is as it is. "The carnal mind is enmity against God: for it is not subject to the law of God, neither indeed can be" (Rom. 8:7). We have all gone our own way, says the prophecy in Isaiah 53. We have gone astray; we have followed our own ideas; we have not listened to the way of God. "All we like sheep have gone astray; we have turned every one to his own way" (v. 6), and this means deliberate rebellion against God. My dear friend, you do not begin to understand yourself and your troubles and your problems and your unhappinesses and your griefs and your sorrows, you do not begin to understand the whole case and condition of humanity and this world in which we are living, unless you grasp that this deliberate rebellion was the original sin, the original temptation.

Here was man, made in the image of God, in paradise and enjoying life in communion with God when the tempter came and said in effect, "Has God said . . .? Do you think it was fair of God to say that? Didn't God say this in order to keep you down and to keep you as only human? He knows perfectly well that if you assert yourselves, you will be equal to him."

And man rose to the bait. Man still rises to this bait. He thinks he is God; he wants to be equal with God. He thinks he knows as much as God, so he resents God's law and defies it and rebels against it. There is no greater sin than the sin of rebellion. And man is as he is today and the world is as it is today and the cross of Christ is as essential today as it has ever been because man is guilty before God. Man's well-being consists of his being blessed by God and in right relationship to him, but as long as he is a rebel and is guilty, he is not blessed by God.

Later on in the book of Isaiah the prophet cries out in agony and says to God in essence, "Why are we as we are? What is the matter?" And he gives the answer, "Behold, the LORD's hand is not shortened, that it cannot save; neither his ear heavy, that it cannot hear: but your iniquities have separated between you and your God" (59:1–2). This world was not meant to be like this. The world as it is today is a manifestation of the wrath of God against the sin and the unrighteousness and the ungodliness of human beings. God has said it everywhere in his law: "The soul that sinneth, it shall die" (Ezek. 18:4). "The way of transgressors is hard" (Prov. 13:15). It does not matter how clever and learned you are, how wealthy and sophisticated, if you are rebelling against God and flouting his laws, if you are guilty of transgression and iniquity, you will be miserable, you will be wretched. Why so much grief and sorrow? Guilt is the problem.

But human guilt is not the only aspect of the problem. Man, we are told in Isaiah 53, is not only guilty, he is also lost. "All we like sheep have gone astray; we have turned every one to his own way." Here again is the whole message of the Bible. Man is not where he was meant to be; the world is not as it was meant to be. We all have this sense within us of being in the wrong place; it is a part of the restlessness we feel. But there is a misunderstanding as to where we *are* meant to be. Where the world thinks we are meant to be is this: wars are banished so we can all go on using our money to buy food and drink and sex and have a marvelous time. That is the world's idea; it is not God's idea. We have gone astray; we do not know where we are, only that we are not where we were meant to be. The world is not enjoying fellowship with God; it is unhappy. Griefs and sorrows sum up the whole of life today, do they not? The world does not understand itself; it does not understand life. It has no purpose; it has no sense of direction and no goal.

So the world has gone astray. It has missed the mark. It has lost the route. It is in a wilderness. This is the whole tragedy, and it is the very essence of the whole problem—life has become pointless, purposeless. What is the meaning of anything? What is the purpose of anything? Can you not see the confusion? What do students do? What is the purpose of being a student? The modern idea seems to be that students go to college to enjoy themselves, and if they are not allowed to enjoy themselves, they grumble and complain. We are here to have pleasure and fun. That is a further indication that men and women have lost their sense of direction and do not know what they are doing or where they are going. All they want is a bit of ease. But then they realize that is not enough because men and women cannot be satisfied with that. There is that in them which cries out for something bigger, something greater, but they cannot find it.

"We have turned every one to his own way." What an extraordinary definition this is of the modern world! It is like sheep who have gone astray. Can you not see this picture? Do you know anything about sheep? Have you ever seen sheep becoming wild, all rushing about, one in this direction, one in another, one going backward, one going forward? Is there anything more ridiculous than a crowd of frightened sheep? But that is the picture that Isaiah gives of humanity as the result of sin. Handel has caught this picture in the music that he wrote in order to depict this very verse. You can see in the music the silly, nodding sheep rushing backward and forward with no purpose, no direction, no plan, in utter confusion. Is not that the world? The world is confused, the world is bewildered, but each person is trying to find a way out, each one is seeking a way of relief. There is humanity with all its learning and sophistication but no direction, no answer, no solution.

I am talking about false religions. I am talking about philosophies and cults. I am talking about all human reasoning and all human ideas. One says this, the other says the exact opposite, and men and women are completely bewildered and fall back upon drink and drugs. Nobody understands; there is no sense in anything. Life is

A tale told by an idiot, full of sound and fury,
Signifying nothing.

WILLIAM SHAKESPEARE, *MACBETH*

"All we like sheep have gone astray." Man is lost like foolish sheep, and in spite of all his civilization, all his educational efforts, all his striving, he cannot find the way out.

But, alas, not only is he guilty and lost, on top of that he is also miserable and sick. "Griefs . . . and . . . sorrows"! Think again of the picture of sheep. We read in the Gospel of Matthew that when our Lord saw the multitudes, "he was moved with compassion on them, because they fainted, and were scattered abroad, as sheep having no shepherd" (9:36). That is how he saw life in this world; that is how he saw man. That is why he came into the world and later said, "The good shepherd giveth his life for the sheep" (John 10:11). What does he mean by this? This is his way of describing this grief and sorrow, this sickness—"sheep having no shepherd." Do you see the picture? Sheep are absolutely hopeless without a shepherd: that is a part of their foolishness. They do not have the understanding that the shepherd has. They do not know where to go to find pasture, so they are not adequately fed. They are thin and scraggly and are fainting because they do not know where the best pasture is to be found.

Not only that, sheep have no protection. Our Lord, again depicting himself as the Good Shepherd, says, "I am the door: by me if any man enter in, he shall be saved, and shall go in and out, and find pasture" (John 10:9). That is a picture of the sheepfold. The shepherd leads the sheep into the fold at night, and then, in order to protect them, he lies down across the entrance. He is protecting them against wild dogs and wolves and other marauding beasts that attack sheep. The shepherd keeps them safe: he takes them in, he takes them out. As well as giving them pasture, he also provides protection and care. And our Lord says in effect, "I have come to do that sort of thing. I am the Good Shepherd." He sees humanity as sheep who are fainting for lack of nourishment and are being attacked by dogs and wolves.

What does he mean? This is a pictorial representation of life in this world. This is what life does to men and women, and the world is fainting today. It does not have the food or nutriment that can build it up and make it strong. As the General Confession puts it, "There is no health in us." Are we healthy, my friends? Are we full of vigor and life? Are we able to stand up to life? Are we conquering, are we mastering, are we full of the energy and power that we were meant to have? Human beings were meant to be God's representatives in the world, lords of creation. Are we?

No. There is no health in us; we are fainting like sheep. Moreover, we are attacked by dogs and wolves. We lose our chastity, our purity, our peace, and our quiet; we lose our ideals; we lose everything that is ennobling. We sink into cynicism and perhaps into despair, and we say, "What's the use of anything?" Or we say, "Let's eat, drink, and be merry, for tomorrow we die" (see Luke 12:19). As a result, like poor, fainting sheep we are merely existing and not living. It is a miserable existence, a fainting existence. Have you ever seen sheep in this condition? You would not take them to market; you would not be proud of them; you would not take your friends to look at them. You would be ashamed of them and would try to conceal them. Why? Because they are not meant to be like that. They are meant to be well-fed. They are meant to be full, strong, and vigorous.

"Understandest thou what thou readest?" asked Philip. The Ethiopian eunuch did not. "Why should anybody suffer like this?" that man may have asked. Because of the condition of humanity. Guilty before God; lost, sick, miserable, unhappy. Grief and sorrow. Failure. Mere existence. We were never meant to be like this, but we have become so. That is why the Son of God had to come into this world.

But even that does not complete the picture. On top of all this, man is perverted and depraved. What do I mean by this? Well, it is a part of iniquity. He is in an unrighteous state; his heart is wrong. This is the most terrible thing about man. It is bad enough that he should be breaking God's law. It is bad enough that he should be transgressing, that he should be falling short of the pattern and the standard. But, my friends, that is not the most terrible thing about us by nature. The most terrible thing about us is that even when we are offered salvation, we do not take it. We resent it. We reject it.

Listen: "Who hath believed our report?" (Isa. 53:1). Here is the question, and here is the "report": "My servant shall deal prudently, he shall be exalted and extolled" (Isa. 52:13). He will "sprinkle many nations; the kings shall shut their mouths at him: for that which had not been told them shall they see; and that which they had not heard shall they consider" (Isa. 52:15). Here is the message, but "Who hath believed our report?" Here is the trouble with humanity, and here in this rejection you see it at its very worst. Man is perverted; he has become depraved. He is offered a way of salvation, but he will not believe it or receive it. He still prefers to trust to his own philosophies, his own knowledge, his own efforts, his own understanding. Here is God's offered way of salvation, but "Who hath believed our report?"

"What!" says the modern man. "You don't mean to say that you still believe that old gospel of salvation? You surely do not still say that we have to believe that Jesus of Nazareth is the Son of God and that he saves us by dying on the cross on Calvary? Do you still believe this myth? It is the funniest joke of all that anybody today still believes that!" But people have never believed it—they did not believe it in the first century. "Who hath believed our report?"

But let us go on—the description is still more detailed. If you really want to know why the Son of God had to die on the cross, if you want to know why this, and this alone, can save you, here is the answer: you see it in the attitude of men and women toward the Son of God who came into the world to deliver and save. What is that attitude? Well, first of all, they did not recognize him. Do *you* recognize Jesus of Nazareth as the Son of God? They did not recognize him when he came. Look at those Pharisees, those doctors of the law, those religious leaders in Israel. They looked at him and said, "Who is this fellow? Who is this carpenter who presumes to teach us?" They asked, "How knoweth this man letters, having never learned?" (John 7:15). They did not recognize him.

And exactly the same, of course, is true of the Greeks who were so proud of their philosophy. Paul says, "Which [God's wisdom] none of the princes of this world knew: for had they known it, they would not have crucified the Lord of glory" (1 Cor. 2:8). Here is God incarnate! Here is the Lord of glory standing as a man among men, speaking such words as had never been heard before, words so amazing that the officers sent by the Pharisees to arrest him said, "Never man spake like this man" (John 7:46). He was doing his mighty deeds, and yet they did not know him. The condition of humanity was such that when confronted by God in the flesh, they did not recognize him.

But it is even worse than that: "He is despised" (Isa. 53:3). They "despised" him. You have put your faith in human beings and in human understanding, human discrimination, human ability. You say all that people need is teaching—if you put the teaching before them, they will rise to it—give people a great example, and they will follow it. But this has all been tried. The Son of God himself has been here, and they despised him: "He is despised and rejected of men." Here is what you must understand and explain to yourself. The world chose a robber rather than the Son of God. Pilate, with a sense of Roman justice and equity, did not want to put our Lord to death. His wife had a dream, and she warned him, and he, not knowing exactly what he was doing, tried to save our Lord from crucifixion. But they cried out, "Away with this man, and release unto us Barabbas" (Luke 23:18). "This man" was the Son of God, the Savior of the world! And yet "Not this man," they said.

"He is despised and rejected of men." Unless you believe in him, you are rejecting him—rejecting his person, rejecting his death upon the cross. Here is the condition of humanity; here is the problem. This is what the world did with him. They ridiculed him, they spat at him, they laughed at him, they jeered at him; they mocked the Son of God who was bearing their sins.

This brings me to my final point, which is this: man is completely helpless to save himself. The cross proves this. People say, "What we want is teaching."

But I say to you that you have had teaching. The law is the teaching of God.

You say, "What we want is to be shown the pattern; we want to be given the rules. Tell us how to live, and we will do it."

The commandments are there, but nobody could keep them. The apostle Paul has put this once and forever in Romans 8:3: "What the law could not do, in that it was weak through the flesh . . ." It is no use giving us laws—we cannot keep them. "And this is the condemnation, that light is come into the world, and men loved darkness rather than light, because their deeds were evil" (John 3:19). Man knows what he ought to do, but he cannot do it—that is the power of sin. "I delight in the law of God after the inward man," says Paul. "But I see another law in my members" (Rom. 7:22–23), and this was dragging him down. It was more powerful than he was. The drives, the lusts, the passions—these are the things that make us break the law of God and prevent us from keeping it.

Indeed, we know that the very Jews to whom the law of God was given misunderstood it completely. The apostle Paul is honest enough to tell us that he misunderstood it himself. He had once thought that he was absolutely perfect as regards the law. He said in effect, "I thought that, but then I saw this little word 'covet,' and when I saw the meaning of this word, I was condemned" (see Rom. 7:7–9). He had thought that as long as he did not actually physically commit adultery, he was not an adulterer, but then the word "covet" came in: "Whosoever looketh on a woman to lust after her hath committed adultery with her already in his heart" (Matt. 5:28). It is not enough that you do not murder a man—if you say, "You fool!" you have already murdered him in spirit (see Matt. 5:21–22). The Jews had misunderstood the law, and they could not keep it.

Men and women can never be saved by teaching. They can never be saved by imitating and following an example. There is no greater folly in the universe today than the whole notion of "the imitation of Christ." How can I who cannot maintain my own standards, still less the Ten Commandments, talk about "imitating Christ"—the one who is sinless, perfect, absolutely holy! He condemns me more than anyone I know. I cannot be saved by law, instruction, teaching, example. My case is too desperate; my condition is too vile. I am guilty. I am lost. I am perverted. I am depraved. I am utterly helpless.

Is there no hope for me? Oh, yes, there is, and this is it: "He was wounded for our transgressions, he was bruised for our iniquities: the chastisement [punishment] of our peace was upon him; and with his stripes we are healed" (Isa. 53:5). So we have peace. My dear friend, our Lord's death on the cross had to happen because of our transgressions, because of our iniquities, because of our utter helplessness and hopelessness. We cannot do anything: he had to come, and he has come, and "He hath borne our griefs, and carried our sorrows" (v. 4). The glory and the wonder of this way of salvation is that it does not ask me to attempt things that are impossible for me; it simply asks me to say:

> Not the labors of my hands
> Can fulfil thy law's demands;
> Could my zeal no respite know,
> Could my tears forever flow,
> All for sin could not atone;
> Thou must save, and thou alone.
>
> Nothing in my hand I bring,
> Simply to the cross I cling;
> Naked, come to thee for dress;
> Helpless, look to thee for grace;
> Foul, I to the fountain fly;
> Wash me, Savior, or I die.

AUGUSTUS TOPLADY (1740–1778),
"ROCK OF AGES"

I say again, he had to come. He had to die to bear the guilt and punishment of our sins, and he has done it.

That is what Philip said to the Ethiopian eunuch, and the man saw it. He said, "I believe it. Can I be baptized?"

"You can," Philip replied, and the man was baptized. Then "he went on his way rejoicing." You will remain a miserable failure with griefs and sorrows, iniquities and transgressions until you believe on the Lord Jesus Christ, and then "thou shalt be saved" (Acts 16:31).

"Understandest thou what thou readest?" Have you seen and understood that it is by dying for you on the cross that the Lord Jesus Christ saves you and reconciles you to God?

16

WITH HIM IN THE GLORY

(1953)
John 17:24

From *The Assurance of Our Salvation*

On March 1, 1968 Martyn Lloyd-Jones had the operation for cancer that saved his life, and on March 1, 1981, thirteen years later to the day, he died. This was rather appropriate as it was both a Sunday, God's day, and also St. David's Day, the national day of Wales.

One of the last messages he gave to his family was "Don't pray for healing, don't hold me back from the glory." He had by now lost the power of speech, so had to scribble the note, and with difficulty as his strength was ebbing fast.

Consequently for us in his family this sermon has a special resonance, since it deals with the glory of God, something that pervaded the Doctor's sermons throughout his ministry and suffused him in the last days of his life.

The series from which we take this is based upon John 17, Christ's High-Priestly Prayer, and it is the last in a four-volume series (also available in one volume, The Assurance of Our Salvation. As well as conveying a powerful sense of God's glory, it also shows the Doctor at his pastoral best and demonstrates that theology can very much be applied to our everyday lives. There was, in his day, a "let go and let God" passive approach to sanctification, and it was, as we can imagine, one that he rejected most strenuously, and, as ever, on entirely biblical grounds. God is working his sanctification in us throughout our Christian lives, but in addition we co-operate with him, taking active steps to grow in our faith, in holiness, and in our love and obedience to God.

In heaven we will be with Christ! But not only that, as the Doctor puts it, all of God's people will be there too! Martyn Lloyd-Jones is there, his wife has joined him, the great host of godly members of her Phillips family *are there too, as are all the Doctor's heroes like Howell Harris, John Owen, and Jonathan Edwards, every one of them now part of the saints in glory, all united in heaven and praising God.*

That is an exciting thought! It should be an enormous comfort for us as well. How often we keep a worldly perspective, preoccupied with the tyranny of the urgent, life's pressures and pains. But one day we will be in a house not made with hands.

We all miss those we love when they die. But if they were Christians, then we can have a very different perspective from that of the world. And this sermon shows us that right doctrine is of permanent use, because not only is it appropriate to remember in times of bereavement, but in fact all the time, as you can now discover. May this be for you as it was for his family in 1981.

Father, I will that they also, whom thou hast given me, be with me where I am; that they may behold my glory, which thou hast given me: for thou lovedst me before the foundation of the world. (John 17:24)

We come here, in verse 24, to a consideration of the last great petition of our Lord and Savior Jesus Christ for his followers and disciples. It is actually the last of the petitions that he offered and is in many ways the end of the prayer. In the final two verses he again just reminds his Father of the character of these people for whom he is praying: "O righteous Father, the world hath not known thee: but I have known thee, and these have known that thou hast sent me. And I have declared unto them thy name, and will declare it: that the love wherewith thou hast loved me may be in them, and I in them" (vv. 25, 26). It is, then, the last of the great petitions, and at the same time in a remarkable and extraordinary way it sums up in itself the entire prayer, so that as we look at it we shall not only be considering the special new request, we shall also be reminding ourselves of certain things that we have been considering regularly as we have worked our way through this glorious and tremendous chapter.

Now as we come to look at verse 24, we must all surely agree that the main trouble with us (I am speaking of Christian people) is that we do not realize the truth about ourselves. In this Christian life there are many problems and difficulties, but more and more it seems to me that most of our problems, if not all of them, arise simply from the fact that we fail to realize and to understand and to appreciate as we ought what is the real truth about us as Christian people. In the Scriptures we have great words such as these in this verse, these exceeding great and precious promises, and they are all for us. They are meant for us; they were spoken for us. Many of them are descriptions of us, and yet how little do we grasp this fact, how little do we seem to realize the truth that is enshrined in them, and how slow we are to apply these things to ourselves! I have increasingly come to the conclusion that somehow or other our trouble lies in the fact that we do not read our Scriptures properly; that is, we tend to read them without meditating upon them, without taking a firm grip of them and grasping them for ourselves and realizing that these truths are truths about us. It seems perfectly clear that if only we did that, our entire lives would be revolutionized, indeed our whole demeanor would be entirely changed. You cannot read the New Testament without coming to the conclusion that God's people are meant to be full of the spirit of joy and rejoicing. One of our Lord's last words with respect to them was that they might know his joy and peace; that seemed to be his supreme concern, as it is here in this verse. And yet how slow we are to realize these things. We are content to think of ourselves in ways that are far removed from the New Testament description of the Christian, and our experiences are correspondingly far removed from what our Lord has depicted here.

I wonder how many of us can truthfully say that we are rejoicing with "joy unspeakable and full of glory" (1 Pet. 1:8) in the Lord Jesus Christ. We are exhorted to "rejoice in the Lord always," says the great apostle in Philippians 4:4, "and again I say, Rejoice." I suppose the final charge that will be brought against us all is the way we have so misinterpreted our blessed Lord by giving the impression that we are living a weary and laborious life, struggling hard against difficulties and obstacles. Indeed, far too often the impression is given that those who are outside Christianity and the church seem to be much happier. Now we know that is merely a matter of appearance and that in reality such people are not happy at all but profoundly miserable, but by appearance alone you might often gain the impression that they are happier than many of God's people. And the answer to all that is to realize the truth about ourselves, to realize who we are, to realize what we are, to realize everything that the New Testament tells us about ourselves.

In working through this chapter we have been doing that constantly, and now we are going to look at one of the most extraordinary and glorious things of all. Here is our Lord's last petition for his people: "Father, I will that they also, whom thou hast given me, be with me where I am; that they may behold my glory, which thou hast given me: for thou lovedst me before the foundation of the world." He is about to leave these followers of his; he is going to the cross, to its agony and its shame; he is going to death and to burial, to the resurrection and to the ascension, but his concern is about them, and that is what he prays for. So let us look together at this summary of the main teaching of the entire chapter.

First of all, let us look at the One who prays for us. This is the first thing always, the thing we need to grasp before everything else. Here is someone praying to God for us; we people are being prayed for. So who is this who is praying for us? Well, the very terms that he himself uses in this verse tell us who he is. He does not hesitate to address the almighty and eternal God as "Father," suggesting at once an intimate relationship. In the first verse also he begins by saying, "Father, the hour is come; glorify thy Son, that thy Son also may glorify Thee." "Father": he is indeed none other than the Son of God. The next word we must look at is the word "will." "Father," he says, "I will"—a most astounding word. He does not say "I request" or "I petition" or "I desire," and it is unfortunate that the Revised Standard Version has translated it as "desire," for that is not the word, it is much stronger. He says, "Father, I will," and we must not reduce that. In other words, here is someone who can come into the presence of the eternal God and say, "Father, I will that these may be with me where I am," at once suggesting, of course, an equality with God; with reverence he says "I will" to the almighty Father.

And then, of course, the other phrase that tells us exactly the same thing about him is this phrase "before the foundation of the world": "for thou lovedst me before the foundation of the world." He has said that before, earlier in this prayer: "And now, O Father," he says in verse 5, "glorify thou me with thine own self with the glory which I had with thee before the world was." We must not stay with this now, but unless we grasp it, we shall not be able to learn the great lessons of this phrase. He is praying there for us, because, remember, he is not only praying for his immediate followers: "Neither pray I for these alone, but for them also which shall believe on me through their word" (v. 20). He is praying for Christians in all places and at all times, and the One who is praying there for us is none other than the eternal Son of God. That is the whole basis of our standing and our position; we are Christians today because he came from heaven to earth and took upon himself the likeness of sinful flesh and did all that is recorded of him in the Gospels. A Christian, therefore, primarily, by definition, is one who is being prayed for by the eternal Son of God.

Furthermore, you cannot help noticing at the same time his concern for us. If only we realized that when we are besieged and attacked by the devil and sin and temptation! As we face certain difficulties in the Christian life that trouble and perplex us, and also the difficulties that we have with ourselves and with other people, our tendency is to feel that we are quite alone and that no one understands. But to all that the answer is that here is the Son of God under the very shadow of the cross, knowing what is before him, and yet his great concern, his primary concern, is for his people. You would have thought he would be spending all his time praying for himself, but if you look at this prayer you will notice that only the first five verses are devoted to himself; the remainder are devoted entirely to this intercession of his on behalf of his followers. There is nothing that is more important for us to grasp than the fact that our Savior is the eternal Son of God, that he prayed for us on earth, and that at this moment he is interceding for us at the right hand of God's glory and power in heaven.

What, then, does he say about us? We have seen the truth about the One who prays, so the second thing we must ask is, what is true of us? Once more we find the answer in this phrase that our Lord has used frequently in this prayer: we are described as "whom thou hast given me." "Father, I will that they also, whom thou hast given me, be with me where I am." Christian people are those whom God the Father has given to his Son. You remember how he puts it earlier when he says in verse 6, "Thine they were, and thou gavest them me; and they have kept thy word." I do not know of anything more comforting than this. I, as a Christian, am one of God's chosen people. This is the great doctrine of the Scriptures; you find it everywhere, and our Lord actually repeats it seven times in this last prayer to his Father. These are the people whom God had chosen before the foundation of the world, people belonging to God, and he has given them to his Son, the Lord Jesus Christ. Is there anything more wonderful than this?

251

Then you note that we are the special object of God's interest and concern. He knew us even before we were born. Before he ever made man or created the world, he had these people whom he had chosen, and he gave them to the Son. As we have seen, there was a great meeting of the Trinity in eternity, and the Father gave these people to the Son, and he sent his Son on this great mission of preparing them for the eternal enjoyment of God.[1] That is what Christianity means, just that; that is why the Son of God ever came into this world. All mankind had sinned and had fallen away from God; all were outside God's life and love. God sent his Son into the world to do certain things for these people whom he had given to him, and everything that the Son did in this world he did for these people, he did for us. God sent him for that purpose. As our Lord himself has already pointed out, "Thou [the Father] hast given him [the Son] power over all flesh, that he should give eternal life to as many as thou hast given him" (v. 2). So he is able to turn to his Father and say, "I have glorified thee on the earth: I have finished the work which thou gavest me to do" (v. 4), and now he says he is going back to the Father.

Now if you are a Christian, that is what is true of you. All along you have been the special object of God's interest and concern; he has loved you to the extent that he even sent his Son from heaven to earth for you, even to the death of the cross, that you might truly be one of his people, that you might have a new nature, a new life, that you might be fitted for standing before him and enjoying him throughout eternity. "They also, whom thou hast given me." Then you notice that negatively we are contrasted with the world. Our Lord has done this throughout the prayer: "I pray for them: I pray not for the world, but for them which thou hast given me [out of the world]; for they are thine" (v. 9), and now he goes on in verse 25, "O righteous Father, the world hath not known thee"—so he is not concerned about them at this point—"but I have known thee, and these have known that thou hast sent me." "These"—who are they? They are obviously not of the world, they are separated, taken out of this present evil world and are given to our Lord as God's chosen and special people.

Now the aspect of this that I would stress at this point is the comfort of it all, the comfort of knowing for certain that we are in this wonderful and blessed relationship to God. Do we meditate upon this truth? Do we think about it? Do we rejoice in it as we should rejoice? Let me repeat, we see here the very Son of God just before the end, and this is the thing that is uppermost in his mind, these people "whom thou hast given me," these people for whom he is going to die, these people he is going to save by giving his life as a ransom for them. "Father," he says, "I will" this thing concerning them. But the question is, do we recognize ourselves? Do we know ourselves in these terms? Is it not the case that far too often we think of ourselves as men and women who decide to be righteous or to be Christian? We have taken it up, and we are going to do this. But before you and I were ever born we were chosen of God and given to the Lord Jesus Christ. He came into the world because the Father had given you and all other Christians to the Son, in order that he might rescue and redeem them; and he has come and has done that, and you are one of his people purchased by his precious blood. Oh, the tragedy of failing to realize these things, the tragedy of trusting to ourselves and our own activities so much that we lose sight of the most precious truth of all!

We have considered, then, the One who prays and the people for whom he prays, and now our third question must be, what does he pray for us? You will remember that in going through this chapter we have seen certain petitions: he prays that we may be kept from the evil that is in this world and from the Evil One at the back of it all, that we may be kept from the devil and his machinations, that we may be kept from his subtle power and jealousy and everything that he would do to separate us from God. Our Lord prays that we may be kept from that, and then, positively, he prays that we may be sanctified, that we may be made more and more fit for God. And that is the way to look at our lives in this world as Christians. This world is a preparation for the next; we are being prepared for glory—that is sanctification. We are being separated from the world and sin; we have been separated to God and brought more and more into fellowship and communion with him: "Holy Father, sanctify them through thy truth." And then he prays that we may maintain the spiritual unity into which he has brought us by the rebirth and the gift of the Holy Spirit. This is not a mechanical, external unity but an inner, spiritual, vital, organic unity, and he prays that it may be preserved. And having prayed all that, he comes to this last and most glorious prayer of all in which he expresses his will.

In other words, in this prayer our Lord has dealt with our past, he prays for our present, and he also deals with our future. The Christian life is a life that is catered for in its entirety, that is the great glory of it.

The past shall be forgotten,
A present joy be given;
A future grace be promised,
A glorious crown in heaven.

OSWALD ALLEN (1816–1878),
"TODAY THY MERCY CALLS ME"

So says the hymn, and here our Lord is now, looking into the future, looking in through the veil, and giving us a glimpse of what awaits us. You see how in every respect he has catered for us. He has interceded on our behalf while we are still alive in this world, but he does not stop at that; he goes on, and as he wills this for his followers, he incidentally teaches us with respect to our own glorious and wondrous future. What, then, is the future that awaits us as Christians? Let me remind you again of our tragic failure to realize the truth about ourselves. What is it that awaits us when we come to die? I want to put this message to you by way of contrast at this point. As I was preparing this very message I happened to read a passage in a daily newspaper under the heading "These great words." And the "great words" were these:

I love to consider a place which I have never yet seen, but which I shall reach at last, full of repose, and marking the end of these voyages, and security from the tumble of the sea. This place will be a cove set round with high hills on which there shall be no house or sign of men, and it shall be enfolded by quite deserted land; but the westering sun will shine pleasantly upon it under a warm air. It will be a proper place for sleep. The fairway into that haven shall lie behind a pleasant little beach of shingle, which shall run out aslant into the sea from the steep hillside, and shall be a breakwater made by God. The tide shall run up behind it smoothly, and in a silent way, filling the quiet hollow of the hills, brimming it all up like a cup—a cup of refreshment and of quiet, a cup of ending. Then with what pleasure shall I put my small boat round, just round the point of that shingle beach, noting the shallow water by the eddies, and the deeps by the blue colour of them, where the channel runs from the main into the fairway. Up that fairway shall I go, up into the cove, and the gates of it shall shut behind me, headland against headland, so that I shall not see the open sea any more, though I shall still hear its distant noise. But all around me, save for that distant echo of the surf from the high hills, will be silence; and the evening will be gather-

ing already. Under that falling light, all alone in such a place, I shall let
go the anchor chain, and let it rattle for the last time. My anchor will
go down into the clear salt water with a run, and when it touches I shall
play out four lengths or more, so that she may swing easily and not drag,
and then I shall tie up my canvas and fasten all for the night, and get me
ready for sleep. And that will be the end of my sailing. (Hilaire Belloc)

"These great words"! Thank God they are not from the Scriptures. They
are what the world calls great words, and I suppose they are very beautiful in a literary sense, but I thank God that I am not called to preach literature. I will grant, if you like, the beauty of the language, but I cannot
think of anything that produces such a striking contrast to the text we are
considering together now. Is that the end? Is that what death means for the
Christian, to be alone—no man or anybody else nearby—all alone, turning
a little boat around the comer of the headland from the mighty ocean into
this little eddy and there alone you fall asleep and end the voyage? I cannot
imagine anything more terrible than that; that is pessimism, that is despair,
this desire to be alone. My friend, if you are a Christian, that is not what
awaits you. Rather it is this: "Father, I will that they also, whom thou hast
given me, be with me where I am." You see the contrast—the Christian
desire is *not* to be alone, regarding that as supreme bliss, it is to be where
Christ is—"where I am." Oh, how I thank God for the Christian gospel!

Where are we going? Are we going into some silent place surrounded
by wonderful hills and the shimmer of the light upon the waves? No, that
is not the gospel! We are going where Christ is: "to be with Christ; which is
far better" (Phil. 1:23). To the Christian death does not mean being alone;
it means going on to be with Christ. That is what he said, you remember,
to the thief dying by his side upon the cross: "Today shalt thou be with me
in paradise" (Luke 23:43). You are not going into some little eddy and there
be alone and put down the anchor and fall asleep but rather "to be with
Christ; which is far better."

And you notice that our Lord is very concerned here to impress upon
us that not only shall we be with him but that we shall *all* be with him:
"Father, I will that they also, whom thou hast given me, shall be with me
where I am." I believe this actually means the total aggregate of Christians,
the whole company of the redeemed. All of us together will be with him;
we do not look forward to being alone at last, no longer buffeted by other

people and thinking, "Thank God, at last I'm alone!" That is a travesty of the gospel that merely appeals to the natural mind because of the beauty of its language. What the Christian looks forward to is this:

Ten thousand times ten thousand
In sparkling raiment white,
The armies of the ransomed hosts
Throng up the steeps of light.
'Tis finished, all is finished,
Their fight with death and sin,
Fling open wide the golden gates,
And let the victors in.

HENRY ALFORD (1810–1871),
"TEN THOUSAND TIMES TEN THOUSAND"

The very essence of the Christian position is that Christians want everybody to share what they have, and they look forward to heaven and to being with all the ten thousand times ten thousand. That is heaven; not to be alone, thank God, but to be among this ransomed throng of the redeemed, safely gathered in, all who have been with us here on earth sharing Christian fellowship, joining with us in song. The saints who have gone before us, the saints who come after us—we all will be there together. What a wonderful vista, what a vision of glory! That is what he wills, "that they"—all of them—"may be with me where I am."

And what will we be doing there? Well, this is what he says: "Father, I will that they also, whom thou hast given me, be with me where I am; that they may behold my glory, which thou hast given me." It is a great word, that word "behold"; to behold means to gaze upon as a spectator, but it also means to gaze upon some extraordinary sight, something quite exceptional and unusual. We often have that kind of experience, do we not? Maybe we are out walking, and suddenly we turn a corner and see some marvelous sight; we behold, we gaze, we stand and look—it is there, in our Lord's phrase, multiplied by infinity. But this word goes even further than that. It is a continuous word—"that they may continually behold my glory"; we go on beholding! That is not the whole of heaven, of course, but it is perfectly clear from the Scriptures, and especially from the book of Revelation, that this is one of the main things in heaven—to look at the Lord Jesus Christ, to gaze and gaze upon him, to behold him, yes, and especially, he says, to behold his glory.

Now this is very important. He says, "that they may behold my glory, which thou hast given me." We must understand this clearly. Again, as we saw in our last study, it obviously cannot mean his inherent eternal glory as the Son of God, because that was not given to him. He is from eternity the eternal Son of God, coequal with his Father in glory and in everything else, so it cannot mean the glory that is inherent in the Son of God as the Son of God. The glory of which he speaks here must be the glory that was given to him after he returned from earth into heaven with his human nature. You see, he came out of heaven and took on himself human nature. He went back into heaven as the God-man. He did not leave human nature behind when he went back to heaven, he took it with him, so that one who is truly human is at the right hand of God's authority and power in heaven. He went back as the God-man, and a special glory was given to him as the God-man and the Savior of his people.

Paul deals with that in Philippians 2, in his great statement about the incarnation. You remember how he tells us that our Lord had gone back to heaven, and then he says, "Wherefore God also hath highly exalted him." Paul has talked about how our Lord "made himself of no reputation" as a man, he humbled himself; "wherefore," because of this, "God also hath highly exalted him, and given him a name which is above every name: that at the name of Jesus every knee should bow, of things in heaven, and things in earth." That is the special glory that God has given to his Son because of what he has done for us men and women and for our salvation.

What our Lord wills here is this: he speaks to his Father and says in effect, "Father, I am looking forward to this." As the author of the epistle to the Hebrews puts it, "who for the joy that was set before him" (Heb. 12:2); he knew what was coming. So here he turns to his Father and says, "Father, I will . . ." "They have seen me here in the flesh. They have seen me as a man of sorrows and acquainted with grief. They have seen me as one who had no place to lay his head. They will see me with the crown of thorns upon my brow, and they are going to look upon me with blood oozing out of my hands and my side. They have seen me in the days of my humiliation and have believed on me, Father, and I ask that they will also see me in my glory and will gaze and gaze upon me as I truly am and as I shall be."

257

That is what is awaiting you and me. But let me go on and complete this, for I find in 1 John 3:2 that to see this glory of his also means to share it: "It doth not yet appear what we shall be: but we know that, when he shall appear, we shall be like him; for we shall see him as he is." In other words, you cannot look at this glory without its being reflected in you; to look at it means to be like it, to be transformed. Paul says the same thing when he says, "We look for the Saviour, the Lord Jesus Christ: who shall change our vile body, that it may be fashioned like unto his glorious body, according to the working whereby he is able even to subdue all things unto himself" (Phil. 3:20–21). In other words, we look forward not only to seeing and beholding him and looking at his glory but also to being changed into the likeness and image of his glory.

And still more wonderful of all is the very fact that our Lord wills this for us, which means that it is going to happen to us for certain. You see, it is at this point that we do not understand ourselves, how we can be what we are as Christians. Do you know that you, a humble child, an ignorant Christian, who may feel you are more of a failure than anything else, buffeted by the devil, tossed here and there, do you know that I can tell you now that you are destined to experience these things of which we have been thinking? When you come to die, you will be with Christ. You will see his glory; you will behold it and will become like him and enjoy the glory forever·and ever. Paul puts it in this way in Romans 8:29–30: "For whom he did foreknow, he also did predestinate to be conformed to the image of his Son, that he might be the firstborn among many brethren. Moreover whom he did predestinate, them he also called: and whom he called, them he also justified: and whom he justified, them he also glorified." In the council of God this has already happened; it is certain. You and I, wherever we are at this moment, are going to look into the face of Jesus Christ in all his glory and be made like him and enjoy him through all eternity. That is his will for us, and because he wills it, it is absolutely certain.

The conclusions we draw from this are quite inevitable, are they not? If we all realized these things, would we go on living as we do? Would we be as concerned as we are about this world and its passing pleasures and its glories, its states and pomp and positions? Would we give the time we do give to such worldly things and so little to this? If we really realized what we are told here, would we be apologetic, sometimes almost afraid for people to know we are Christians? Would we be like that if we believed this, if we knew it was going to happen? But if we are Christians this *is* going to happen; it is absolutely certain. It is more certain than anything under the sun today that we shall behold him and his glory and become like him.

Whatever, then, you may be doing, put this at the forefront of your mind; think about it in a way that you have never done before; never let a day pass but that you remind yourself of who and what you are. You are one of God's people—"thine thy were, and thou gavest them me." In summary Jesus was saying, "I have done for them the work that thou gavest me to do, and I am coming back to thee." "Father, I will that they also, whom thou hast given me, be with me where I am; that they may behold my glory, which thou hast given me." Hold that before yourself day by day, start your day with it, remind yourself of it constantly. "Set your affection on things above, not on things on the earth" (Col. 3:2), "for our light affliction, which is but for a moment, worketh for us a far more exceeding and eternal weight of glory; while we look [we gaze steadfastly] not at the things which are seen, but at the things which are not seen: for the things which are seen are temporal; but the things which are not seen are eternal. For we know that if our earthly house of this tabernacle were dissolved, we have a building of God, an house not made with hands, eternal in the heavens" (2 Cor. 4:17–5:1).

So let us always "nightly pitch our moving tents, a day's march nearer home."[2] Oh, do not think of the end of your life in this world as sliding out of the ocean into some little eddy where at last you can be alone. Rather, think of it as going to be with him and with all the ransomed saints, to see and meet people again who were pilgrims with you in this world, and to join with them in singing praises unto him who loved you to the extent of dying for you and rising again to save you. Think of yourself among the ransomed hosts, the ten thousand times ten thousand, singing forever and ever the praises of the Lamb who once was slain and who has redeemed us. What a heritage! What a promise! What a hope! What a glory! Blessed be the God and Father of our Lord and Savior Jesus Christ. Amen.

17

MORE THAN CONQUERORS

(1968)
John 4:28–30

This was the last Sunday morning sermon Martyn Lloyd-Jones preached in Westminster Chapel as its minister.

From *Living Water*

Deeds speak louder than words. This well-known saying is also true, according to Dr. Lloyd-Jones, of evangelism, if one looks at the way in which Christianity was spread in the days of the book of Acts.

A preacher can give his all in a sermon, but if the congregation members are not living lives transformed by what they hear from Sunday to Sunday, then the impact of the gospel on their friends and colleagues is bound to be somewhat lifeless. A pastor can be faithful week by week in proclaiming the good news, but his flock needs to be living the kind of Christian lives that gets those non-Christians they invite to church through the door.

This particular sermon related the impact that the conversion of the woman at the well (the woman of Samaria) had upon the people in her town. As she had been notorious—the very fact that she had to use the well when no one else was there tells the story—her following of Jesus would have been a truly amazing event.

However, most conversions are not that dramatic. As the years go by from the time of our own conversion, those who knew us before and after dwindle in number. If we were young when converted, then most of the people we know will only have known us as Christians.

So what kind of impression do we leave on those around us? What should mark us as Christians in relation to our friends in need of the gospel?

This is a very practical sermon, while at the same time suffused with doctrine. As was always the case with the Doctor, he used one Scripture to prove the validity of others. In this sermon he quotes aptly and power-fully from the Psalms and from 2 Corinthians 4 as well as from the book of Acts. Doctrine and application are never mutually exclusive, and this doctrinally down-to-earth sermon shows that very neatly. Such a sermon can also be evangelistic, since a non-Christian listening to it would realize that the gospel is clear about two matters: (1) without Christ there is no inner peace, and (2) all the solutions of the world are, as ever, completely hopeless.

Without the Doctor or his congregation realizing it, this would prove to be the last morning service he would ever lead at Westminster Chapel. (His last ever sermon there, "Why Christ Had to Suffer," is Chapter 15 in this book and was preached that evening.) But this sermon shows what a difference the gospel makes to our peace within as Christians and the way in which that sense of inner peace can attract many to the gospel. What a glorious note it was upon which to retire!

The woman then left her waterpot, and went her way into the city, and saith to the men, Come, see a man, which told me all things that ever I did: is not this the Christ? Then they went out of the city, and came unto him. (John 4:28–30)

There have been various periods in our history when the masses outside the church have been indifferent to her message. It is at such times that the witness of the individual Christian is greatly enhanced. Today we are living at such a time. But why are people today largely outside the church? Is it be-cause we are failing in our witness as individual Christians? Is it because we are somehow or other different from the woman of Samaria so that those who know us are not attracted, not interested, not concerned about listen-ing to the gospel? This is a very important matter. It is not merely a matter of duty that we should consider this question—it becomes a thorough test of our whole position as Christians. There is something wrong with the Christian who cares simply about himself or herself and has no concern whatsoever about those who are outside.

That is the background to our consideration of verses 28–30, which we are dealing with in a very practical way. Having considered the motives that impelled the woman of Samaria to fetch her fellow townspeople—motives that have always impelled Christian men and women—we are now considering the way in which we bring people to our Lord, and this, again, is all-important. In the case of this woman, all she had to do was invite people to come out of the city to meet our Lord, since he was there by the side of the well. We cannot do that, but the principles are perfectly clear, and there are many guidelines in the Scriptures. Once we leave the four Gospels and go on to the book of Acts and the epistles, we find the people in the position that we are in today, and there is abundant teaching with regard to this whole matter.

We have been emphasizing the importance of what we are. We are bound to start here because what we are is altogether more significant than what we do. We are in a century that is activistic, and part of its trouble is that, forgetting principles, people rush off into action. So it is essential that we should remind ourselves that though we may do this, that, and the other, if we ourselves are not right, we are wasting our time, and people will not listen to us. "What you are," they say, "speaks more loudly than what you say." And they are interested in what we are.

So we are considering the kind of impact that we as Christians should be making upon others. As we have seen, the book of Acts records that ordinary Christians, scattered abroad by persecution, spread the gospel. They were in contact with other people, and it was what these others saw in the Christians that aroused the desire to be like them. This is the way that God has always used so strikingly for the extension of his kingdom. What staggered the ancient world was the quality of life of the Christians. Therefore this is a subject that we should consider very carefully.

So what are the characteristics of the Christian? Christian men and women are serious people. They are followers of one who was "a man of sorrows" (Isa. 53:3). They do not take the superficial, giddy view of life that so many have in the midst of tragedy. They are bound to be serious, they cannot help themselves, and they realize the seriousness of what they are doing. They know something of what the apostle Paul experienced when he went to Corinth "in weakness, and in fear, and in much trembling" (1 Cor. 2:3). The days are evil, and it is only Christians who really have an understanding of the times.

But we must hasten to say that Christians also have joy, a joy that no one else has. The seriousness and the joy are not incompatible; they go together.

It is a serious joy or a joyful seriousness. It is not solemnity; it is not dullness. The last thing the Christian should ever be is dull. A dull Christian is a contradiction in terms.

But let me suggest some further qualities that, it seems to me, are particularly important at a time such as this. The Christian is one who always conveys a sense of peace. We can use many other words for this—a sense of tranquillity, a heart that is at rest. You see the relevance of this at the present time. The words that really describe the world as it is today are the words of the prophet Isaiah: "But the wicked are like the troubled sea, when it cannot rest, whose waters cast up mire and dirt" (Isa. 57:20). Is not that the modern world? Oh, the restlessness of this age! The hurry, the tension, the excitement, the lack of stability. It is a time of trouble, a time of confusion, a time of uncertainty. Its waters cast up mire and dirt, and we see that in our newspapers and on our televisions. It is part of the restlessness.

That is the world in which we live, and that is the description of the wicked. Now we give that word *wicked* much too restricted a meaning. The term means all those who are not Christians. And they are "like the troubled sea," carried about hither and thither, having no center, no central stability, and at the same time, of course, troubled in mind and troubled in spirit.

I need not dwell on this. It has been talked about at great length. This restlessness is the outstanding characteristic of the present age. It is an age that has to live on drugs, tranquilizers, and medications and depends on artificial means to get to sleep. Commonly used words in our vocabulary today are the words *tension* and *stresses* and *strains*. And on top of that there is the mania for pleasure. It is all because of this restlessness, the turmoil of life, and the complete failure to deal with it and to understand it.

Now that being the state and condition of the world, it is obvious that the Christian is to be the exact opposite. The sense of peace that Christians have is one of the most wonderful proofs of the Christian faith, and it is this, when it is seen in us, that attracts others, because, I say again, the world is always more ready to listen when it sees an example than when it hears mere talk. It is familiar with the talk.

The cults, of course, thrive on the condition of the modern world and are always offering easy remedies. But people have tried them and their philosophies and are tired of it all. They just find that it does not work. This is what is so significant today. People have only turned to drugs and other forms of escapism because they have lost hope in what the world has to offer them and have lost confidence in human reason and understanding. They have to escape, they say. The world cannot help; there is nothing there. This is a very serious matter. As we said earlier, politically the world tends to turn to dictatorship in a time of restlessness and uncertainty.

All this gives us as Christians an exceptional opportunity. We have the opportunity to show that though we are in the same world and subject to the same pressures, yet we are essentially different, and the big difference is expressed in a line from a hymn by Anna L. Waring: "a heart at leisure from itself." That sense of tranquillity, of peace, of being at rest is the greatest thing of all.

It is my contention that the Christian alone is capable of this. I do not want to weary you with an analysis of all this, but we are aware of the teaching of the Stoics. As in the days when our Lord was here, so now and in every time of strain and stress this philosophy tends to come. But Stoicism does not teach a heart at rest; it is mere resignation, a mere refusal to face things. That is not true rest; it is a form of repression. If you have the willpower and the health to follow this philosophy, you may give the impression of having a kind of rest in your life, but you do not really have it. Merely to hold things down is not to be at peace. There is no solution there, only grim determination just to go on in spite of everything. I grant you that there may be something quite noble about it, something that at times can even appear to be heroic, but it is always negative, and in any case it is of no value to others because it is entirely dependent upon the willpower and ability of the person concerned.

Some people are born with a phlegmatic kind of temperament. They do not react as others do; they seem to be rendered more insensitive to things that happen. But like the Stoic, the phlegmatic person has nothing to give to anyone else.

But that is not the position of Christians. The reason for their peace, of course, is that they have a solution, an understanding of life. This has not come from anything in themselves; they have received it from the Word of the Lord. To quote Matthew Arnold, the Christian is someone who is able to "see life steadily and see it whole," and that is the only thing that gives inward peace and rest. The Christian is no longer frantically looking for some solution or for some understanding. It is the search for understanding that causes the restlessness. The book of Acts describes this perfectly. One of the most sophisticated cities and societies in the ancient world was Athens, the mecca of philosophy, where all the philosophers went. It was the seat of learning and of understanding, and, of course, the great object there was, as the book of Acts tells us, "either to tell, or to hear some new thing" (Acts 17:21).

Why was that the characteristic of the life of Athens? It was because of the perplexities created by the whole problem of life and living. They were trying to understand, and they could not. The philosophers were canceling one another out, and none of them was really satisfactory. And as the secular historians tell us, the rate of suicide among the philosophers was higher proportionately than in any other section of the community. So, you see, the whole society was restless, and it is just the same today. People are on edge; they are tense and under a tremendous strain. You see it in their faces.

So here is our opportunity, and here is the test for us. Do we have hearts at leisure from themselves? Do we have an inward peace? If we have, it inevitably shows itself. We read of our blessed Lord that "he could not be hid" (Mark 7:24), and this peace, too, simply cannot be hidden. This is a great psychological point, of course. What we are inside always shows itself. It shows itself in our faces, in our eyes, in the very atmosphere that we carry with us. There are certain people whom we cannot meet without immediately feeling at rest. We cannot analyze this; we just know it, we are at once conscious of it. Of course, we can all put on appearances, can we not? We can smile and appear to be very content when everything is wrong inside. But here is something different. This peace is not playacting; it is not merely on the surface.

People of the world see through all the playacting because that is how they live themselves, but when they come across Christian people, they know at once that they are different. They see this inward peace; they recognize that Christians have what is called "the quiet heart." This is what the Quakers, in particular, have always been concerned about, and to that extent they are absolutely right. They have tended to turn this into a philosophy and into a cult, and in a very subtle way, because of their departure from the orthodox Christian faith; it becomes for them just a refined form of Stoicism. But the quiet heart itself, the tranquil heart, "a heart at leisure from itself," that they are seeking is always right.

Nothing so opens the door of opportunity as that you and I should have this sense of inward peace and rest. In this way we can influence others and bring them to the Lord Jesus Christ, for our whole testimony is that we are not like this by nature, that some of us were as far removed from this as it is possible for a human being to be. We do not have some sort of bovine stolidity. No; we have been given this peace by the grace of God. Our Lord said, "Peace I leave with you, my peace I give unto you: not as the world giveth, give I unto you. Let not your heart be troubled, neither let it be afraid" (John 14:27). This is the peace of God. And what he has done for us, he can do for others.

Then there is something further, which leads logically and directly from that and is an extension of it, but I put it separately because I think one must. People must be able to see that we have inner reserves. I draw the distinction because they must first see that we are at peace. After that they see that we continue to be at peace in spite of what happens to us. This is an important distinction because the great test of life is what we are like when things go wrong.

Very many people give the impression of having inward peace and tranquillity when everything is going well. We can, most of us, put up a very good show when we are well and hale and hearty and young, and everything is prospering, and the sun is shining in the heavens; most of us are fairly good under such conditions. We have wonderful theories and say we will do this, that, and the other. But the test comes when everything goes wrong. Then people find that they have nothing at all, and they break down. That is where the opportunity for the Christian comes in at the present time because never have the outward stresses and strains been greater than they are at this moment.

Our Lord dealt with that once and forever at the end of the Sermon on the Mount in the parable of the two houses. Here is a man who rushes to build his house without a foundation, and he is very amused that the other fellow is so slow. He has his house up before the other man has dug his foundation. "What a fool! This is marvelous! This solves all my problems." Oh, the marvel of shortcuts! But then the rain descends, and the floods come, and the wind blows, and the whole building collapses. That is so typical of the world—its theories and ideas cannot stand up to the test.

And here again the Christian is essentially different. This is one of the most profound tests that we can ever apply to ourselves. It is the great test between believism and faith, between taking up religion and being taken up by it, between having it in your head and having it in your heart, in your spirit, at the center of your life. The whole point about Christian men and women is that they are not easily disturbed or shaken by what happens; they are no longer dependent upon circumstances for their happiness and their joy. This is absolutely basic. What has happened to us as Christians is, as it is put so frequently in the New Testament, that we have been delivered from "this present evil world" (Gal. 1:4) and "translated . . . into the kingdom of his [God's] dear Son" (Col. 1:13). Now when Paul says that we have been delivered from "this present evil world," he does not merely mean that we are delivered from its practices, from its habits and customs. These words mean much more. They mean that we have been delivered from the world's way of thinking, from its outlook, from its whole understanding of life and living and the purpose of it all. This is one of the things that is most striking about the Christian. Those who are not Christians, by contrast, are dependent upon what happens to them; they are dependent upon their surroundings and circumstances.

Now there is no need to prove this; it is shouting at us. Why do people spend so much money on drinking and on smoking and on pleasure? It is obvious, is it not? They cannot live without it. They are dependent upon it. They are dependent upon other people; they are dependent upon the state of their health; they are dependent upon success. They are in the hands of circumstances and conditions and the things that are happening around them. The result is that when there is an adverse change in their circumstances, and everything is collapsing, they have nothing to fall back on. There is no sense of having an inward reserve; there is no satisfaction within. They have been kept going by the things outside. The life of the unbeliever is indeed like a bubble—you keep it going, you go on blowing, and then if you cannot for some reason, it collapses and is gone.

Here is one of the greatest and most glorious differences between the Christian and the non-Christian. Here is one of the great differences between the child of God and the one who is not a child of God. The psalmist says:

Unto the upright there ariseth light in the darkness: he is gracious,
   and full of compassion, and righteous.
A good man sheweth favour, and lendeth: he will guide his affairs
   with discretion.
Surely he shall not be moved for ever: the righteous shall be in
   everlasting remembrance.
He shall not be afraid of evil tidings: his heart is fixed, trusting in
   the LORD.
His heart is established, he shall not be afraid. (Ps. 112:4–8)

Now that is the Old Testament. Here is a man writing at least a thousand years before the coming of the Son of God into this world, and yet he is able to say that, and it was true. That is the secret of those great men of the Old Testament—the patriarchs, the psalmists, the prophets, and others. And yet we know that we are in a superior position. They were children of God, yes, but they did not have the knowledge that we have. "He that is least in the kingdom of heaven is greater than he [John the Baptist]"—in position and in understanding (Matt. 11:11); and yet there it is in the Old Testament. And so we ask ourselves this question: are we afraid of evil tidings? The world is as it is because its heart is not fixed, because it is not established in the very center.

Or let me put it another way. The book of Proverbs says, "The name of the LORD is a strong tower: the righteous runneth into it, and is safe" (18:10). In other words, the righteous have a place into which to retreat. When the enemy is attacking powerfully outside, and God's people feel their defenses are being penetrated, and they are tending to lose ground, they are all right, there is no panic. Here is this tower—"a strong tower"—that is impregnable, and "the righteous runneth into it, and is safe." He enters into the fortress, and he knows that no enemy can ever penetrate it.

That is from the Old Testament, but this is obviously so true of Christian men and women. It differentiates them from non-Christians; they have inner resources. And is there anything more glorious and more wonderful about this life than this very fact that there is within us a place that is absolutely impregnable no matter what the world may think or do? And does it not become obvious that the real reason why so many are outside the church is that they do not see people like this inside the church? They say, "Ah, these people, they go to this place on Sunday, and they affect an interest, but I have watched them when things go wrong and when troubles come, and they are no different from the rest of us. They are just as panicky, and they obviously do not know what to do." Those are the words that are used. They say, "What's the value of all their churchgoing?" And that is a perfectly fair criticism. It is no use talking about the Christian faith if that is how you behave. They say, "What's the value of your faith if it can't help you at the time of trial?"

The New Testament is full of this teaching. Let me give one or two of these glorious examples in order that we may all examine ourselves and, I trust, be filled with a sense of shame and realize that the first thing we must do is put ourselves right and become the sort of people about whom anyone meeting us will say, "I would give the whole world if only I could be like you!"

Let me give you a great example: look at the apostle Paul. Here he is in prison. First-century prisons were dank, damp, horrible in every sense, and Paul is suffering. But one afternoon he is brought out of prison to give a little bit of entertainment to a king and a queen and a Roman governor. They ask him about the Christian faith, and Paul gives them the account of his conversion. Then Paul says, "King Agrippa, believest thou the prophets? I know that thou believest." Agrippa then says to Paul, "Almost thou persuadest me to be a Christian." Do not misunderstand that. Perhaps a better translation is, "Do you think that with just a little talk you can make me a Christian?" But here is the important point. Paul then says, "I would to God, that not only thou, but also all that hear me this day, were both almost, and altogether such as I am, except these bonds" (Acts 26:27–29).

I think that is one of the greatest statements ever made. Here is a man, a prisoner with the chains hanging from his wrists, and he is addressing the king and the queen and the Roman governor. They are at liberty, enjoying life, while he is in a prison. And yet this prisoner is able to say, "I would give anything if only you people could be as I am. Oh, I wish you had the inward peace and the rest that I am enjoying! I wish that you could have the experience that I am having in that prison cell! Oh, that you were as I am!"

Here is a man who is entirely independent of his circumstances—they make no difference to him. He has inner reserves; he has something here that is bigger than the whole universe. It does not matter what man may do to him—he wishes that all others would be as he is. He does not want them to be in bonds, he does not want them to suffer, but what he does want them to have is the rest, the peace, the quiet, the satisfaction that he has. He wants them to discover that the truth is, whatever happens to Christian people, it all ministers to the life they have been given through the Lord Jesus Christ by the Holy Spirit.

Let the apostle himself teach you. He himself gives us the explanation. He tells us why he was able to speak as he did on that occasion to Agrippa and Festus. In a passage in 2 Corinthians 4 he quite honestly and frankly gives us an account of the difficulties that he has been going through. Yet he says this:

> But we have this treasure in earthen vessels, that the excellency of the power may be of God, and not of us. We are troubled on every side, yet not distressed; we are perplexed, but not in despair; persecuted, but not forsaken; cast down, but not destroyed; always bearing about in the body the dying of the Lord Jesus, that the life also of Jesus might be made manifest in our body. For we which live are always delivered unto death for Jesus' sake [those were the things that were happening to him, but notice the great contrasts. What is the explanation?]. . . . For which cause we faint not; but though our outward man perish, yet the inward man is renewed day by day. (vv. 7–11, 16)

My dear friends, this is the question: do you know the difference between the outward man and the inward man? Are you living your life entirely on the outward level? So many people are. They live on talk and gossip and excitement and pleasure. It is all outside, and inside there is an emptiness. That is not Christianity. What makes a Christian a Christian is the inward life, new life from God, "the life of God in the soul of man" (Scougal). Christians are "partakers of the divine nature" (2 Pet. 1:4). There is an inward man, and this inward man is entirely independent of the outward man and is being renewed day by day.

And then Paul continues, "For our light affliction"—all that has been happening to him, all that he has been describing, he calls a "light affliction"—"which is but for a moment . . ." What does he mean by "but for a moment"? Does he know that the persecutions are going to stop? Does he have second sight? Is this sympathetic understanding? Does he know that all his circumstances are suddenly going to change and all is going to be well? Is that what he means? Of course not! That is his view of life in this world. For the Christian it only lasts "a moment." Of course, for the non-Christian, life in this world is everything. And when physical death comes, that is terrible; it is the end of all things: "Death is coming! I'm getting older. I must do everything I can to keep young—rejuvenation! I'll go to the end of the earth, get an operation, a new heart!"

What a tragedy! That shows the emptiness of the heart. But what about this "light affliction, which is but for a moment"? What does it do? It "worketh for us a far more exceeding and eternal weight of glory." This word "worketh" is most important. It means "produces," "creates," "stimulates." The "light affliction, which is but for a moment," all these terrible things that are happening, are creating within the apostle and increasing and enhancing within him "a far more exceeding and eternal weight of glory." How do they do it? Well, Paul says, the secret is, "while we look not at the things which are seen, but at the things which are not seen."

What another vital distinction this is! What do you spend your time looking at? Are you always looking at something outside? Do you live through the winter by thinking of your summer vacation plans—is that how you get through? Many people are like that. Now let us be reasonable about these things. I am not saying that you should not plan your summer vacation, but what I am saying is that you should not live on that. Some people are always talking about their schemes and plans and proposals as if they cannot enjoy the present moment. They have nothing within them. "We look not at the things which are seen, but at the things which are not seen." The whole secret of Christian men and women is that they see "the things which are not seen," and they can see them wherever they are. Within a prison cell they see them. They are not outside; they are inside.

And so the more adverse and cruel and trying the circumstances, the more they remind Christian people of their imperishable souls and of the Lord Jesus Christ, who had similar experiences when he was in this world. They remind Christians that the Lord has gone on to prepare a place for them and will come again and receive them unto himself. The apostle goes on to put it like this: "For we know that if our earthly house of this tabernacle were dissolved, we have a building of God, an house not made with hands, eternal in the heavens" (2 Cor. 5:1; cf. 4:7–11, 16).

So the more you are afflicted and tried by things that happen to you from the outside and the malice of men, the more it drives you to realize that you do not belong to this world, that you are bigger than it, that you belong to Christ, you belong to heaven, you belong to glory—"a far more exceeding and eternal weight of glory."

The trouble with all of us is that we think so little about that glory; we are looking so much at the outside, at the seen, the visible, that we do not gaze upon the unseen, the eternal, the glorious, which God in Christ is preparing for us. We do not heed the exhortation of Paul to the Colossians: "Set your affection on things above, not on things on the earth" (Col. 3:2). So when afflictions and trials come, they force us to do what we had foolishly not been doing. We cannot enjoy the outside because it is all against us at the moment, and that, therefore, reminds us of the inside, the unseen, the eternal, the spiritual. And the moment we begin to think in that way, we are immune to what happens outside. This builds up, and we see the eternal more and more gloriously, and we know we are going on to it. So even if they kill us, what have they done? They have simply introduced us to that glory at an earlier point than we had expected. "Though our outward man perish, yet the inward man is renewed day by day."

Now, my dear friends, it is the people who give this impression who conquer the world. These are the people who act as magnets, drawing others to the Lord Jesus Christ. The apostle Paul was full of this; clearly it was one of the most important things of all to him. For your encouragement, let me remind you of what he wrote to Timothy. Timothy was so like us. He was nervous, apprehensive, troubled, anxious about the care of the churches, and now he gets a message to say that Paul is not only in prison but is likely to be put to death at any moment. So as well as being worried about himself, Timothy is worried about Paul, and the apostle has to write to him. Look here, says Paul, "God hath not given us the spirit of fear"—that is what we have by nature, and the world is in the grip of the spirit of fear. What has God given us? ". . . but of power, and of love, and of a sound mind [discipline]" (2 Tim. 1:7).

Then Paul goes on to say:

Be not thou therefore ashamed of the testimony of our Lord, nor of me his prisoner: but be thou partaker of the afflictions of the gospel according to the power of God; who hath saved us, and called us with an holy calling, not according to our works, but according to his own purpose and grace, which was given us in Christ Jesus before the world began, but is now made manifest by the appearing of our Saviour Jesus Christ, who hath abolished death, and hath brought life and immortality to light through the gospel: whereunto I am appointed a preacher, and an apostle, and a teacher of the Gentiles. For the which cause I also suffer [I am suffering] these things [I am in prison, and I have been treated very cruelly and in a most unjust manner; then comes that blessed word "nevertheless"]: nevertheless I am not ashamed [I am not troubled, I am not taken unawares, I am not grumbling and complaining, and you must not. Why not?]: for I know whom I have believed, and am persuaded that he is able to keep that which I have committed unto him against that day. (vv. 8–12)

Well, there it is, my dear friends. To use again the language of the great apostle, the Christian does not merely manage to get through; that is what the Stoic does. Here is the Christian perspective:

Who shall separate us from the love of Christ? shall tribulation, or distress, or persecution, or famine, or nakedness, or peril, or sword? As it is written, For thy sake we are killed all the day long; we are accounted as sheep for the slaughter. Nay [this blessed protest, the inner man begins to speak], in all these things we are more than conquerors through him that loved us. For I am persuaded, that neither death, nor life, nor angels, nor principalities, nor powers, nor things present, nor things to come, nor height, nor depth, nor any other creature, shall be able to separate us from the love of God, which is in Christ Jesus our Lord. (Rom. 8:35–39)

Oh, beloved Christians, are you giving everyone the impression that you have inner reserves, that your inner man is growing day by day and is independent of circumstances—of chance, of war, it does not matter what it is—and that all they do is increase this "far more exceeding and eternal weight of glory"? Believe me, when the Christian church, as insignificant as she is today, is filled with people who give that impression, the world will come streaming in, for it is the one thing that it cannot discover because it is only to be found in our blessed Lord and Savior Jesus Christ.

SOURCES

Acts: Chapters 1–8. 3 vols. Wheaton, IL: Crossway, 2013. First published in 6 volumes by Banner of Truth (as *Authentic Christianity: Sermons on the Acts of the Apostles* [1999–2006]) and Crossway (as Studies in the Book of Acts [2000–2007]). Chapter 15, "Why Christ Had to Suffer," used by permission of Crossway and The Banner of Truth Trust.

The Assurance of Our Salvation: Exploring the Depth of Jesus' Prayer for His Own: Studies in John 17. Edited by Christopher Catherwood. 4 vols. in 1. Wheaton, IL: Crossway, 2000. First published in 4 volumes by Kingsway and Crossway, 1988–1989. Chapter 16, "With Him in the Glory," used by permission of Crossway.

The Cross: God's Way of Salvation. Edited by Christopher Catherwood. Eastbourne: Kingsway, 1986. Wheaton, IL: Crossway, 1986. Chapter 12, "He Is Our Peace," used by permission of Crossway.

Evangelistic Sermons at Aberavon. Edinburgh: Banner of Truth, 1983. Chapter 2, "The Narrowness of the Gospel," used by permission of The Banner of Truth Trust.

God's Way of Reconciliation: An Exposition of Ephesians 2. Grand Rapids, MI: Baker, 1972. Chapter 8, "The Christian Message to the World," used by permission of The Banner of Truth Trust.

The Gospel in Genesis: From Fig Leaves to Faith. Wheaton, IL: Crossway, 2009. Leominster: Day One, 2010. Chapter 13, "Where Art Thou," used by permission of Crossway and Day One.

Great Doctrines of the Bible. London: Hodder, 1996–1998. Wheaton, IL: Crossway, 2003. Chapter 7, "My Purpose and Method," used by permission of Crossway.

The Kingdom of God. Wheaton, IL: Crossway, 1992. Chapter 11, "The Only Hope," used by permission of Crossway.

Living Water: Studies in John 4. Wheaton, IL: Crossway, 2009. Chapter 17, "More than Conquerors," used by permission of Crossway.

Preaching and Preachers. London: Hodder & Stoughton, 1971. Grand Rapids, MI: Zondervan, 1972. 40th anniversary edition: *Preaching and Preachers: The Classic Text with Essays from Mark Dever et al*. Edited by Kevin DeYoung. Grand Rapids, MI: Zondervan, 2011. Chapter 1, "No Substitute," used by permission of Hodder & Stoughton.

Revival. Basingstoke: Marshall Pickering, 1986. Westchester, IL: Crossway, 1987. Chapter 9, "The Purpose of Revival," used by permission of Crossway.

Romans: The Sons of God: An Exposition of Chapter 8:5–17. Edinburgh: Banner of Truth, 1974. Chapter 10, "The Spirit Himself Bears Witness," used by permission of The Banner of Truth Trust.

Seeking the Face of God: Nine Reflections on the Psalms. Wheaton, IL: Crossway, 1991. Chapter 14, "Seeking the Face of God," used by permission of Crossway.

Spiritual Depression: Its Causes and Cure. London: Pickering & Inglis, 1965. Grand Rapids, MI: Eerdmans, 1965. Chapter 6, "Mind, Heart, and Will," used by permission of Eerdmans.

Studies in the Sermon on the Mount. London: Inter-Varsity, 1959–1960. Grand Rapids, MI: Eerdmans, 1959–1960. Chapter 5, "Practicing the Sermon on the Mount," used by permission of Inter-Varsity and Eerdmans.

Truth Unchanged, Unchanging. 3rd ed. Bryntirion: Evangelical Press of Wales, 1990. Wheaton, IL: Crossway, 1993. Fearn, Ross-shire: Christian Focus, 2013. Chapter 4, "Is the Gospel Still Relevant," used by permission of Crossway and Christian Focus.

Why Does God Allow War? A General Justification of the Ways of God. 2nd ed. Bryntirion: Evangelical Press of Wales, 1986. Wheaton, IL: Crossway, 1994, 2003. Chapter 3, "The Final Answer to All Our Questions," used by permission of Bryntirion and Crossway.

NOTES

Chapter 2: The Narrowness of the Gospel

1. Preached on the evening of Dr. Lloyd-Jones's first visit to Westminster Chapel, December 29, 1935, and earlier at Sandfields.

Chapter 10: The Spirit Himself Bears Witness

1. C. H. Spurgeon, *The New Park Street Pulpit*, vol. 7 (1861), 294.

Chapter 15: Why Christ Had to Suffer

1. Algernon Charles Swinburne, "Hymn to Proserpine."

Chapter 16: With Him in the Glory

1. See *Saved in Eternity*, vol. 1 (Wheaton, IL: Crossway, 1988).
2. James Montgomery, "At Home in Heaven."

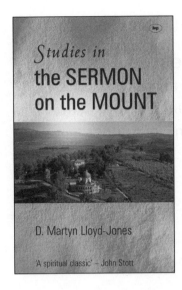

Studies in the Sermon on the Mount

D. Martyn Lloyd-Jones

ISBN: 978-0-85110-583-3
656 page paperback

With characteristic insight, Dr D. Martyn Lloyd-Jones here offers
a detailed and comprehensive exposition of one of the best known
but most frequently misunderstood passages of Scripture – the Sermon
on the Mount.

The Sermon on the Mount, says Lloyd-Jones, is not a code of ethics
or morals; it is a description of what Christians are meant to be. With
his eye always on both Scripture and life, he explains and applies Christ's
teaching for Christians struggling to live like Christ.

Originally delivered as sermons, the sixty studies in this devotional
classic provide a fine example of clear, consecutive expository preaching
from one of the greatest preachers of our time.

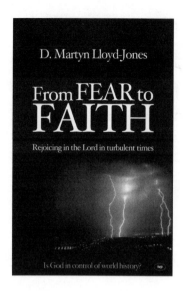

From Fear to Faith

*Rejoicing in the Lord
in turbulent times*

D. Martyn Lloyd-Jones

ISBN: 978-1-84474-500-5
76 page paperback

Is God in control of world history?

The country was on the brink of a devastating invasion. Famine threatened. Violence and social injustice filled the land. Habakkuk the Old Testament prophet had every reason to sink into despair. Where was God in these turbulent times?

D. Martyn Lloyd-Jones was one of the twentieth century's foremost preachers and Bible teachers. The parallels he draws between the message of Habakkuk and the crisis-ridden West are still powerfully relevant to our own times. Here is the secret of the problem of history. No event, however catastrophic, fails to find a place in God's loving purpose for humanity. Habakkuk's great assertion of faith, in the midst of enormous personal upheaval and emotional strain, can be ours: 'Yet I will rejoice in the Lord ... The Sovereign Lord is my strength.'

Available from your local Christian bookshop or **www.thinkivp.com**

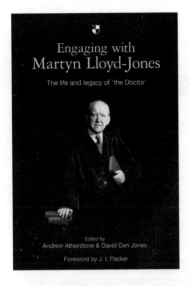

Engaging with
Martyn Lloyd-Jones
The life and legacy
of 'the Doctor'

Andrew Atherstone and
David Ceri Jones (editors)

ISBN: 978-1-84474-553-1
376 pages, large paperback

The figure of D. Martyn Lloyd-Jones (1899-1981) dominates the history
of British evangelicalism in the twentieth century. As perhaps the greatest
non-conformist statesman of his generation, 'the Doctor' is best known as
a preacher and mentor of young preachers. From the pulpit of Westminster
Chapel in London and other platforms, he called the evangelical movement
back to a robust reformed Christianity, with a passion for biblical conviction
and Spirit-empowered revival. His impact upon evangelicalism was
immense, and his legacy remains deeply influential.

By building on, and engaging with, the work of earlier biographers and
theologians, this valuable collection of new studies seeks to advance
our understanding of Lloyd-Jones' life and legacy in a number of fresh
directions. The topics covered are: the interwar Calvinist resurgence,
Wales, revival, the charismatic controversy, ministerial education,
fundamentalism, Barth, Rome, the Anglican secession crisis, and the
Protestant past. The volume concludes with a chronological bibliography
of Lloyd-Jones' writings.

The contributors are Andrew Atherstone, Ben Bailie, David W. Bebbington,
John Coffey, Philip H. Eveson, David Ceri Jones, William K. Kay, John Maiden,
Robert Pope, Ian M. Randall and Robert Strivens.

Available from your local Christian bookshop or **www.thinkivp.com**

For more information about IVP
and our publications visit

www.ivpbooks.com

Get regular updates at **ivpbooks.com/signup**
Find us on **facebook.com/ivpbooks**
Follow us on **twitter.com/ivpbookcentre**

Inter-Varsity Press, a company limited by guarantee registered in England and Wales, number 05202650. Registered office IVP Bookcentre, Norton Street, Nottingham NG7 3HR, United Kingdom. Registered charity number 1105757.